Praise for *Trying Disc Injury Cases*

"This is a monumental work that is a must-have for all trial lawyers who handle disc cases. Never has a book taken such a deep dive into the reasons why, and how, the defense approaches our cases with the degenerative defense. [Simon] doesn't hold back and shares all of his battle-tested methods to defeat this classic defense tactic."

—Mauro Fiore, Jr., Consumer Attorneys Association of Los Angeles board member, Dordick Trial College board member, voted Super Lawyer, and *Running with the Bulls* contributing author

"Robert Simon is brilliant! This is a must-read for any lawyer representing a client who sustained a disc injury. Not only does he meticulously explain what to expect from the defense, but more importantly, Mr. Simon gives you invaluable gems on how to empower the trier of fact favorably for your client. Well done, Mr. Simon!"

—Hon. John M. Pacheco (retired), mediator with over four decades of experience in civil and family law

"If you're seeking expert tips from someone who truly understands the day-to-day realities of the trenches in today's courtrooms, Bob Simon is an invaluable resource. His working-class background and personal experiences lend him exceptional credibility with jurors. His advice is both practical and substantive, grounded in the recognition that courtroom dynamics often differ significantly from what's on paper. He knows what he's talking about. Take heed."

—Hon. Jacqueline A. Connor (retired), mediator and arbitrator with over 25 years of judicial experience in resolving complex legal and factual issues

"While spinal injuries can affect the literal bones in a back, they inflict greater harm on the 'backbones' in our communities who work hard each day to show up and support their loved ones. Disc injuries have long been the target of tort reform narratives and dishonest defenses relying on junk science. Our clients are called liars and malingerers simply because their injuries exist beneath the surface of the skin, invisible to the naked eye. Simon's book is the antidote. This book thoroughly examines the strategies employed in disc injury cases and provides a clear framework for dismantling dishonest defenses. Simon excels at distilling complex medical concepts into digestible lessons for every attorney, reinforcing the critical point that there is no substitute for hard work and knowing the medicine. This book is essential reading for any trial lawyer interested in mastering the medicine and has become required reading for every new lawyer I hire."

—Andrew Garza, partner and trial attorney at Claggett, Sykes & Garza, LLC

"This book should be required reading for every plaintiff's personal injury attorney. Most injured car crash victims suffer from exactly the type of injuries covered in this book. Most personal injury attorneys are also not doctors. The book very successfully bridges the gap with practical, real-world tips on how to defeat the insurance company's nonsense and succeed in spinal injury/chronic pain cases. Thank you, Mr. Simon, for writing such a practical and well-written book."

—Carol O. Cadiz, attorney at O'Connor Cadiz Accident and Injury Law

"Bob Simon masterfully outlines the common tactics defense attorneys use to downplay the value of cases, targeting both clients and plaintiff's attorneys. In his signature no-nonsense style, Bob debunks these myths with clarity and precision, delivering a powerful message that makes you realize just how much more these cases are truly worth. I particularly appreciate his straightforward approach in dismantling the insurance companies' nonsense—it's refreshing and packed with facts that make you say, 'Yes, this case is worth far more.'"

—Jennifer Gore, founder and attorney at Atlanta Personal Injury Law Group

"Robert Simon's new book on litigating disc injury cases is a very easy, informative read. The straightforward discussion and analysis of the tactics of successfully litigating a case provides good advice to plaintiff and defense counsel, such as the importance of truly understanding the nature of the injuries and keeping the presentation to the jury simple and understandable. While at times disparaging of defense counsel and insurance companies (he is, after all, a plaintiff's attorney), the book provides insight into 'how to' litigate a case, with valuable suggestions for both plaintiff and defense counsel who try those cases. Plaintiff attorneys will gain valuable techniques and approaches, and defense counsel will be better armed to defend a case by educating themselves on them."

—Hon. Joe W. Hilberman (retired), *LA Daily Journal* Top Neutrals and Los Angeles Chapter ABOTA Jurist of the Year for 2008

TRYING DISC INJURY CASES

Defeating the Degeneration Defense

Robert Simon with Peter Lowry, MD, and Orlando Micheli, MD

TRIAL GUIDES™

Trial Guides, LLC, Portland, Oregon 97210

ISBN: 978-1-951962-72-2

Trial Guides, LLC Attn: Permissions

2350 NW York Street Portland,

OR 97210 (800) 309-6845

www.trialguides.com

Developmental Editor: Tina Ricks

Production Editor: Travis Kremer

Assistant Editor: Amanda Fink

Cover Designer: Alexandra Starkovich

Original Interior Template Design by Laura Lind Design

Printed and bound in the United States of America.

Printed on acid-free paper.

Table of Contents

Publisher's Note ix
Foreword xi
Acknowledgments. xv
Introduction. xix
Educating Yourself About the Medicine xxv
About the Cases in This Book xxix

PART I. Developing Your Case & Anticipating the Defense

1. Spine 101 1
2. Diagnosing Spine Injuries. 25
3. Building Your Spine Case through Science. 39
4. Common Defense Arguments 61
5. Teaching an Old Defense Attorney New Tricks 77
6. Telling Your Client's Story. 101
7. Gathering the Evidence 113

PART II. Witnesses in Deposition & Trial: Why Less Is Always More

8. Treating Doctors: Deposition as Direct Examination 131
9. Defense Experts: Deposing to Prepare for Cross-Examination 151
10. Deposing Defense Doctors: Depositions for Use at Trial. 167
11. Defense Biomechanical Experts: Depositions for Use at Trial 201
12. Defense Medical Billing Experts: Depositions for Use at Trial 223
13. Responding to Defense Doctors: Deposition & Cross-Examination 243

PART III. The Trial

14. Pretrial Motions: Before the Courtroom 257
15. Venues, Jury Pools & Voir Dire: Finding the People. . . . 267
16. Opening Statement. 283
17. Plaintiff Direct Examination 295
18. Cross-Examination 307
19. Closing Argument 309

Conclusion 335
Appendix A: Outline for Plaintiff's Direct Examination. 337
Appendix B: A Deeper Look into the Radiology Room 353
Appendix C: Glossary of Medical Terms. 371
About the Authors. 377

Publisher's Note

This book is intended for practicing attorneys. This book does not offer legal advice and does not take the place of consultation with an attorney or other professional with appropriate expertise and experience.

Attorneys are strongly cautioned to evaluate the information, ideas, and opinions set forth in this book in light of their own research, experience, and judgment; to consult applicable rules, regulations, procedures, cases, and statutes (including those issued after the publication date of this book); and to make independent decisions about whether and how to apply such information, ideas, and opinions to a particular case.

Quotations from cases, pleadings, discovery, and other sources are for illustrative purposes only and may not be suitable for use in litigation in any particular case. The cases described in this book are actual cases, and the names and other identifying details of participants, litigants, witnesses, and counsel have been fictionalized except where otherwise expressly stated.

All references to the trademarks of third parties are strictly informational and for purposes of commentary. No sponsorship or endorsement by, or affiliation with, the trademark owners is claimed or implied by the author or publisher of this book.

The author and publisher disclaim any liability or responsibility for loss or damage resulting from the use of this book or the information, ideas, or opinions contained in this book.

Foreword

You have made a great choice in picking up this book. What you are about to read is a guide our civil justice system has needed for a very long time. Over the past fifteen years, I have seen Bob Simon and his allies righteously flip the script and change the way spine injury cases are looked at, handled, and valued—paving a path for the countless humans who deserve full compensation and justice for the changes to their bodies and lives caused by the negligence and wrongdoing of others.

Approximately 3 million people in the United States suffer from whiplash injuries each year. Half of them end up living with chronic pain for the rest of their lives. Sadly, only a small percentage of these humans ever end up being fully compensated. The rest are written off, settled out for cheap, and forgotten. They are classified as "soft tissue" cases, instead of real people with compelling human stories who have suffered real, life-changing injuries. There are different reasons for this sad reality. The most important one is our collective failure as trial lawyers to believe in these cases, invest the resources, do what it takes to go the distance, and dedicate the time and resources needed to teach others. The time to rectify our failure is now.

This wonderful book shines new rays of hope into the pits of darkness where most lawyers get stuck or are otherwise unwilling to go. Having spent what seemed like endless time in those pits, struggling to get out of them over and over again with my clients and oftentimes their families on my shoulders, trust me, I know how dark and difficult things can be. If there is a knight of justice dedicated to keeping his clients out of the pits, fighting the dragons, and dragging them out into the light, then Bob Simon is that champion. If the Mandalorian were a trial lawyer, I know what he would say about this book. He would tell us, *this is the way*. Having spent over two decades trying these difficult cases, educating myself, testing new methods and strategies, and learning from some of the best in our field, I can confidently say that no better tool exists to teach lawyers how to best represent clients who have suffered spine injuries than this book.

By reading the referenced cases and seeing the way the medicine is thoroughly explained in conjunction with how the human stories are told, you will become a lawyer who is capable of winning full justice for the people you convince to trust you. By committing to learning how to do things better and differently, you will learn how to handle neck and back injury cases from the moment you get the first call through prelitigation, discovery, dealing with defense medical examinations, knowing which experts to hire, and (if you are willing to go the distance) how to effectively present these cases and human stories to juries, whether they are liberal, rural, conservative or otherwise.

This book teaches us how to smack down typical defenses such as when the defense expert testifies that the MRI shows nothing but wear and tear or the defense makes its primary focus the unimpressive property damage or gaps in medical treatment. If the radiology room is something you don't know much about, and you want to learn more, you will soon understand things such as the difference between clinical and nonclinical radiologists.

If someone has told you that the merit or value of spine injury cases is determined by the size of the disc protrusions, bulges, or herniations, you'll learn how that is very far from the truth and why. I could go on and on, but the book does a much better job.

I do have a wish that I hope the decision-makers publish, which is that all personal injury/accident billboard lawyers in America buy enough copies of this book to ensure the people they have intaking and working up these cases learn how to do their jobs better. If my wish comes true, I am confident we will see a ripple effect of generational justice over the next few decades with less pain and suffering and a whole lot more life, liberty, and pursuit of happiness.

I am very honored to write this foreword, express my respect and belief in the authors, and insist that every trial lawyer read this book.

I have known Bob Simon and his twin brother Brad since they started their law firm in 2010, a decade and a half ago. I specifically remember how proud they both were handing out pins and hats with their new "Simon Law Group" logo at a lawyer mixer in Malibu. These two brothers had moved out west and started their law practice with nothing but the shirts on their backs. From the beginning, they have always been good and generous people who give back even when they have little or nothing to give. It makes me proud to have grown up with these great humans as a fellow trial lawyer and friend.

In terms of trial work, Bob Simon started his career straight out of the chute, running against the grain and breaking the mold and winning jury trial after jury trial. He tried cases others didn't believe in. Judges told Bob he would lose, defense lawyers laughed, colleagues asked him what the heck he was doing, but Bob kept putting one foot in front of the other. He chose to believe in his clients and do whatever it took to figure out how to win. As young lawyers, we would find ourselves trying cases next door to each other, down the hall, or Bob would be waiting to start a trial as I was finishing or vice versa. I saw him win, I saw him evolve, but most importantly I saw that he never gave up or let anybody beat him down. I have seen Bob, his family, and his partners and law firm put it all on the line, repeatedly standing up for the people and issues they believe in. This book is a precious and beautiful gift to us all.

With gratitude, your friend and ally,
Nick Rowley

Acknowledgments

Robert Simon

For anyone who knows me, they know full well I am all about family and work–life balance. So, to have that balance, our family works together so we can talk law over Christmas! Without my wife, Christine Bullock, constantly inspiring me and pushing me to do better, I would likely still be an associate at some other firm, hoping to try a case year. Without my brothers Brad and Brandon running our firm and managing the litigation, I would likely be pulling my hair out, drowning in discovery. Without my mom and dad telling me it is okay to fail, I would likely still be afraid of my own shadow. Without my sisters Julie and Nicole, who are instrumental to the success of Justice HQ and Attorney Share, I would likely be spread too thin to still try a lot of cases. Without my daughters, Remington (Remi), Penelope (Poppy), and Josephine (Josie), I would not be able to cry for real during every closing argument.

Professionally, there are many to thank who have molded me into the lawyer that I am today. Being a trial lawyer takes a lot of practice, and well, a lot of stealing other people's ideas and weaving them into your own style. So here is a list of people I have stolen from over the years, who have also been huge mentors of mine:

- Ben Swanson
- Nick Rowley
- Brian Panish
- Mauro Fiore
- Randi McGinn
- Brad Simon
- Sevy Fisher

And of course, my go-to for everything law and life, my law-mentor Gary Dordick.

Orlando Micheli, MD

I have been greatly blessed with phenomenal mentors and teachers. It is virtually impossible to sit down, read a stack of books, and have the expectation or achieve the reality of becoming a skilled physician. It is necessary therefore to learn such art from those around us. I, like many others, stand on the shoulders of giants. These giants for me were first recognized at home, as a child, in both of my parents who were high school educators. They taught me that we should be lifelong learners and strive to achieve excellence in the process.

I was frequently ill for most of my childhood. As a child-patient, I learned what it was to suffer. This ultimately provided the drive to become a physician and to alleviate the suffering of others. I am sure that having a sickly child aged both of my parents beyond their chronological years. My mother, as an advanced stage cancer patient, has also been a source of valuable lessons. My father, even though I was a terrible athlete, showed up to all my baseball and basketball games and offered unquestionable support. He also supported me at all my competition shooting matches. Thank you, Mom and Dad, and sorry that I was the sickly bubble boy.

The advice and instruction of Susan Rachlin, MD, shined the light onto the field of radiology. Without her, I would likely be a surgeon of some sort. I would also like to thank the wonderful radiologists at the University of Southern California: Alison Wilcox, MD, Victoria Marx, MD, Sue Hanks, MD, Randy Radin, MD, Jay Gordonson, MD, and Michael Katz, MD. These individuals shaped me as a radiologist. Lastly, and most importantly, I would like to thank my original physician, Jesus of Nazareth.

Peter Lowry, MD

The list of mentors and colleagues to which I owe an overwhelming debt of gratitude is extensive. Like attorneys, radiologists are wordsmiths, and the best radiologists become a vault of clever, efficient phrases and little gems of inside knowledge collected from their sharpest colleagues. I've been lucky to learn from numerous great ones. Many of the concepts I help to present in this book are echoes of my most influential teachers. My highest thanks go to my wife, who is the best radiologist I've ever known and is my most frequent source of genius level material. She does so much for family, friends, and the trainees she mentors that I constantly wonder how (or if) she is working with the same number of hours in the day as the rest of us.

Introduction

Thank you for joining my thought process on handling and trying spinal disc injury cases. This book will not be about the obviously traumatic spine injuries that render our client without the use of legs and limbs. If you only have cases like that, you probably don't need this book.

This book will walk you through how to handle the run-of-the-mill, meat-and-potatoes, spinal disc injury cases we deal with in our everyday practices. The book is also about chronic pain. These are the injuries that the defense calls "soft tissue," that they claim will "heal in three to six months and the rest is just good old degeneration." These are injuries that our clients did not think would be lifelong at the time of the crash. These injuries took some time to manifest, but resulted in epidural injections, a discectomy surgery, or a full-blown fusion. These are the cases that did not have significant property damage to their cars. These are the cases where the defense hires experts to say, "No one can get a disc injury from this type of collision."

I chose these types of cases because I truly believe they are the lion's share of the cases that we handle. And just because the injuries in these cases might be subtle or reveal themselves over time does not mean they are not high-value losses. These cases have real value and have given me some of my largest verdicts.

I grew in Pittsburgh, Pennsylvania (and have the tattoos to prove it). My dad was a truck driver for UPS, and my mom raised me and my four siblings into fine citizens. We grew up strictly working class. We played every sport imaginable and worked several customer service jobs when not in school or on the field. Growing up in a working-class neighborhood, I think, gives me a unique insight into what an injury does to a working-class family. I would see firsthand that if a friend's dad was injured, they wouldn't be able to make rent and would have to move to another school district.

I developed a special passion for fighting for the injured and disabled when my uncle was paralyzed due to a crash. He was a laborer, and my cousins were my age, eleven to fourteen at the time. I saw what their family went through, and how their attorney fought for them. And saw all the frivolous defenses. They tried to say that he was just not that "valuable" because he was "just working class." It was terrible. In the end, however, they won. My uncle and his family had enough money to help them live their lives. I also saw the struggle my uncle had due to complications of this severe injury even after the litigation was done. And learned that money is just never enough to justify the damage done.

I started my firm, Simon Law Group (also known as The Justice Team) with my brothers Brad and Brandon in 2010. Since then, it's become an all-hands-on-deck family affair, with my mother and father helping out on the business end. My parents both moved out to California from Pennsylvania, and they work at our firm. Both my sisters work with us too. We grew from a firm of three in a small, crammed office, to having six office locations, over twenty lawyers, and over fifty non-attorney employees.

My twin brother Brad was born with severe scoliosis and had steel rods implanted into his spine. As kids lying in bed, he would whack me with a stick every time he was in pain, so I knew when to give him another pain pill. We played the NHL '93 video game the whole summer of his surgery because he couldn't get out of bed.

With that background, I take a lot of this stuff personally. Although I can't relate to the extreme amount of physical and psychological pain accident victims go through as they lead altered lives, representing them has allowed me to learn empathy. As trial lawyers, we want to be a receptor for all this and beam those stories back to the jury, so we need to be great storytellers.

I'm writing this book to help provide you with the basis to tell your client's complete story. I have given you mine, to help show that trial attorneys who achieve good results are made from their own experiences, their own life struggles, and (most importantly) their own striving to make a difference for those who have hired them.

At my firm, we handle approximately two hundred spine injury cases every year and try no less than a dozen each year (caveat: we had the same COVID-19 court closures as everyone else, so there was a break during that time). It is our passion. I believe that I have created a straightforward path to success on these types of cases. I've spent years working on these cases, educating myself, trying new strategies, and learning from some of the best in the business.

I personally have tried over thirty spine injury cases just like these—all in a seven-year span. They have resulted in verdicts from $500,000 to $17 million. I have tried them in all types of jurisdictions: from liberal cities to conservative rural areas. My clients have come from every background and many did not speak English. They ranged from nineteen to eighty-four years of age. The damage to their vehicles has been severe to hardly even a paint transfer. In fact, the damage in my $17 million case was so minor you could hardly see it. But in the end, the results have been the same. This book is designed to give you all the tools to achieve the best possible results in your cases.

Getting Results

For the most part, I believe your case is won or lost before you get into the courtroom.[1] It's like producing a movie. You have to do your research and make sure all the pieces are in the right place. If you think a person's pain is real, and not a psychological issue, litigate the case.

The most important piece is your client. If you have a nice client with a good story, and if you can tell that story effectively and make the

1. A note on the jury trial: civil cases aren't going to trial like they used to according to data collected over the past three decades. From 2000 to 2009, civil jury trials dropped 47.5 percent to a 0.5 percent low in 2009, according to the National Center for State Courts. Nonetheless, I continue to believe in the power of the jury system.

jury want to fight for them, that's a solid start. If you have a good client, you can win every case. To have a good, believable client, you have to know their injuries well.

I have built a successful trial practice from learning the medicine and talking to my clients. These are the very basic fundamentals to building your case for trial:

- Understand your client's injuries.
- Keep your case simple.
- Don't buy into the bullshit coming from the defense and their expert.

Understanding your client's injuries is always the first step to successfully trying these cases and can get you a long way with everyone involved. Here's just one example.

In the fall of 2018, I was trying a spine injury case in Arizona federal court. During my closing argument, the judge interrupted me to ask a question, mistakenly referring to me as "Dr. Simon." Later, she asked how I understood the spine and could explain it better than any of the experts.

"I did telemarketing in high school, and I watch YouTube," I told her.

While both of those things are absolutely true, it requires more work than that. This book includes the methods I used to educated myself in the next section, "Educating Yourself About the Medicine." However, I would be willing to bet that since you are reading this book, you likely could answer that question in a similar way. Most of us were former salespeople, bartenders, teachers, concession stand clerks, and grocery baggers. We know how to talk to people in a way that they understand.

I find that most great trial lawyers are a dangerous combination of being both fantastic communicators and highly educated in the items at issue. The latter is where this book really comes into play.

Flow of this Book

We broke this book into three parts:

1. Developing Your Case and Anticipating the Defense
2. Witnesses in Deposition and Trial: Why Less Is Always More
3. The Trial

I believe that the foundation of my success at trial was built on educating myself on the science. As noted throughout the book, understanding your client's specific injuries and sources of pain will help you weed through the landmines the defense will attempt to place throughout litigation and help you to, ultimately, tell your client's complete story at trial.

Built into this book are outside perspectives from both the medical side and the defense side. To help with this, I brought in two radiologists: Orlando Micheli, MD, and Peter Lowry, MD, and former defense attorney Steve Rosen. They offer an insider's understanding of the medicine and the defense's point of view and discuss the importance of many of the concepts we talk about within these pages.

This book is intended to provide you with both the foundation to work on disc injury cases, as well as some insight into the nuances that ultimately bring home the big verdicts.

Let's have some fun.

Educating Yourself About the Medicine

A critical part of being an effective trial lawyer for disc injury cases is educating yourself about the medicine. And while there are some trial lawyers who have formal medical training, most of us do not. It's beyond the scope of this book to try to teach you all you need to know, and for me, developing this knowledge has been the work of decades. Instead, I want to give you the tools you will need to begin and continue your own education.

Watch Depositions

I used to have to travel to watch other lawyers take depositions and spend my time sitting in a conference room in a suit trying to look smart (not to mention time and money on airline tickets and hotels). Now we can just log into depositions. Be sure that the lawyer who is taking the deposition gives notice that they are streaming it as an educational tool for other lawyers. I have yet to get pushback from any defense lawyer or court for streaming a deposition.

Treating Doctors

I think the absolute best way to learn is to sit in on the deposition of a client's treating doctor and listen to them and how they explain things. It doesn't have to be your case. Often, I have lawyers across the country, and ones at Justice HQ, live stream my depositions so they can learn.

Experts

The next best source is to read or watch the depositions of experts. Reach out to other lawyers you trust. They usually have a vault of depositions. I know I do!

Conference Learning

There are a lot of medical-legal and solely medical conferences to attend. I prefer the medical-legal ones because they teach from the lawyer's perspective. It helps with jurors and adjusters. Here are a few of my favorites:

- TBI Med Legal and their webinars (http://tbimedlegal.org).
- Law-Di-Gras (http://law-di-gras.com). Full disclosure: I started this one. But I truly think it's the best.
- Dordick Trial College (http://dordicktrialcollege.com).

Other Sources

- Expert Institute (https://www.expertinstitute.com): this platform tracks experts, the cases they work on, articles they published, malpractice issues, and any motions filed with them. Expert Institute also has a lot of depositions. This is a great resource to learn from.
- The defense doctor's own website. When you get the name of a defense doctor who is hired for a defense medical exam, go to their website. Look them up on YouTube. They will likely be talking about stuff that they will later contradict in your case. This can be a gold mine.

Books & Videos

- Gregory D. Cramer and Susan A. Darby, *Clinical Anatomy of the Spine, Spinal Cord, and ANS*, 3rd ed. (Mosby, 2013).
- Arthur C. Croft, *Whiplash and Mild Traumatic Brain Injuries: A Guide for Patients and Practitioners* (Spine Research Institute of San Diego, 2009).
- Aaron DeShaw, *Spinal Injury Cases* video series, sessions 1–6 (www.trialguides.com).
- Samuel D. Hodge Jr. and Jack E. Hubbard, *The Spine for Lawyers* (American Bar Association, 2014).
- Frank H. Netter, MD, *Netter Atlas of Human Anatomy: Classic Regional Approach*, 8th ed. (Elsevier, 2022).

Papers

- David F. Fardon et al., "Lumbar Disc Nomenclature: Version 2.0," *The Spine Journal* 14, no. 11 (November 2014): 2525–45, https://doi.org/10.1016/j.spinee.2014.04.022.
  - »These terms became so subjective and widely disagreed upon that a task force was created in 2001 to unify the language used by radiologists, surgeons, and non-surgical treating physicians in order to ensure that everyone is on the same page. This is the most updated version of the consensus paper with the recommendations of the combined task forces of the North American Spine Society, American Society of Spine and Radiology, and the American Society of Neuroradiology. These are strict guidelines about terminology in all aspects of spine care. If there is a physician who doesn't use these terms

correctly or doesn't understand them, this is a red flag as to their depth or breadth of knowledge.

- Michael T. Modic and Jeffrey S. Ross, "Lumbar Degenerative Disk Disease," *Radiology* 245, no. 1 (October 2007): 43–61, https://doi.org/10.1148/radiol.2451051706.
- Christian Pfirrmann et al., "Magnetic Resonance Classification of Lumbar Intervertebral Disc Degeneration," *Spine* 26, no. 17 (September 2001): 1873–78, https://doi.org/10.1097/00007632-200109010-00011.
- Maureen C. Jensen et al., "Magnetic Resonance Imaging of the Lumbar Spine in People without Back Pain," *New England Journal of Medicine* 331, no. 2 (July 14, 1994): 69–73, https://doi.org/10.1056/nejm199407143310201.
- Michael A. Adams and Peter J. Roughley, "What Is Intervertebral Disc Degeneration, and What Causes It?" *Spine* 31, no. 18 (August 2006): 2151–61, https://doi.org/10.1097/01.brs.0000231761.73859.2c.
- Kenneth M. Cheung et al., "Prevalence and Pattern of Lumbar Magnetic Resonance Imaging Changes in a Population Study of One Thousand Forty-Three Individuals," *Spine* 34, no. 9 (April 2009): 934–40, https://doi.org/10.1097/brs.0b013e3181a01b3f.

About the Cases in This Book

Since this book is intended to provide you with a practical and functional approach to handling disc injury cases, I have included the following two case studies. I reference these cases throughout the book, and I thought it would be important to provide you with a little background on each. These are both cases that I tried to favorable verdicts.

Michael Johnson v. Jonathan Brown

Michael Johnson was a Division I basketball player who held, and still holds, many records during his time playing. But when I met him in 2012, he couldn't even pass a ball anymore, let alone shoot around with his young son. That's because a rear-end accident that occurred under seven miles an hour changed the trajectory of his entire life at the age of forty-three. He was eating so many pills to numb the pain that he lost count. Imagine planning your whole day around when to take medication. One of the plates in his spine was backing out, necessitating another surgery. An extruded disc went into his spinal canal, so every time he swallowed, he experienced trouble.

Johnson was hit from behind by a guy who was fumbling for his radio. He felt like crap the next day, complaining of pain going down his left arm and down his left lower back. An MRI confirmed Johnson's subjective complaints with objective findings in the scan. Johnson had never had a single complaint of neck or back pain in his life before this accident and he was seeing a doctor regularly. There were no problems with his lumbar spine or cervical spine whatsoever. There were long gaps in treatment after the crash, however, when he would travel.

Johnson had lower-back fusion surgery, but when they fused his lumbar spine, the surgeon missed with the screws—twice. They missed the vertebrae, which meant he wasn't completely fused. He continued to have chronic pain. One of those screws was a millimeter away from his aorta, which runs along his spinal column and could have killed him if it had punctured the aorta.

He also had cervical fusion surgery, but was in extreme pain, and had difficulty swallowing. After I came in to represent him, I got him to one of the best neurosurgeons—someone I would let operate on my own spine if I needed it. He had to go back and have his surgery redone. It was an all-day procedure in which Mr. Johnson was cut open from the front so all his damaged hardware could be taken out. Then he was flipped over, so the doctors could re-fuse him with new hardware. He incurred almost $700,000 in medical bills. Over $400,000 was for this procedure alone!

Of course, the defense made no good offers. At trial, their accident reconstructionist/biomechanical expert actually said, based on studies that are not peer reviewed, that a person cannot get a disc injury from a rear-end collision. They attempted to show he was a liar, an exaggerator, and had all attorney-referred care paid for with a lien on this case, all with a crash that was less severe than a pillow fight. They told the jury to give him $15,000.

The defense experts even contradicted each other. The defense's spine surgeon said it was okay that one of those screws was just one millimeter away from his aorta. Then the defense radiologist testified that the screws were a problem and should probably have been taken out.

In 2014, a Los Angeles jury returned an award of $16.4 million. We waived past and future lost earnings; this verdict was solely based on past and future medical bills and pain and suffering ($15 million). The defendant's new trial motion was denied, and with costs and prejudgment interest, the judgment to date is over $18 million. The defense appealed, and on the heels of the appellate decision, the entire matter was settled for a confidential amount.

An important note about pain and suffering. This is a generic term, and it is different in each state. In many states these damages are capped, so you have to get creative on increasing the special damages, or economic harms. Pain and suffering are the human harms, or noneconomic damages. Check your state law. For instance, in Colorado these are generally capped. However, damages for "disfigurement" are not capped. So you have to ensure your argument fits the jury instructions.

Mr. Johnson used his compensation to continue getting treatment for his injuries and ongoing symptoms. He has created a better life for himself and his son. Not only did he make his immediate family's life better, he is now an advocate for the injured. He remains a good friend and an inspiration.

I'll be getting into the granular details of the Johnson trial throughout this book.

Note from Dr. Orlando Micheli

I was fortunate enough to be involved as the expert on this case. Though I will touch more on the details of important insights and key points as an expert and share some intel with you about how I approach these cases, this case highlighted the importance of several key principles from an expert's perspective.

We Experts Need to Know the Clinical Records Well

This is our job as experts. I was able to elicit critical information in my review of the clinical record. For example, Johnson reported in one doctor visit that after his cervical spinal fusion that he was having trouble swallowing. This was not evaluated. Zero effort was placed in looking into this complaint. Johnson later mentioned it once in a primary medical doctor visit. This immediately caught my attention as the esophagus is in the surgical incision area and, after a minimal investigation, I determined that the hardware plate in the cervical spine was not positioned well and was actually putting mechanical pressure on the esophagus. This was undoubtedly causing his difficulty with swallowing. I was able to confirm my suspicion of this diagnosis with a very basic maneuver in a simple physical examination. If I had ignored the clinical records, like most radiology defense experts, this key piece of information would have undoubtedly gone undiagnosed.

There is a vast amount of treasure buried in the clinical record if you are willing, able, and qualified to dig. As another example, in this case I noticed that multiple hardware screws were malpositioned. In addition to the screw close to the aorta that Bob mentioned earlier, there was a lumbar screw that had transversed the right common iliac vein and undoubtedly would have been a potential source of significant intra operative bleeding during removal. The screw could have left a big hole in this large vein, putting the patient at enormous risk. In this case, I was able to speak to the operating surgeon who performed the hardware removal so that the surgery could be performed in a safe and effective manner. I advised the operating surgeon that during removal, they should consider the involvement of a doctor like me (an interventional radiologist) who could repair this potentially nasty vascular injury using minimally invasive techniques. I have known patients who have nearly died from undiagnosed iliac venous bleeding. It can be scary stuff.

Use Your Expert as a Strategist

Before you depose the opposite experts, talk to your expert. If your expert possesses the appropriate understanding of the case, you should acquire insight and learn what questions you should ask. This will help form your argument and prove your case. For example, in the Johnson case I made sure to tell Bob to ask each expert about the malpositioned screws. This clearly was a heads-up play as it resulted in a difference of opinion on the opposite side. Your expert should be able to provide you with a greater understanding of the medical care given to your client, how it could be better, and what questions you should ask to pin the opposite side down on what care is appropriate and why. If your expert fails to possess this complex, multi-dimensional knowledge, find another expert.

Paulina Atlantic v. B&D Transport

Paulina Atlantic was sixty years old when a tractor trailer hit her from behind. She was in the process of moving from California to Texas to live with her son and grandson. Instead of calling 911, the driver fled and called his brother, who owned the trucking company. Ms. Atlantic and another woman remained trapped in the car until the emergency services extricated them using jaws of life.

Ms. Atlantic went to the ER where they diagnosed her with a lumbar sprain. They did CT scans which showed no acute fractures, and she was discharged. She went on to Texas and started seeing a chiropractor. Her lower back pain remained the same, so she was referred to a spine surgeon. She also complained of numbness in her left leg. She actually fell in the shower and was bruised from the fall. While the defense claimed that she was clumsy, the real reason was that she had leg weakness due to her disc injury, which caused nerve problems in her leg and made it to go numb. The spine surgeon ordered an MRI, and it showed degenerative disc disease in her lower spine, causing stenosis, that was greater in her right leg than her left leg. Paulina ended up having a single-level fusion surgery, with good result, from a Los Angeles neurosurgeon on a lien. Her medical bills were approximately $300,000. She needed another $300,000 in the future for an adjacent segment surgery and pain management.

During the litigation we heard the same old song and dance:

- "She is a nurse. These injuries are just cumulative wear and tear from her job and aging."
- "This is all just chiropractic care."

- "The MRI does not show acute findings, there are no signs of trauma, and she is all over the place on describing her pain."

There was no serious offer. They hired a medical doctor who examined her and opined all of the above. He actually blamed her injuries on the fall in the shower. This doctor avoided the facts and the medicine showing that the disc injury was pinching a nerve in her lower back causing numbness and weakness down her leg. They hired a billing doctor to say all the bills were excessive, not realistic, and the doctors should only be given Medicare rates. They argued she was "too old to return to work" anyway. The defense likes to use the argument that once someone is Medicare eligible, usually around sixty-five to sixty-seven, they retire, and any wages claimed after that point are not realistic. You know what I think is not realistic? That most people ever have the luxury to stop working. This resonates well with the jury. Especially when the defense attorney is in his seventies and so is the judge!

At trial, we waived her lost earnings claim. The number was not significant, and we believed that the noneconomic loss of not being able to work, her feeling of uselessness, was greater than her actual lost earnings. The defense went all-in that the surgery was only due to her pre-existing condition, that the surgery was not warranted, and if it was, it was caused by her fall in the shower. They asked the jury to give at most $250,000. The jury in the end compensated Paulina with $3.8 million.

The facts in Atlantic are pretty standard for many of our cases; and the results tend to be the same, regardless of venue. This case was tried in a "conservative" venue. But how do we get these results time and time again? What is the secret sauce? What does the defense continue to miss when evaluating these cases? You.

PART I

Developing Your Case & Anticipating the Defense

In this part, we will discuss how to develop your case for success during trial. By doing so, you also set yourself up to maximize settlement value for the client if the insurer is willing to make a reasonable offer.

In my practice, we see new clients come through the door two ways: they either just got in a crash and need help; or they are being represented by another attorney who wants us to handle the litigation and try the case. No matter how the case comes through the door, our first step is always the same: identify the client's symptoms and make sure we have the right doctors taking care of them.

The next step is to look at your case closely and find the weak spots that the defense will find and pounce on. Knowing your defense attorney may be a good start. If you haven't worked with that particular defense counsel before, reach out to the plaintiffs' community to get a sense of that defense attorney's playbook. Chances are, they carry the same style and the same games from case to case.

The next few chapters cover common themes the defense uses in spinal cases. For the most part, it's always a game of playing your science versus their confusion tactics.

1

Spine 101

By Orlando Micheli, MD & Peter Lowry, MD

Introduction to the Spine

The spine is composed of many elements and has numerous complex articulations and joints. These complexities can make the spine confusing—even intimidating—to the lawyers, physicians, and radiologists who are involved in disc injury cases. One useful approach to reviewing anatomy is an "inside-out approach" that starts with the deep structures and progresses outward. So, we will begin with the bones.

Bones in the Spine

A good framework for understanding vertebral anatomy is to consider the two main goals of the bones of the spine:

1. Support the weight of the head, neck, and upper body.

2. Protect the spinal cord and nerve roots as they course from the base of the brain to the pelvic region.

The vertebrae vary widely in size and structure throughout the cervical, thoracic, and lumbar segments in order to accomplish these goals. We will revisit the segmentation of the spine—and why it is important—later in this chapter.

We will first discuss the anatomy of a single vertebral level, and then how each level articulates with the levels above and below. Picture, in your mind's eye, a single vertebra. It can be divided into the vertebral body, which is the large, weight-bearing mass of bone *anteriorly* (in the front), and the ring structure and extensions from it located *posterior* (in the back) to the vertebral body, collectively known as the posterior elements.

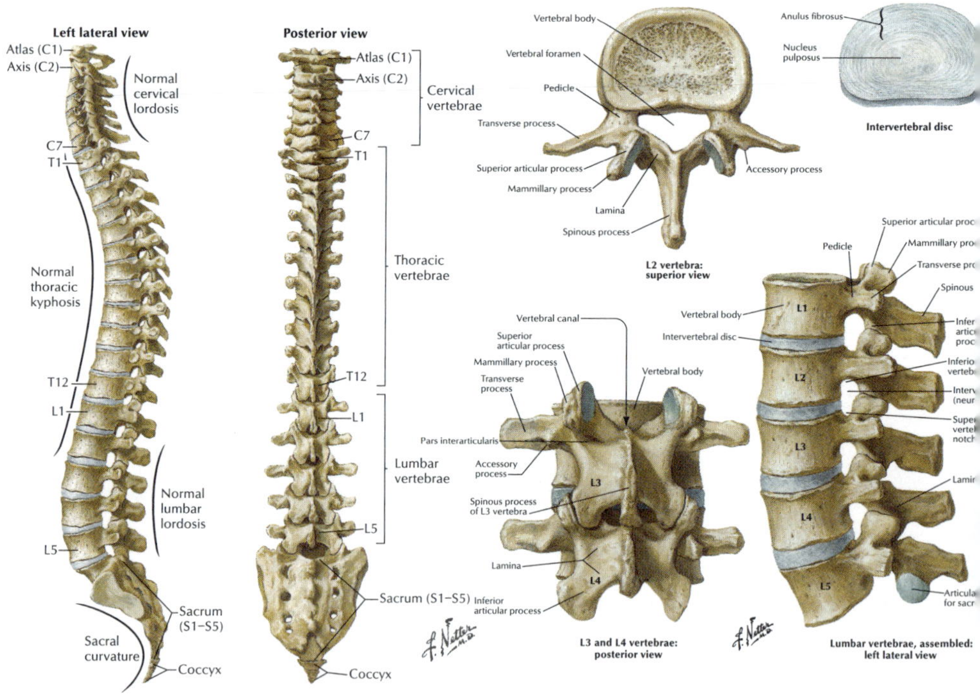

Figure 1-1. Vertebral Column, Lumbar Vertebrae & Intervertebral Disc
(Netter illustrations from www.netterimages.com © Elsevier Inc. All rights reserved.)

Shown above are illustrations of a lumbar vertebra for reference. The vertebral body, the large cylindrical portion of each vertebra that provides weight-bearing support throughout the spine, is located anteriorly and is roughly oval shaped when viewed from above or below, and roughly rectangular when viewed from the front or side. The posterior elements are comprised of the following:

- pedicles (singular: pedicle)
- laminae (singular: lamina)
- facet joints
- transverse and spinous processes

Recall that one of the two goals of the bones of the spine is to protect the spinal cord. It accomplishes this by surrounding the spinal cord with a ring of bony structures. The opening in the center of this bony ring, where the spinal cord is located, is called the spinal canal. At most levels in the spine, the spinal canal is roughly pentagonal in shape—with the vertebral body forming the anterior border, the cylindrical pedicles forming the left and right sides, and the laminae forming the angled sides posteriorly.

There are several bony extensions from this ring shape. Each level of the spine has a single spinous process that extends posteriorly from the junction of the laminae in the midline, and is angled slightly inferiorly toward the feet, serving as an attachment for ligaments as well as muscles and tendons which all help to support and move the spine. There are also two transverse processes, one on each side, which extend laterally from each pedicle. These also serve as an attachment point for ligaments, tendons, and muscles that assist in lateral bending and stability.

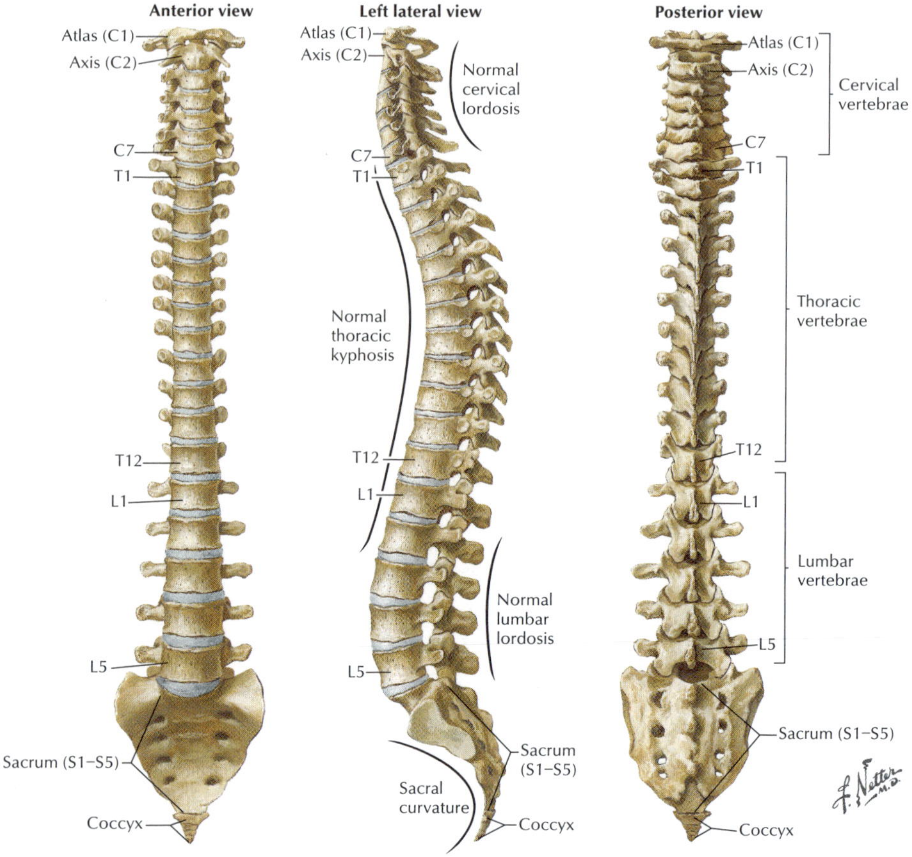

Figure 1-2. Vertebral Column

(Netter illustration from www.netterimages.com © Elsevier Inc. All rights reserved.)

The spine is divided into three segments, which are discussed in greater detail below.

- The segment in the neck is known as the *cervical* spine.
- The segment in the upper and mid back is known as the *thoracic* spine.
- The lower segment, often referred to as the "small of the back," is known as the *lumbar* spine.

The cervical spine has seven vertebrae, numbered C1 through C7. The C1 vertebra articulates with the base of the skull, at what is known as the *craniocervical* junction. The C7 level is the lowest cervical level and articulates with T1 at the C7-T1 level, which is also known as the *cervicothoracic* junction.

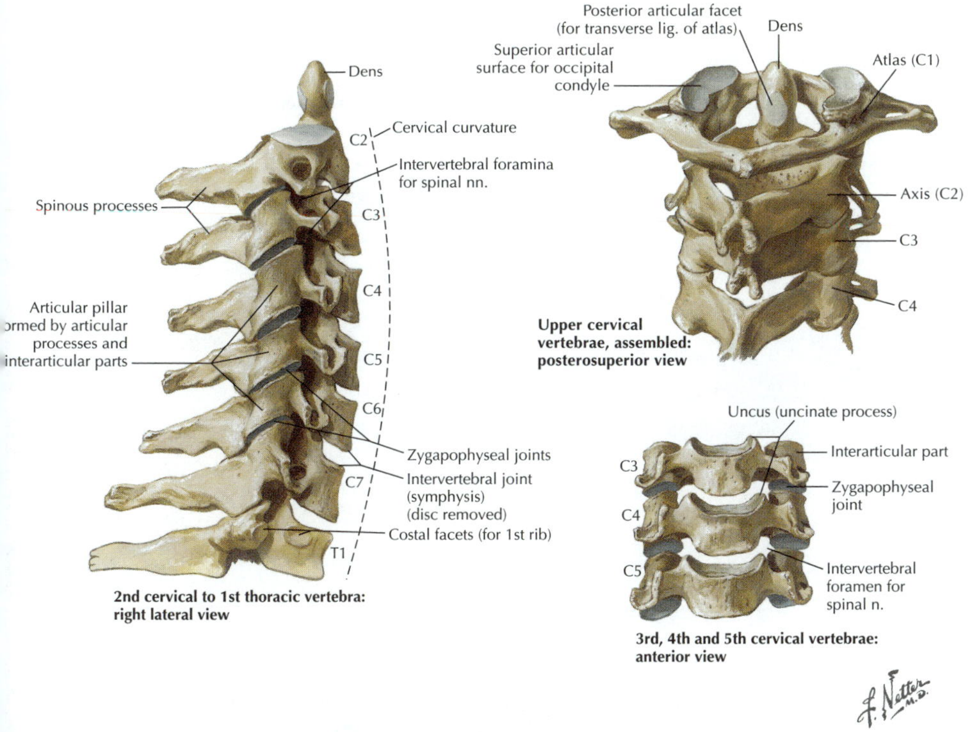

Figure 1-3. Joints of the Cervical Spine

(Netter illustration from www.netterimages.com © Elsevier Inc. All rights reserved.)

There are twelve thoracic vertebrae, numbered T1 through T12. Each of these thoracic levels adjoins with paired ribs which are also attached to the sternum at the anterior aspect of the chest, creating the chest cage and limiting motion in the thoracic spine compared to both the cervical and lumbar segments. The T12 vertebra, which is the lowest level of the thoracic spine, articulates with L1 (the uppermost lumbar vertebra) at the *thoracolumbar* junction.

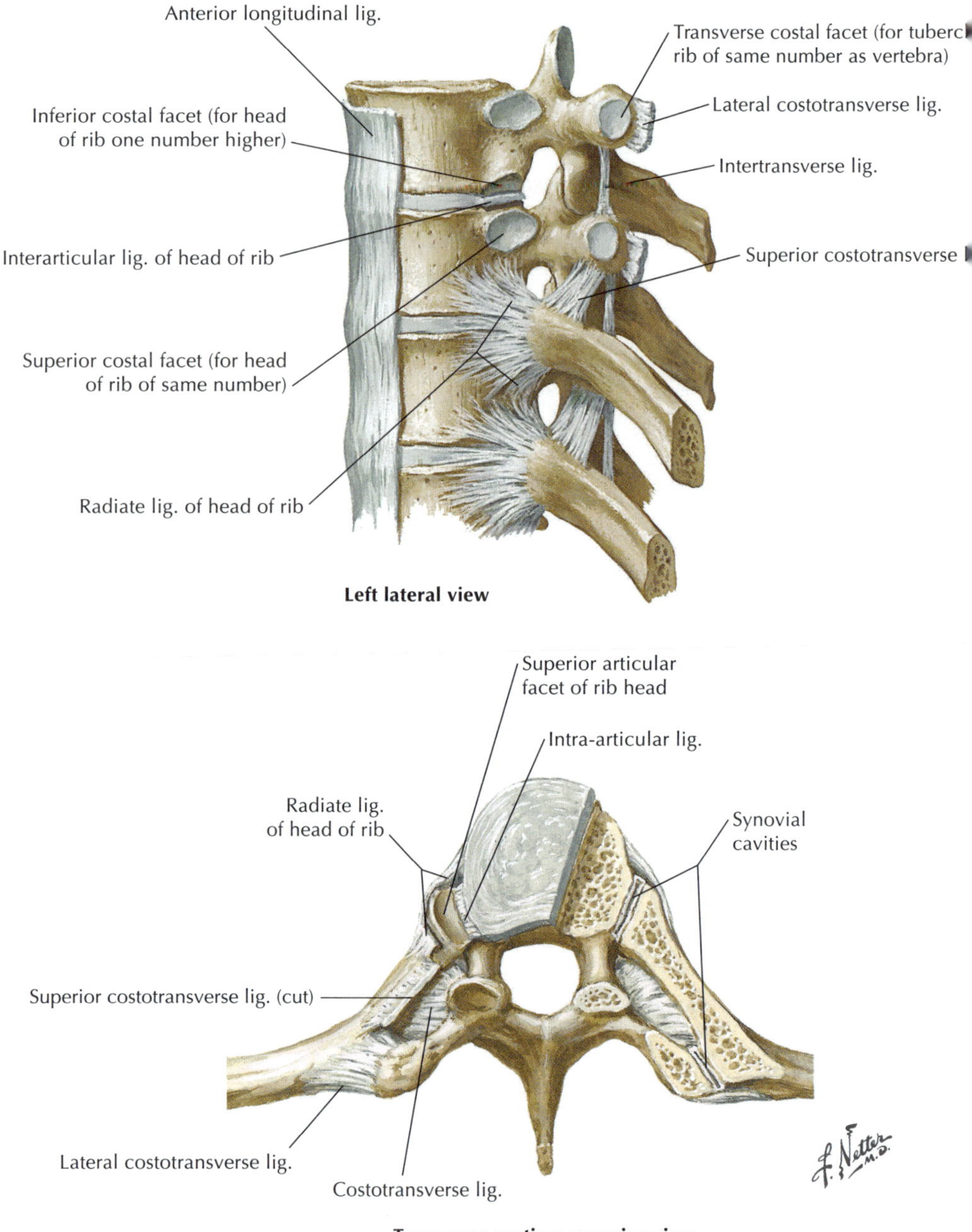

Figure 1-4. Joints of the Thoracic Spine

Finally, the lumbar spine is comprised of five vertebrae, numbered L1 through L5 from top to bottom. Because each level of the spine must support all the weight above it, vertebrae become progressively larger the farther down the spine they are. Lumbar vertebrae are larger than their cervical and thoracic counterparts, for example. You can see in figure 1-5 that each of these vertebrae has a single spinous process posteriorly, and two transverse processes, one on each side.

Anatomical Variations

In most people, the five lumbar vertebrae are all similarly shaped, without ribs and without bony contiguity with the rest of the sacrum. However, you may hear about *transitional anatomy of the lumbar spine*, wherein one of the levels resembles either a thoracic vertebra at the top of the lumbar spine (with ribs, for example) or a sacral segment (contiguously fused with the sacrum, either partially or completely) at the lowest level of the lumbar spine. In these cases, keeping terminology consistent can be difficult. Radiologists and surgeons use terms to clarify this phenomenon, such as *sacralized L5* or *lumbarized S1,* that attempt to keep everyone on the same page for diagnostic and treatment purposes.

Still, mistakes occasionally happen when a patient has atypical anatomy–something to be aware of in legal cases. Additionally, transitional anatomy at the lumbosacral junction can affect the mechanics of the spine at one of its most-often injured levels. In these cases, biomechanical standards no longer apply! Those standards are based on standard anatomy, and it can be critical to know that atypical anatomy may predispose someone to significant injury under much lower external forces. Suffice it to say that in the lumbar spine, anatomy *can* become a bit strange, and in these cases, a discussion with your retained medical experts should clarify both the terminology and the implications of the anatomic variant with respect to the case.

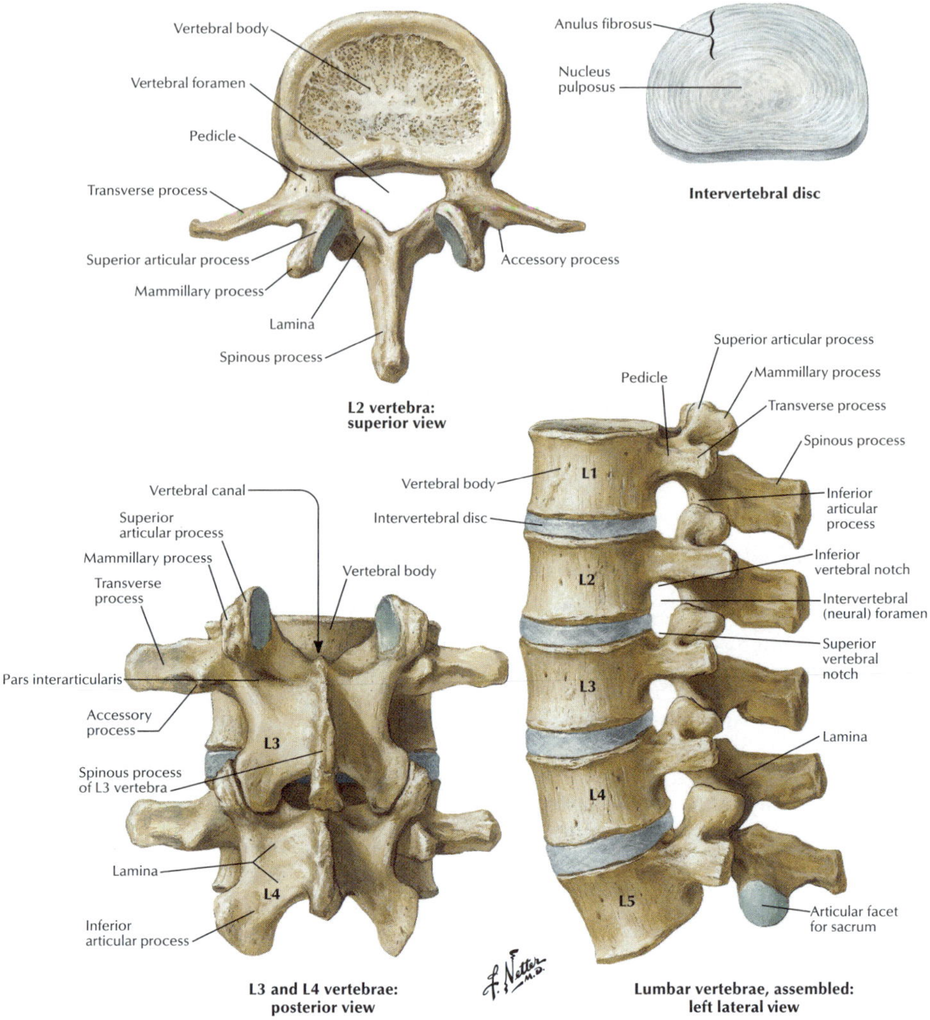

Figure 1-5. Lumbar Vertebrae & Intervertebral Disc

(Netter illustration from www.netterimages.com © Elsevier Inc. All rights reserved.)

The *sacrum* is a triangular shaped bone that articulates with both the lumbar spine (at the *lumbosacral* junction, traditionally L5-S1) and the pelvis (at the *sacroiliac* joints, often abbreviated as the SI joint). The sacrum therefore serves as a transition point, shifting the weight of the trunk and upper body from the vertically oriented spine laterally to the pelvis, where it is then transferred through the legs to the ground.

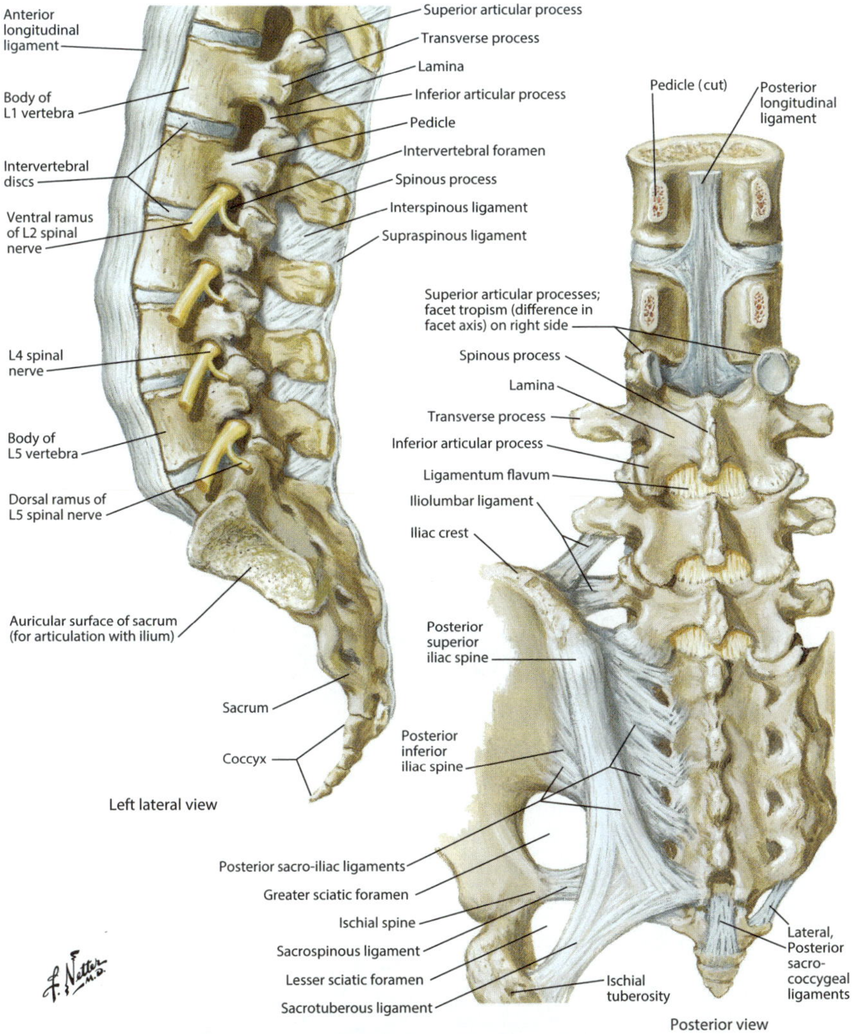

Figure 1-6. Vertebral Ligaments: Lumbosacral Region

(Netter illustration from www.netterimages.com © Elsevier Inc. All rights reserved.)

With the exceptions of the *craniocervical* junction and C1-C2 articulation, the vertebrae are separated from each adjacent vertebra by an *intervertebral* disc. This disc serves as a shock absorber between vertebrae, cushioning what is termed *axial loading*, which can be thought of generally as the force of gravity when standing or sitting upright. The discs are named for the vertebrae which border it—for example, the disc that separates the cervical levels C3 and C4 is the C3-C4 disc. Often the second letter is eliminated, so the disc separating the L4 and L5 levels of the lumbar spine is often referred to as L4-5.

Each spinal level is also separated above and below from its neighboring levels by a joint on either side of the posterior elements called the *facet joints*. Facet joints are small articulations between slight upwardly and downwardly directed extensions (processes) of the posterior elements known as the articular processes. Facet joints are slightly curved and are angled differently at different levels in the spine, but most often they layer obliquely on adjacent levels like shingles on a roof. Facet joints help to guide and limit forward to backward and lateral bending and rotation of the spine.

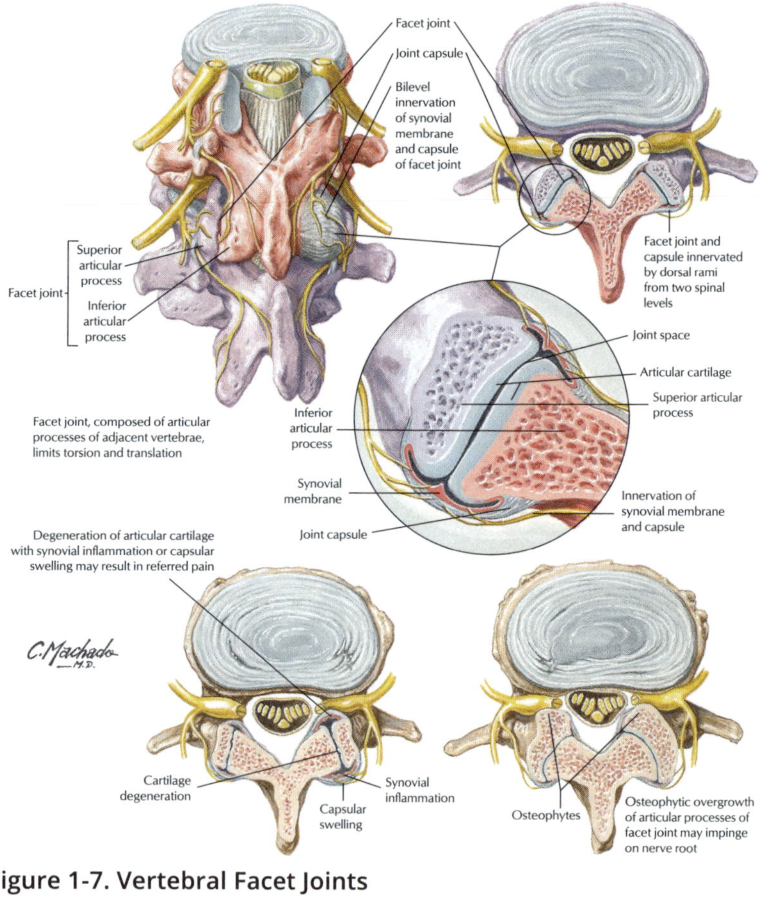

Figure 1-7. Vertebral Facet Joints

(Netter illustration from www.netterimages.com © Elsevier Inc. All rights reserved.)

Connecting all of these levels together is a network of ligaments. The ligamentous anatomy at the junction between the base of the skull and the C1 level, and at the C1-C2 level, is unique and exceedingly complex. This includes many ligaments oriented in different planes to allow for rotation of the head and to limit the extent of motion at these levels. Throughout the remainder of the cervical spine, as well as in the thoracic and lumbar spine, the ligaments are structured in a much more uniform way. Anterior to these vertebral bodies lies the *anterior longitudinal ligament.* The *posterior longitudinal ligament* is located at the posterior aspect of the vertebral bodies and helps to form the anterior part of the spinal canal. At the posterior aspect of the spinal canal is the *ligamentum flavum.* These three ligaments—the anterior and posterior longitudinal ligaments and the ligamentum flavum—are all large, broad ligaments that provide significant stabilization of the vertebral column. Additionally, there is a network of ligaments that connects the posterior elements of the spine, including the *interspinous ligaments*, the *supraspinous ligaments*, and the *intertransverse ligaments.* In addition to the *joint capsules* at each facet joint, these ligaments serve to stabilize the spine posteriorly.

The Spinal Canal

Now that we have discussed the bones and ligaments that provide the structure of the spine, we will describe the contents of the spinal canal. The spinal canal, as you recall, is the pentagon-shaped space enclosed by the vertebral body and posterior elements. Within it, there is an envelope type membranous structure called the *dura*, which contains the nourishing cerebrospinal fluid. Floating within this fluid is the spinal cord, which is comprised of nerve fibers that relay signals between the brain and every part of the body. At each level of the spine, the spinal cord sends out a nerve root to each side of the body. Much like the wiring in a house, these nerve roots carry all the information and instructions for structures at that level of the body. And much like the wiring in a house, if any portion of this wiring is damaged (in a spinal injury, for example), the structures that wiring supplies can malfunction.

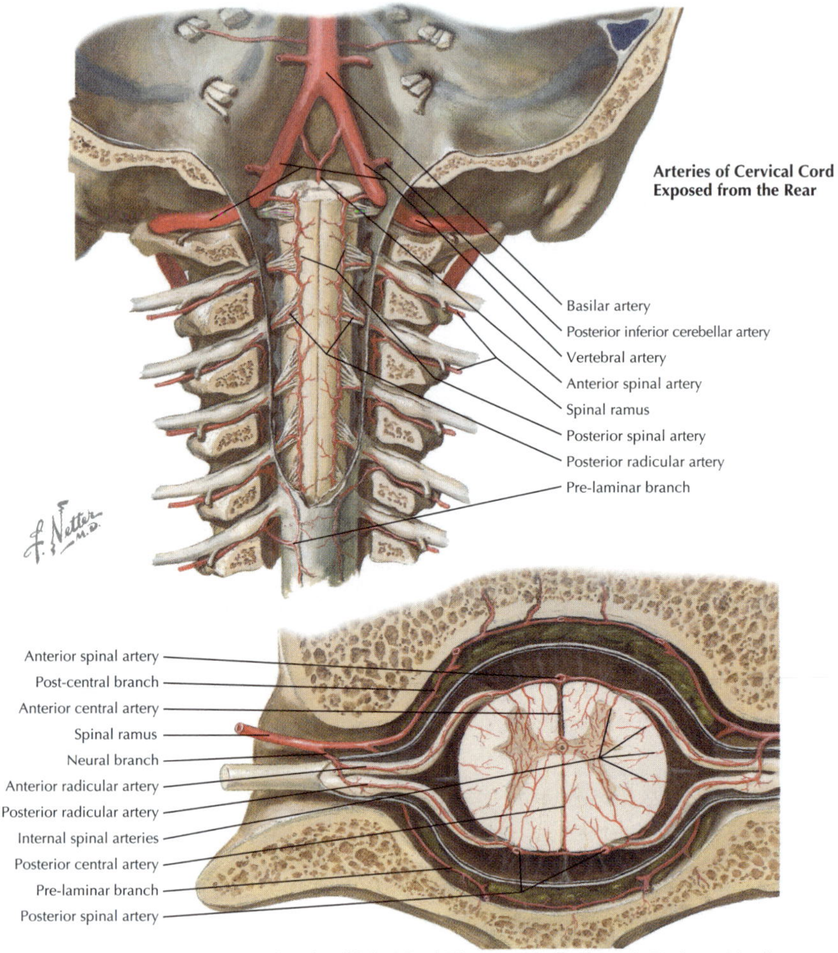

Figure 1-8. Anterior & Posterior Spinal Arteries & Their Distribution
(Netter illustration from www.netterimages.com © Elsevier Inc. All rights reserved.)

One interesting misconception about the spinal cord is that it runs the entire length of the spine. This is not true—while the spinal cord begins at the base of the brain, it ends in the upper lumbar region at about the L1 level, varying slightly from person to person. Below this, the spinal canal contains only a bundle of nerve roots called the *cauda equina* (horse's tail). One of these nerve roots still exits the spinal canal on each side at each level of the lumbar spine, just as with other levels of the spine, and supplies structures that correspond to that level. This becomes important since the lower lumbar levels are often injured; and while there is no such thing as a spinal cord injury at L4-L5, for example, an injury to these nerve roots can have devastating consequences.

Spinal Injuries

So how do spinal structures get injured? Let us count the ways…

Fractures

First, the bones of the spine, including the vertebral bodies and all of the parts of the posterior elements, can break. Just like any bone! Except when vertebral bodies break, they most often don't break into two pieces along a clearly visualized fracture line, as a long bone would. Instead, they collapse under the weight of the load applied. When they collapse, they change in shape from roughly rectangular to somewhat narrowed anteriorly, causing it to be shaped like a wedge.

These types of fractures can be traumatic, like from a car accident, but they can also be related to an underlying weakening of the bone as is seen in osteoporosis. Spinal compression fractures such as these often result in the spine bending forward, which is associated with significant morbidity and decreased life expectancy. Spinal compression fractures can also result in externally observable deformity, with the associated social and career consequences.

The posterior elements of the spine (which we learned about in the previous section—the side and back bony structures) can also be fractured. This can lead to an unstable condition for the patient and can put both the structures of the spinal canal and surrounding structures such as arteries at risk of further injury.

Because of their unique shapes, the C1 and C2 vertebrae fracture in unique ways. At C1, there are named fracture patterns including *hangman's* and *Jefferson fractures*, which are due to distraction and compressive injury, respectively. At C2, the odontoid process can fracture, and depending on the location of the fracture, this is divided into type I, II, and III fractures. These are pictured in figure 1-9.

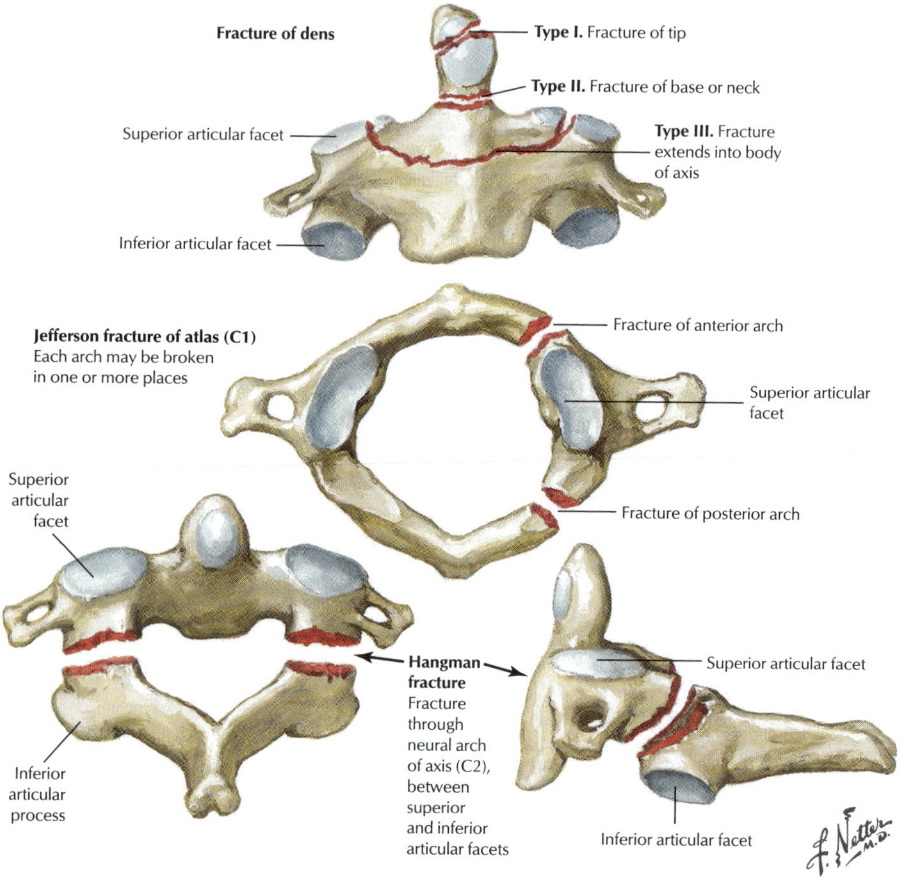

Figure 1-9. Cervical Vertebral Fractures

(Netter illustration from www.netterimages.com © Elsevier Inc. All rights reserved.)

Disc Injuries

To discuss disc injury, it is helpful to consider the jelly-doughnut analogy often used to describe disc anatomy. Think of the disc as a jelly doughnut.

There is an outer, thicker, and more durable ligamentous part known as the *annulus*. This is like the outer, breaded part of the jelly doughnut. Inside is a jelly-like internal substance known as the *nucleus pulposus*.

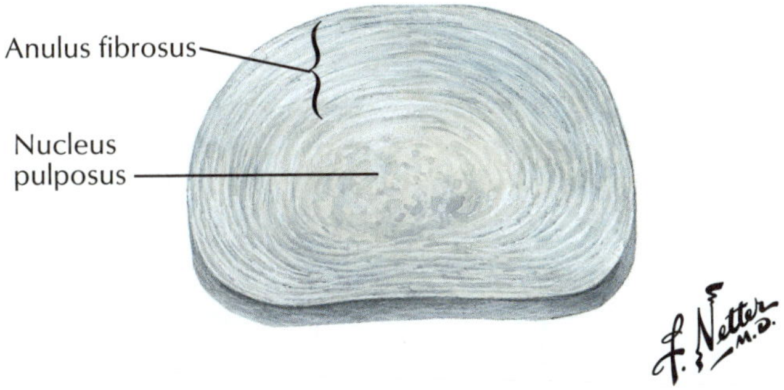

Figure 1-10. Intervertebral Disc (A)

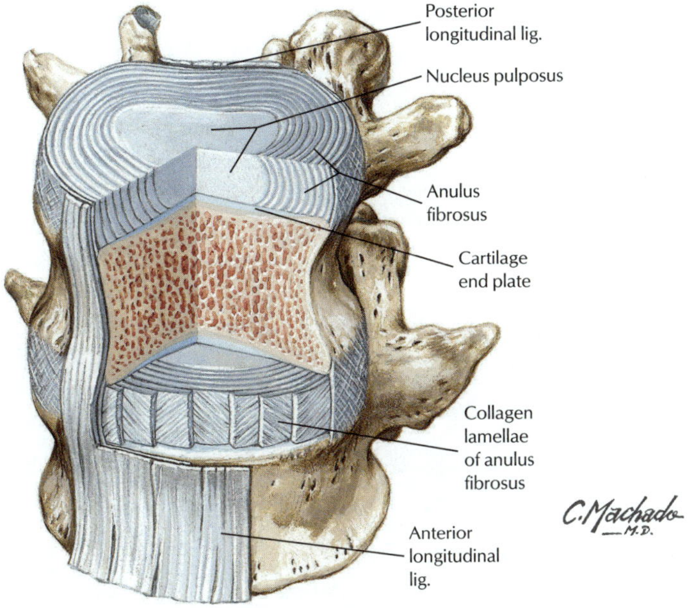

Intervertebral disc composed of central nuclear zone of collagen and hydrated proteoglycans surrounded by concentric lamellae of collagen fibers

Figure 1-11. Intervertebral Disk (B)

The annulus, when it is durable and intact, contains the nucleus pulposus. When everything is normal, the disc works almost like an air-filled car tire to help cushion impacts to the spine.

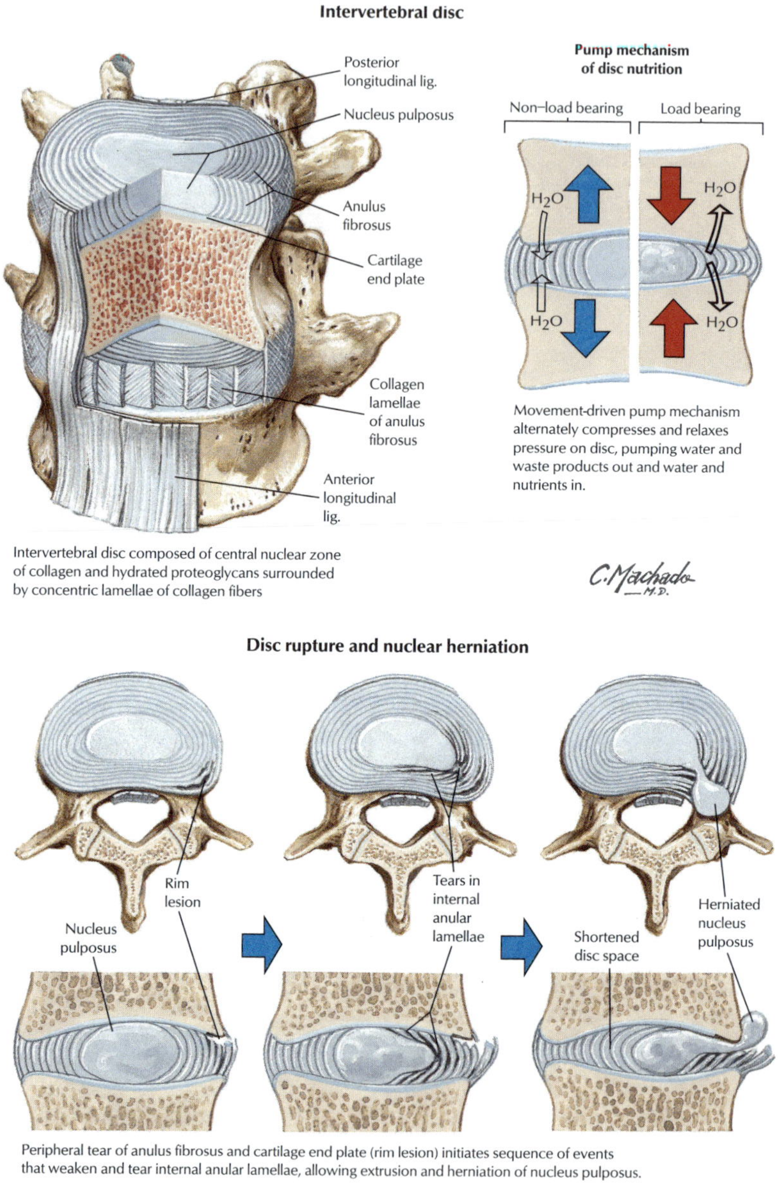

Figure 1-12. Intervertebral Disc with Pump Mechanism & Disc Rupture & Nuclear Herniation

When the annulus is injured (when the bread portion of the jelly doughnut is torn), the nucleus pulposus can ooze out of the center of the disc. The disc then often will lose its normal height and lose its ability to provide the normal amount of cushion for the spine as well—similar to having a flat tire on a car. Complicating matters even further, the nucleus pulposus—that jelly-like substance normally contained centrally in the disc—has to go somewhere. So it squeezes out from the rupture in the annulus and can lead to narrowing of the spinal canal or the space around the nerve roots, and can impinge on these vital structures or cause inflammation around and within the nerve roots themselves, resulting in pain or dysfunction.[1]

Disc Herniations

Broadly, these injuries are informally known as *herniated discs*. However, in a spine CT or MRI report, these injuries should be categorized further in both type and extent.

Disc herniation terminology is, for many people, the most confusing aspect of spine injury evaluation. Using MRI, we are able to see things that had not been previously possible, so a whole litany of terms have been introduced, refined, and agreed upon in the medical community. This disc nomenclature absolutely *will* be a part of your case, rearing its head again and again throughout discovery, deposition, and trial.[2]

Disc bulging can be thought of as stretching or laxity of the annulus (the bread part of the jelly doughnut). None of the fibers are torn, and there is no leaking out of the nucleus pulposus material. Disc bulging

1. For more about nerve roots, see the section titled "The Spinal Canal" earlier in this chapter.

2. David F. Fardon, Alan L. Williams, Edward J. Dohring, F. Reed Murtaugh, Stephen L. Gabriel Rothman, and Gordon K. Sze. "Lumbar disc nomenclature: version 2.0," *The Spine Journal*, 14, no. 11 (Nov. 1, 2014): 2525–2545. These terms became so subjective and widely disagreed upon that a task force was created in 2001 to unify the language used by radiologists, surgeons, and non-surgical treating physicians. The most recent update, published in 2014, forms the basis of what should be expected from spine radiology reports.

simply describes a saggy disc which has lost at least some of the elasticity the annular ligaments normally provide.

If the annulus is torn, this is broadly described as a *disc herniation*, which can be broken down into three types depending on size and severity.

Disc Protrusion

Disc protrusion is the first type of disc herniation. It is defined as a disc herniation in which "the greatest dimension between the edges of the disc material presenting beyond the disc space is less than the distance between the edges of the base of that disc material that extends outside the disc space"[3] In other words, if it looks like you could push the herniated portion of the disc back into place with your finger, that's probably a disc protrusion.

Disc Extrusion

Disc extrusion is the second, slightly more severe form of disc herniation. A disc extrusion is defined as a herniated disc in which "in at least one plane, any one distance between the edges of the disc material beyond the disc space is greater than the distance between the edges of the base measured in the same plane."[4] Basically, if the herniated portion of the disc is taller than the disc itself, and it looks like pushing it back in would be a complex maneuver, it is likely a disc extrusion.

Disc Sequestration

Disc sequestration is the third and most severe form of disc herniation. Regarded as a subtype of disc extrusion, a disc sequestration is a disc herniation that develops into a separate glob of a disc fragment. In the consensus nomenclature paper, it is defined as a herniation "when no

---

3. *Id.*

4. *Id.*

continuity exists between the disc material beyond the disc space and that within the disc space."[5] Put simply, a sequestered disc is an island of disc material no longer connected to any disc. These can become so severe that it can be difficult to determine which disc the fragment came from in the first place.

Common Locations of Disc Injury

Because the thoracic spine is stabilized by the ribcage, most of the motion of the spine occurs in the cervical and lumbar segments. Due to this, thoracic spine discs are injured far less frequently than cervical or lumbar discs. In the cervical spine, C5-6, C6-7, and C7-T1 are commonly injured. In the lumbar spine, disc injuries at the L4-5 and L5-S1 levels are the most common.

The bony anatomy of the spine influences disc herniation anatomy in another way. Because the posterior elements of the spine limit how far backward someone can bend (anatomically termed *extension*), but there are no solid bony obstructions preventing forward bending (*flexion*), the discs are routinely subjected to more compressive force anteriorly than posteriorly. And if you squeeze a jelly doughnut on one side, the contents herniate out the opposite direction—so it makes sense that most disc herniations are directed posteriorly toward the spinal canal.

The location of any posterior disc herniation is further broken down into zones: central, subarticular, foraminal, and extraforaminal. Though they are nonstandard according to the *Spine Journal* consensus paper, you will almost certainly also come across the terms *paracentral* and *far lateral* in radiology reports or surgical notes. Central herniations are exactly as they sound—aimed exactly in the center of the spinal canal. If you can imagine the disc as a clock face, central disc herniations would be centered at the 6:00 position of the disc as viewed on a normal MRI. Paracentral herniations are located just to either side of this. Not far, but not right in the middle either—think roughly the 5:30 or

5. *Id.*

6:30 position. Moving outward from the central and paracentral zones, the next zone is termed the *subarticular* zone, which extends from the lateral edge of the spinal cord to the bony pedicle. Incidentally, the vast majority of traumatic herniations occur in the subarticular zone, as the posterior longitudinal ligament is weakest in this region. The foraminal zone is exactly the width of the bony pedicle, where the nerve root exits from the spinal canal. *Extraforaminal* herniations are defined as any herniation lateral to the pedicle.

Radiculopathy & Radicular Pain

Disc injuries can result in a range of symptoms that can vary in intensity and location. Because there are pain-sensing nerves called the *sinuvertebral* nerves that go to (*innervate*) the intervertebral discs, there is often pain at the site of injury, which may additionally radiate slightly around the affected level.

Disc herniations may also be associated with a specific type of pain, called *radiculopathy* or *radicular pain*, which is indicative of nerve compression by the herniated portion of the disc. Radicular pain is a type of *referred pain* that the brain senses as pain coming from a different location than the actual injury. For example, if a nerve root is compressed by a foraminal disc herniation at one of the cervical levels, the pain would feel as if it were coming from the area where the nerve ends in the fingertips, not where it is actually pinched. Regions of the body which sense referred pain mapped to specific levels of the spine are called *dermatomes*, and the map which illustrates these is called a *dermatome map*. They can extend into the arm and hand (*cervical radiculopathy*), around the chest and abdomen (*thoracic radiculopathy*), and into the pelvis, legs, and feet (*lumbar radiculopathy*). While it is helpful to correlate a patient's pain with a dermatome map, it is also important to know that there is some mild variability in the precise dermatomal anatomy from person to person. In other words, a patient with an injury that compresses the L5 nerve may have symptoms that cross into what is normally L4 or S1 territory. Don't let opposing expert witnesses convince you that this is an absolute!

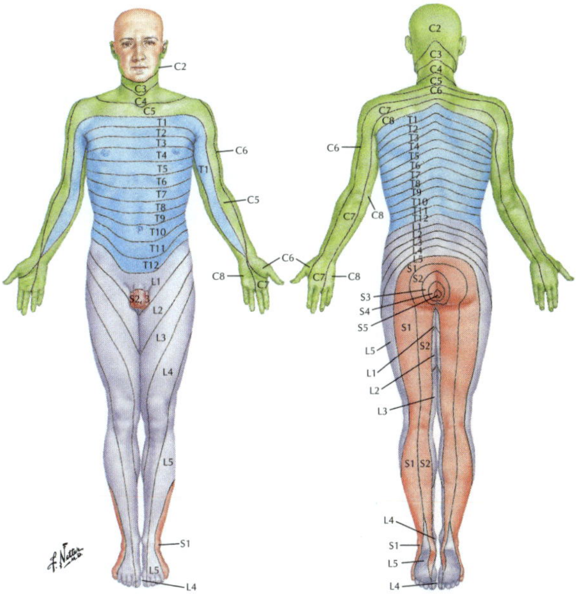

Levels of principal dermatomes

C5	Clavicles	**T10**	Level of umbilicus
C5, 6	Lateral sides of upper limbs	**L1**	Inguinal or groin regions
C8, T1	Medial sides of upper limbs	**L1, 2, 3, 4**	Anterior and inner surfaces of lower limbs
C6	Thumb	**L4, 5, S1**	Foot
C6, 7, 8	Hand	**L4**	Medial side of great toe
C8	Ring and little fingers	**L5, S1, 2**	Lateral and posterior surfaces of lower limbs
T4	Level of nipples	**S1**	Lateral margin of foot and little toe
		S2, 3, 4	Perineum

Figure 1-13. Adult Dermatomes Dermal Segmentation

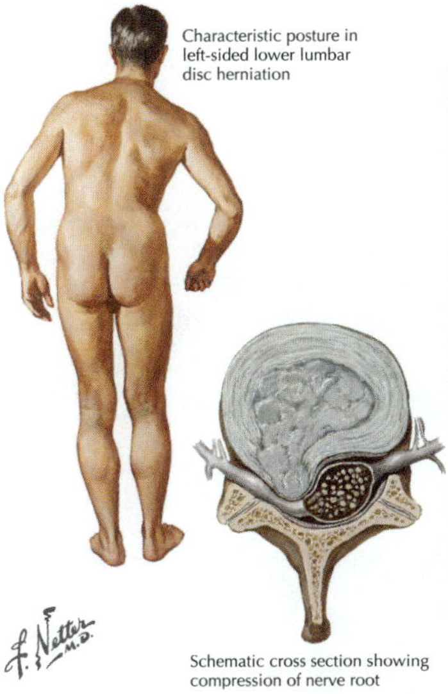

Clinical features of herniated lumbar nucleus pulposus

Level of herniation	Pain	Numbness	Weakness	Atrophy	Reflexes
L3, L4, L5, S, L5 **L4-5 disc; 5th lumbar nerve root**	Over sacroiliac joint, hip, lateral thigh and leg	Lateral leg, first 3 toes	Dorsiflexion of great toe and foot; difficulty walking on heels; foot drop may occur	Minor	Changes uncommon in knee and ankle jerks, but internal hamstring reflex diminished or absent
L4, L5, S **L5-S1 disc; 1st sacral nerve root**	Over sacroiliac joint, hip, posterolateral thigh and leg to heel	Back of calf, lateral heel, foot to toe	Plantar flexion of foot and great toe may be affected; difficulty walking on toes	Gastrocnemius and soleus	Ankle jerk diminished or absent

Figure 1-14. Lumbar Disc Herniation: Clinical Manifestations

Other potential symptoms include bladder or bowel instability, which can be associated with compression of the nerves at the lowest part of the spinal cord at approximately the T12-L1 levels, called *cauda equina syndrome*. Because this level has the origin of all of the lumbar nerve roots, injury to this level may be catastrophic. However, it is important to remember that these nerve roots continue inferiorly in the spinal canal and exit at lower levels, so some symptoms of true cauda equina syndrome can be mimicked by injuries that compress nerve roots at lower lumbar levels.

Ligament Injuries

Ligament injuries in the spine can occur in isolation of, or in combination with, injuries to the vertebrae, posterior (back or behind) elements, and/or discs; and they can have significant impact on the stability and function of the spine. Ligament injuries are broadly classified as either a sprain (defined as stretching of the ligament without any tear) or a ligament tear/rupture. For the purposes of discussing injuries to the ligaments of the spine, it is helpful to consider the commonly used three-column model of the spine.

The anterior (front) column is comprised of:

- the anterior longitudinal ligament
- the anterior disc annulus
- the anterior two-thirds of the vertebral body

The middle column is comprised of:

- the posterior longitudinal ligament
- the posterior disc annulus
- the posterior one-third of the vertebral body

The posterior column includes:

- the ligamentum flavum
- the *interspinous* and *paraspinous ligaments*
- the posterior elements of the spine (including the facet joints)

Injury to any single column is not associated with spinal instability, but injury to two or more columns results in an unstable injury that very often requires surgical stabilization.

X-ray and CT imaging does not usually play a significant role in the imaging of ligament injuries, but the presence of a ligament injury and instability can be suggested by a special set of X-rays called *flexion-extension views*. In this type of X-ray series, often colloquially called *flex-ex* views, the patient is asked to bend forward for one image and backward for another. Comparison between the two images at each level can suggest the presence of underlying ligament injury if there is shifting of vertebrae by more than 2 mm between the two views.

This shifting is called *spondylolisthesis*, which can be modified to show directionality using the terms *anterolisthesis* (forward shifting) and *retrolisthesis* (backward shifting). The presence of spondylolisthesis greater than 2 mm at any level is one cause of *spinal instability*, which often necessitates placement of surgical hardware to stabilize the spine. New spine surgery techniques are continually evolving. Traditionally, a stabilizing surgery would necessitate spine fusion. However, there are now several other surgical approaches which stabilize the spine but do not technically qualify as a true fusion.

Ultimately, these ligament injuries are best visualized by MRI, where they can be identified as either *edema* (fluid) spread throughout the ligaments in the case of ligament sprain, or complete disruptions of the ligaments in the case of complete tears (most often seen in the anterior or posterior longitudinal ligaments). Ligament injuries are most often associated with pain at the site of the strain or tear, which is often described as dull, achy, or throbbing. However, these injuries can also be associated with significant inflammation surrounding the strain/tear, which can lead to referred pain as well. Overall, ligament injuries in the spine can vary widely in severity and extent, but their presence is important to identify as it may significantly alter the patient's clinical course, and necessary treatment.

Key Takeaways

- The spine is divided into three segments: the cervical spine (neck), the thoracic spine (mid back) and the lumbar spine (lower).
- Most typical spinal injuries involve the disc and soft tissues, but if there is a fracture, the vertebrae will compress rather than snapping in two pieces like a long bone.
- Disc bulging is not a herniation, but rather the stretching of the annular ligaments.
- Disc herniations are categorized as protrusion, extrusion, and sequestration.
- Symptoms of disc injury may include pain at the site of injury, as well as radicular pain corresponding to any associated nerve compression or spinal cord/cauda equina impingement resulting from disc herniation.
- Ligament injuries in the spine can be thought of using the three-column model, wherein injury to two or more columns denotes an unstable injury. This unstable injury can result in ongoing symptoms, permanent impairment, and may require stabilization surgery.

In the next chapter, we discuss diagnostic imaging, technology, and how lawyers can be the most competent advocates for their clients.

2

Diagnosing Spine Injuries

By Orlando Micheli, MD & Peter Lowry, MD

A Note from Robert Simon

Now that you have an introduction to the anatomy of the spine, and a forever-altered outlook on jelly donuts, it's now time to look at how doctors diagnose spine injuries.

In this chapter, we will cover how to use diagnostic technology, as well as subjective information, to help your clients get the medical answers that they need, and to help you look smarter than the other side. To understand your client's injuries, it is first important to understand the scope and limits of diagnostic technology—as well as the general dynamics of the reading room and the potential influences of some radiologists.

To help with this next step, we give you, once again, wise words from Dr. Lowry and Dr. Micheli.

Picture This: Imaging Explained

To obtain a complete understanding of the extent of their injuries, the spine patient will often undergo multiple imaging exams. We will explain these in basic terms.

X-Ray

The first radiology exam that a patient usually undergoes is an X-ray—also called a *radiograph* or sometimes referred to as a *plain film*. These show bony detail well, but they are extremely limited in the level of detail that they can show regarding disc or ligament injury. In other words, these can be very useful to look for fractured bones, which is often the use case in the emergency room setting. Additionally, X-rays are often taken of the cervical or lumbar spine with the patients in different positions (termed *dynamic* or *stress* views) to analyze how the spine moves. Flexion-extension views and lateral-bending views are commonly used in this way to assess for hidden instability. Indeed, because CT scans and MRIs (discussed below) are performed with the patient lying on the imaging table in a supine position, those more detailed studies can mask instability that simple, dynamic X-rays can diagnose.

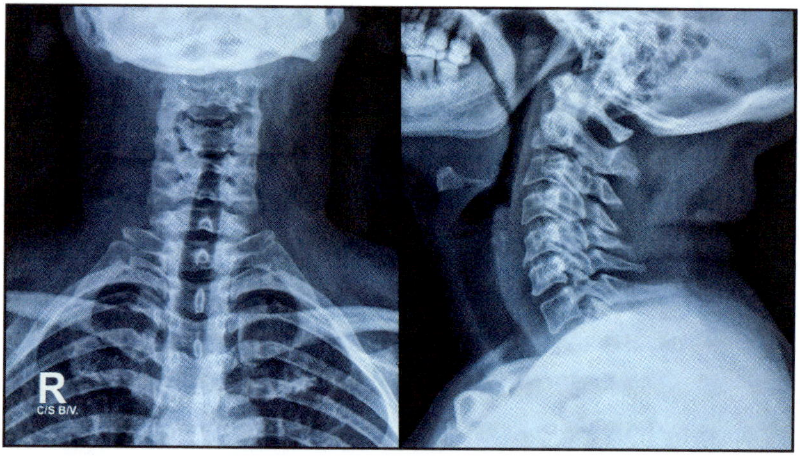

Figure 2-1. Example X-Ray
(Image © 2024 Salah Uddin. www.istockphoto.com)

CT Scan (Computerized Tomography)

If the patient's injuries are initially serious, the ER will often skip X-rays entirely and move straight to a CT scan. Think of a CT scan as an X-ray machine that spins around the patient, taking X-rays from all angles. These scans are then put together into a three-dimensional image that can be viewed in slices and oriented in any direction that you need. The standard imaging planes are *axial* (a horizontal slice through the body, which is viewed as if we were looking upward from the patient's feet), *sagittal* (looking at the patient from the side), and *coronal* (looking from the front). These images are even better than X-rays at evaluating bony structures, and furthermore, can also give some information about the soft tissues of the spine. Their utility in evaluating the soft tissues is not nearly as good as MRI.

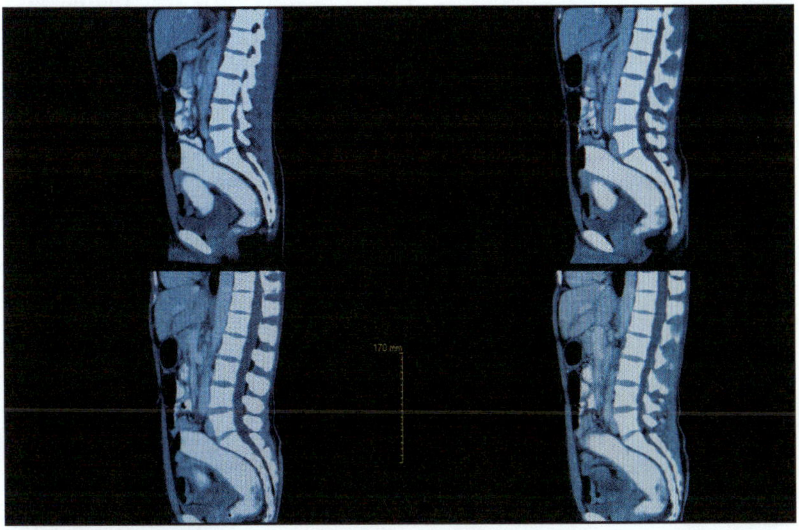

Figure 2-2. Example CT Scan

(Image © 2014 Praisaeng. www.istockphoto.com)

MRI (Magnetic Resonance Imaging)

The king of spine imaging, though, is MRI. It can provide information about the discs, spinal cord, nerve roots, and all of the ligaments and muscles surrounding the spine, which CT scans and X-rays simply cannot do. Even more, it can be used to determine the age and degree of the healing of fractures, and even find subtle early compression fractures that CT scans miss. Spine MRI, even among radiologists, can be a bit of a minefield. To describe why, it helps to take a step back and give some background into what an MRI is, and how it works.

The fact that MRI exists is, in our opinion, one of the clearest examples of human genius. In the simplest terms, MRI works by sending out an electromagnetic pulse, in the setting of a very strong magnetic field.[1] When these magnetic fields and electromagnetic pulses are applied to the human body, they have an amazing effect. Water molecules in every structure in the body are magnetically charged in an asymmetric fashion; so like the needle of a compass, one part of the molecule has a slight positive charge and the opposite side has a slightly negative one. When the magnetic pulses from MRIs hit the body, they force every single water molecule in the body to line up in the exact same way, as if they were standing at military attention. Then the pulse is removed, the water molecules are allowed to "relax," and they fall back into their normal tumbling randomness.

This relaxation occurs at different rates in different tissues of the body. Amazingly, we can measure this process and create maps of these signals, which become the pixels in the MRI through sophisticated computer processing. The pixels are different shades of white, gray, and black depending on the rate at which the molecules fall back to randomness—which in turn depends on the surrounding tissue characteristics. For example, water molecules in a muscle cell do this at a

1. Incidentally, if you have had an MRI, the loud jackhammering noises are the repetitive sending of these pulses over and over.

different rate than water molecules in the discs of the spine, which also have a different rate from those within bone.

But there's more!

Water molecules in normal muscle fall back into randomness at a different rate than water molecules in abnormal muscle. And even more confusingly than that, the parameters of the electromagnetic pulses can be adjusted to emphasize or de-emphasize certain tissue types, disease states, or injuries within tissues. The number of permutations that can occur given all these variables is astronomical.

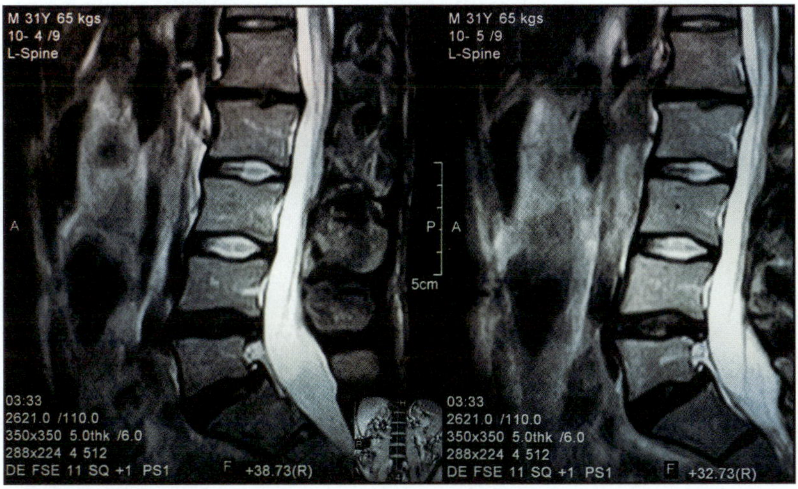

Figure 2-3. Example MRI
(Image © 2017 Marko Rupena. www.istockphoto.com)

More About MRIs

To simplify things a bit, we should first note that MRIs are organized into sets of images called sequences. Each sequence is designed to make certain things brighter and certain things darker within the grayscale images that MRIs produce. It can be helpful, then, to think of an MRI as a visual game of Twenty Questions. The reason that MRIs take a long time is that we look at the same anatomy (for example, the lumbar spine) multiple times, with each sequence asking a specific set of questions. In a typical spine MRI performed to evaluate back pain, we obtain T1, T2, and STIR (Short Tau Inversion Recovery) sequences.[2]

The T1 Sequence

Things that are bright on T1 are fat, blood (but not blood moving within blood vessels), and protein. T1 images have been called the *anatomy sequence* because they often differentiate things very clearly. The T1 sequence, then, is often used by radiologists to find their way and to figure out what structure they are looking at on one of the other sequences. One caveat regarding T1 sequences is that the spinal cord and nerve roots are not well seen, as they are dark gray in color and the cerebrospinal fluid that surrounds them is also dark gray to black in color.

The T2 Sequence

T2 sequences can be thought of as a *water map*—the brighter the structure, the more the water content. Fat has a significant amount of water within it, so fat is bright on T2 as well. Intervertebral discs in the spine, when they are healthy, also contain a great deal of water. T2 then becomes a critical sequence for examining disc health.

The STIR Sequence

Short Tau Inversion Recovery (STIR) sequence images are also very helpful in spine imaging. The goal of STIR sequence imaging is to show fluid within structures that are not normally supposed to have fluid present. When an acute injury occurs, the injured area swells (much like if someone swings a hammer and hits their thumb). This swelling is

2. For the purposes of this discussion, it is sufficient to note what is "bright" on each sequence, and how it is used to evaluate the back pain patient.

fluid and located in the tiny spaces between cells, called the interstitial spaces. In T2 imaging, fat and swelling often look similar. It can be nearly impossible to tell if a certain area is bright because it has been injured or if it is bright simply because there is fat there.

STIR sequence images are like T2 images, except they are designed to turn fat to a near black color to de-emphasize it. Turning fat to a near black color makes any swelling within the tissues stand out as bright white against a near black background—making it easy to see. Using the STIR sequence then, we can find swelling in and around the spinal cord and nerve roots, within the muscles or ligaments that stabilize the spine, and even within the bones themselves in the setting of a fracture.

Many radiologists (myself included) use the STIR sequence as the first stop when looking at a spine MRI. It simply tells the radiologist where to look, and pay more attention to, for underlying injury.

The King's Powers (& Limitations)

So just how good is MRI technology? Provided the study is performed well with the appropriate technique, and the patient is able to remain still, it's pretty damn good![3] One caveat that you may encounter is that "open MRI" studies use a different shape and much weaker strength of magnet, and the resolution and quality of these are lower than a normal MRI. Most MRI studies are performed with a magnet strength of 1.5 T (Tesla). At some specialty centers, even more high-end MRI machines can use magnets of 3.0 T. In contrast, open MRIs use a magnet strength

3. Ryan D. Muchow, Daniel K. Resnick, Matthew P. Abdel, Alejandro Munoz, and Paul A. Anderson, "Magnetic Resonance Imaging (MRI) in the Clearance of the Cervical Spine in Blunt Trauma: A Meta-Analysis," *The Journal of Trauma and Acute Care Surgery*, 64 no. 1 (January, 2008) 179-189. This large study involving spine trauma patients and imaging findings. The study found near a 21 percent incidence of abnormalities discovered on MRI that were *not* able to be detected on X-ray or CT scanning. Furthermore, in the acute trauma setting, MRI showed a 97 percent sensitivity, and a 98.5 percent specificity with a negative predictive value of 100 percent. A conclusion was drawn that a negative (showing no traumatic abnormality) MRI can be considered the gold standard for removing a trauma patient's cervical collar, aka "clearing the cervical spine."

of 0.2 to 0.5 T. The result of this is a decreased signal to noise ratio that, in layman's terms, translates to a blurrier and less detailed image. Thus, you may find that a client presents with an open MRI study that doesn't show the full extent of their injury, and subsequent findings on conventional MRI studies may not be "new" but rather were missed by the poor quality of the previous open MRI.

Additionally, MRIs are performed with the patient lying down supine, and are therefore non-weightbearing studies. As we discussed in the disc anatomy and injury sections, gravity and cushioning are significant aspects of disc function. If we position the patient supine, we change the forces that the disc normally experiences when the patient is sitting or standing upright. Therefore, it is important to remember that *normal MRI studies may underestimate the degree of disc bulging or herniation* (by up to 26 percent), as well as the associated narrowing of the spinal canal or neural foramina.[4] While upright MRI exists, it is very uncommon, and we do not know of any rigorous study that has evaluated the accuracy of normal supine MRI compared to upright MRI. It is sufficient therefore to recognize this mechanical limitation of MRI in general.

Lastly, since a human must interpret an MRI, the report itself is not perfect. MRIs are not like laboratory tests, something that is put in a machine and a numerical answer comes out on the other end. Instead, radiologists interpret MRIs—and differences in the interpreting radiologist's style, opinions, and knowledge (among many other factors)

4. D. Weishaupt, M.R. Schmid, M. Zanetti, N. Boos, B. Romanowski, R.O. Kissling, J. Dvorak, J. Hodler, "Positional MR Imaging of the Lumbar Spine: Does It Demonstrate Nerve Root Compromise Not Visible at Conventional MR Imaging?" *Radiology* 215, no. 1 (2000): 247–53, https://pubmed.ncbi.nlm.nih.gov/10751495; F. Alyas, D. Connell, A. Saifuddin, "Upright Positional MRI of the Lumbar Spine," *Clinical Radiology* 63 (2008): 1035-1048. https://www.standupmrioffltlauderdale.com/pdf/UprightPositionalMRI_ClinicalRad2008.pdf.

come into play in how that radiologist interprets images. The same MRI can be read many different ways.[5]

Several studies have examined some form of the question: if we take a patient and perform several MRIs of the lumbar spine in a relatively short period of time, can we expect similar results and similar diagnoses? Well, that is exactly what was evaluated in *The Spine Journal.*[6] A sixty-three-year-old woman with a history of low back pain and L5 radicular symptoms was evaluated in a period of three weeks, utilizing ten different MRI studies of the lumbar spine. The reported results were then tabulated and assessed for variability and error. Two of the study's authors were "spine radiologists" from different institutions, and independently reviewed the examinations and then came to a final diagnosis by consensus.[7] Across all ten study examinations, there were found to be forty-nine distinct findings.[8]

So we can state that, on MRI studies, the information is right there, in the images, almost always. But there is sufficient variability to make interpretations and radiology reports significantly different *a lot* of the time.

---

5. According to a study performed by highly qualified radiologists at Massachusetts General Hospital on abdominopelvic CT interpretation, there was disagreement between radiologists in more than 30 percent of cases. In addition, CT studies previously interpreted by the same radiologist had a disagreement rate of around 25 percent.

6. Richard Herzog, et al., "Variability in Diagnostic Error Rates of 10 MRI Centers Performing Lumbar Spine MRI Examinations on the Same Patient within a 3-Week Period," *The Spine Journal* 17 (2017) 554–61; Michael C. Fu, et al., "Interrater and Intrarater Agreements of Magnetic Resonance Imaging Findings in the Lumbar Spine: Significant Variability across Degenerative Conditions," *The Spine Journal,* October 2014, 2,442–48; John A. Carrino, et al., "Lumbar Spine: Reliability of MR Imaging Findings," *Radiology* Vol. 250, no. 1, (2009).

7. This was utilized as the exam key for comparison to the individual MRI reports. An error of interpretation in each individual MRI examination was considered to be present if a difference was encountered between the consensus exam key.

8. The authors found that the true-positive rate for these findings (sensitivity) was 56.4 percent +/-11.7 percent and the false-negative rate (misses) was found to be 43.6 percent +/-11.7 percent.

To help address this variability, most people grade things on a mild-moderate-severe scale, and will place things between these somewhat arbitrary levels, adding "mild to moderate" and "moderate to severe." I have worked with a radiologist for whom these five levels were insufficient, and he would break things down further into "mild to mild-to-moderate," "mild-to-moderate to moderate," "moderate to moderate-to-severe," and "moderate-to-severe to severe." In my opinion, this is the height of absurdity and unintentional comedy. It serves to illustrate, however, that people add their own spin to their interpretations. Understanding this becomes hugely important both medically and legally.

The Smoking Gun?

You've studied the anatomy, the disc herniation nomenclature , and are familiar with the spine. Opposing counsel can't make the disc injury disappear—it's right there on the MRI, plain as day! But they can blame the other guy… degenerative disease.

It's been studied, and studied, examined a million different ways, and then a million more. How can it be determined whether a disc herniation is related to the injury? And what in the world does *subacute* mean? OK, here we go. Briefly.

First, there are numerous studies that attempt to quantify the prevalence of degenerative disease, both symptomatic and asymptomatic, throughout the population for different age groups. Most of these studies find that at least some degree of degenerative disc disease is fairly prevalent, with one large study demonstrating a prevalence of 87 percent in individuals over the age of fifty.[9] A significant percentage of degenerative disease is either asymptomatic or minimally

9. Kjaer, P., J.L.O. Korsholm, et al. "Degenerative Cervical Spine Disease in a Large Population-Based Cohort Study." *Spine* 31.14 (2006): 1601-1607.

symptomatic. Thus, the presence of degenerative disease is expected, and it is not surprising to find that it exists. However, there are MRI findings that suggest whether a disc injury is acute, as opposed to chronic and degenerative.

Acute Disc Herniation

1. **High-Intensity Zone (HIZ):** presence of a bright signal on T2-weighted images indicating a tear in the annulus fibrosus.
2. **Disc Fragment Signal Intensity:** more commonly demonstrates isointense or hyperintense signal on T2-weighted images compared to chronic herniations, which are lower in T2 signal secondary to desiccation.
3. **Modic Type I Endplate Changes:** acute trauma can lead to Modic type I changes (edema) which are hyperintense on T2 and hypointense on T1-weighted images.
4. **Disc Contour:** the shape of the herniation can be more irregular and less well-defined in acute cases.
5. **Soft-Tissue Edema:** presence of surrounding soft tissue or muscle edema corresponding to recent injury.
6. **Contrast Enhancement:** post-contrast CT or MRI imaging can show peripheral enhancement of the herniated fragment due to inflammation or granulation tissue in acute or subacute cases.
7. **Decreases in Size on Subsequent Imaging:** an acute herniation is associated with inflammation at the time of MRI, which along with subsequent desiccation and scarring may significantly decrease the size of the herniation in the months after the initial injury.

Chronic Degenerative Disc Disease

1. **Disc Desiccation:** loss of disc height and decreased signal intensity on T2-weighted images.
2. **Osteophyte Formation:** bony growths at the vertebral body endplates, which take months to years to develop and therefore suggest long-standing degenerative changes.
3. **Modic Type II or Type III Changes:** similarly to endplate osteophytes, Modic type II (fatty degeneration) or type III (sclerotic changes) take months to years to develop and suggest long-standing degenerative disease.
4. **Disc Contour:** more rounded, well-defined margins of the herniation are typical of chronic processes.
5. **Calcification:** calcification within the disc or herniated fragment suggests a chronic process.
6. **Ligament Hypertrophy:** thickening of the posterior longitudinal ligament or ligamentum flavum.

More than that, degenerative changes can actually predispose to injury. If there is degenerative disc disease and facet joint arthritis at C5-6 and C6-7, for example, the mechanics of those levels are affected. They don't move as well, and because of that, any external force (like a car accident) puts more strain on adjacent levels than they would otherwise be subjected to. Thus, in an accident, the adjacent C4-5 (above the degenerative segment) and C7-T1 (below) levels are more likely to suffer acute injury. If we find a disc herniation at either of those two levels that has some of the acute features described above, it can be suggested that it is more likely acute.

After any acute injury, the body attempts to heal. Disc injuries heal poorly overall because intervertebral discs do not have a blood supply. Disc herniations do often gradually shrink somewhat in size after the acute injury, however. One interesting side effect of the medical care and insurance procedures that patients have to go through is that MRIs are not obtained very quickly after the initial accident. Instead, MRIs are often obtained weeks to months after the initial injury. This time frame, often called the *subacute period*, is a frequent source of questions during deposition and trial. The mechanisms and scope of imaging findings with healing are beyond the scope of this book. Suffice it to say that there is a great deal of variability in the speed with which each individual patient will heal, and to what extent their initial injury resolves.

As we will see later, building the case involves identifying these findings, but also correlating them with the rest of the story. Does the herniation correlate with the area of the patient's pain, particularly if it new-onset pain, or a change in the type or location of pain? Did the pain decrease with treatment directed at that level? Please see the following chapters for further discussion of this manner of putting it all together.

Key Takeaways

Having a basic understanding of the imaging that your client has received is important. You should also be aware of the limitations of certain modalities. For example, X-rays and CT scans are not great for visualizing the intervertebral discs, for this, you need MRI. Also, the timing in which the client receives the MRI is important. If we are looking for acute findings after an accident and the MRI is performed six months after the incident, it may not show such findings. Your expert should be able to let you know and explain such things. This is important.

A Note from Robert Simon

In the next chapter, we get to the heart of this section: how to apply what you've learned so far in trial.

3

Building Your Spine Case through Science

Now that you've had an introduction to the anatomy and imaging used for spinal disc injuries, it's now time for the fun part: how to use the information you've gained to learn more about your case and research it properly.

In this chapter, we cover many of the nuances of spinal disc injuries. You will learn what to look for from both your clients and their treating doctors. This is where you put together all those puzzle pieces to create a picture for the jury and scare the defense attorneys along the way.

One of our first hires was a patient care coordinator who was with a very well known orthopedic surgeon. He became our case manager, patient care coordinator, and now partner in most of what we do. His name is Eric Heath. If you ever need in-depth education on injuries, patient care, or need your case manager tried, he has immense insight. As you grow your practice, you should find your Eric Heath.

Seeing through X-Rays & MRIs

Routine X-rays are taken to see if there is an obvious bone problem (such as an acute fracture). X-rays can obviously be valuable in many cases, including spine cases. However, as doctors Lowry and Micheli note in the previous chapter, they are extremely limited.

Since X-rays are so limited, juries are more inclined to give substantial weight to MRI evidence. This is great if the objective findings are significant, but it can be challenging when the objective findings in the MRI are limited. As lawyers, we have to be prepared to show the jury that MRIs don't tell the whole story.

As we've previously discussed, it's important to be able to convey that spinal motion is simply not observed on MRI. Patients are imaged while they're lying down and not moving, but that's not how they live their lives. You can't look at an MRI and accurately say "this patient doesn't have symptoms." When an MRI is taken, the patient is in a static position. So if a patient's disc pinches a nerve or fires pain receptors in small nerve fibers when they move in a certain way, it won't show up on a static MRI. Diagnostics are a tool, but not the entire story.

There are two types of scans: *static* and *dynamic*. A static image, taken with an X-ray, CT scan, or MRI, shows one moment in time while the patient is totally still. With both CT and MRI, the person is on their back. An active scan shows a series of images as the patient moves from one position to another, and so it shows more depth and detail of the various parts of their anatomy while in motion.[1]

A lot of people focus too much on the findings of the spine MRI. However, we've all had cases where there's a relatively normal MRI but the client is in a ton of pain. So, what do you do with a client who is in excruciating pain, but their MRI doesn't pick up the root of the problem? Keep looking. The pain may not be coming from a disc herniation that is visible on an MRI. I usually refer the client to

1. *See* chapter 2, "Diagnosing Spine Injuries" under the section titled "X-rays."

another specialist. The kind of specialist is going to vary depending on the client's injuries. This could be an orthopedic specialist or a pain management specialist.

When dealing with substantial pain (particularly in the lower back) that doesn't seem to have corresponding MRI findings, I find that it is often a sacroiliac joint (SI joint) problem. This is the area at the lowest part of the spine, but off to the side towards the hip.[2] When the pain is not related to the SI joint, it's often other joint pain, or an issue with instability of the spine. A lot of lawyers miss these injuries because they don't pay attention to their client's symptoms, and they don't know the anatomy well enough to point the client in the right direction. A lot of lawyers assume there is a soft-tissue injury, but that's not always true. So keep looking.

As doctors Micheli and Lowry discussed in the previous chapter, dynamic or flexion-extension X-rays can also be performed to provide information about relative motion or stability of anatomic structures and can be a big help in explaining why your client continues to suffer. So it's important to be aware of this technology and use it when necessary. A client could have a perfectly normal static MRI but be in a ton of pain, and the only way to see if they have instability in their spine is to do a dynamic or flexion-extension X-ray.

Instability from Ligament Damage

Look for terms such as *spondylolisthesis* (when vertebral bodies are moving abnormally because of the potential structural compromise). Some people see words like this and gloss over them, but slow down! That could be your whole case.

A hypermobility or instability of the spine can often create pain for your client. If the vertebrae are slipping (hypermobility) or there is spinal instability, this may be a clinical indication for fusion surgery.[3]

2. *See* chapter 1, "Spine 101."

3. *See* the section titled "Ligament Injuries" in chapter 1.

Spinal instability means that the vertebra are slipping in relation to one another due to ligament and/or disc injuries, and the spine is unstable. Radiologists can determine the severity of a hypermobility or instability by measuring the translation of the vertebral body in comparison to the vertebra below. This hypermobility or instability after an injury can impinge on the nerve root, spinal cord or cauda equina. This usually occurs due to a ligament injury, but can also indicate one or more fractures.

Again, the radiologist read is a window into the bigger picture. The radiologist will be looking at the dynamic X-rays, which are X-rays taken with the patient in different positions, and you will see if the vertebra are slipping forward or backward abnormally. The MRI will not be nearly as important if you have this finding. If you have flexion/extension views showing dynamic instability, there is legal justification for damages as these are often caused by trauma.

Disc Injuries & Dermatomes

In regard to disc injuries, the defense likes to play a game where they pretend that a plaintiff must have perfect radicular pain down the perfect dermatome, which is constant, never waxes and wanes, and matches perfectly with an MRI finding.[4] This is one type of pain that can occur from a disc injury and is referred to as *discogenic pain*. There can also be referred pain in other areas from a disc injury. In practice, if you ask any doctor, pain that only follows a strict dermatome pattern is almost never the case. This is just another example of how learning the medicine will help you.

Imaging is often the foundation of any spine injury case, but it's not everything. The key to successfully trying these cases is ensuring that the right diagnostic imaging is conducted to match findings to your client's symptoms. And once you have that imaging it's important to know what to look for.

---

4. *See* "Radiculopathy and the Dermatome Map" later in this chapter.

General Spine Reports: Size Doesn't Matter

Some lawyers try these spine cases thinking they have to prove an acute, one-time disc herniation of "significant size." You don't.

Inexperienced lawyers will often tell me when looking at their client's MRI report, "well, there's a 3 mm or 5 mm herniation—so I have a solid case."

My response is usually the same, "sorry, but that doesn't really mean anything." You must look much deeper into the findings to really understand the injuries that your clients are suffering from. To truly advocate for your clients, you need to review the MRI reports and understand what you are looking at. This is what's covered in the next few sections—how to read MRI reports and what to make of them. Typically, you're not going to see images, you're going to get a written report from a doctor. Below is an example of what a typical MRI report on a disc case might look like. When you get a written MRI report from a radiologist, this is how to begin to make sense of them.

Sample MRI Report

PATIENT NAME: [Redacted] DOB: [Redacted]
EXAM DATE: [Redacted]
MODALITY: MRI
EXAMINATION: MR CERVICAL W/O

IMPRESSION

1. Mild reversal of normal cervical lordosis can be at least partially secondary to muscle spasm. Multilevel disc, facet, and uncovertebral disease of the cervical spine:

- At C2–C3, 3 mm central posterior disc osteophyte complex narrows the anterior thecal sac compatible with mild central spinal canal stenosis. There is no evidence for neural foraminal narrowing.
- At C3–C4, broad-based 2 mm posterior disc osteophyte complex and mild bilateral facet and uncovertebral hypertrophy are noted with mild bilateral neural foraminal narrowing. There is mild central spinal canal stenosis.
- At C4–C5, 2 mm posterior disc osteophyte complex and bilateral facet and uncovertebral hypertrophy cause mild right and minimal left neuroforaminal narrowing. There is narrowing of the anterior thecal sac.
- At C5–C6, 3 to 4 mm posterior disc osteophyte complex and mild ligamentum flavum buckling are noted with minimal cord deformity compatible with mild to moderate central spinal canal stenosis. There is minimal, 1 to 2 mm, retrolisthesis of C5-C6 which is likely chronic and degenerative in nature. There is no evidence for cord signal abnormality. Bilateral facet and uncovertebral hypertrophy and bony spurring cause moderate to severe right and at least moderate left neuroforaminal narrowing.
- At C6–C7, 1 to 2 mm posterior disc osteophyte complex and ligamentum flavum buckling are noted with mild central spinal canal stenosis. Bilateral facet and uncovertebral hypertrophy cause mild bilateral neuroforaminal narrowing.

2. Additional findings in the body of the report.

CLINICAL INDICATION

Neck pain radiating to bilateral upper extremities status post motor vehicle accident 2 months ago. History of surgery 2 years ago.

COMPARISON

None available to me at this time.

TECHNIQUE

Study was performed per routine institutional protocol on a 1.5 Tesla Magnet. Sagittal T1, T2, STIR, axial T1, oblique sagittal and axial T2-weighted images of the cervical spine.

FINDINGS

Minimal reversal of normal cervical lordosis at C5. Bone marrow signal is mildly heterogeneous with no focal aggressive appearing mass. There is no acute fracture or traumatic misalignment. Multilevel disc desiccation and disc height loss involving the cervical spine as well as mild anterior and posterior disc osteophyte complexes are noted. Posterior fossa structures are suboptimally evaluated. There is no evidence for cord signal abnormality.

At C2–C3, 3 mm central posterior disc osteophyte complex narrows the anterior thecal sac compatible with mild central spinal canal stenosis. There is no evidence for neural foraminal narrowing.

At C3–C4, broad-based 2 mm posterior disc osteophyte complex and mild bilateral facet and uncovertebral hypertrophy are noted with mild bilateral neural foraminal narrowing. There is mild central spinal canal stenosis.

At C4–C5, 2 mm posterior disc osteophyte complex and bilateral facet and uncovertebral hypertrophy cause mild right and minimal left neuroforaminal narrowing. There is narrowing of the anterior thecal sac.

At C5–C6, 3 to 4 mm posterior disc osteophyte complex and mild ligamentum flavum buckling are noted with minimal cord deformity compatible with mild to moderate central spinal canal stenosis. There is minimal, 1 to 2 mm, retrolisthesis of C5-C6 which is likely chronic and degenerative in nature. There is no evidence for cord signal abnormality. Bilateral facet and uncovertebral hypertrophy and bony spurring cause moderate to severe right and at least moderate left neuroforaminal narrowing.

At C6–C7, 1 to 2 mm posterior disc osteophyte complex and ligamentum flavum buckling are noted with mild central spinal canal stenosis. Bilateral facet and uncovertebral hypertrophy cause mild bilateral neuroforaminal narrowing.

At C7–T1, there is no significant central spinal canal stenosis. Minimal right neuroforaminal narrowing is noted.

Please note that this study is suboptimal for evaluation of the neck soft tissues and vasculature.

Your client may have a visible disc herniation but, if it is not close to any nerves, it might not cause any issues.[5] Your client could have a 1 mm herniation that is compressing a nerve and causing pain after an injury. We are all made differently. Don't worry about the size of the herniation, worry about how it is affecting the structures around it and the client's symptoms.

---

5. Again, remember that a disc herniation may not demonstrate an impact on the nerves on the MRI because the client is lying down, not impacted by gravity, and not moving. This often does not accurately represent the impact on the nerves or spinal cord when the client is standing, sitting, moving or lifting in their daily activities.

Impingement & Stenosis

There are other clues you should look for your clients' MRI and medical reports—words such as *impingement* or *stenosis* are a lot more telling than the estimated measurement of the herniation.

Spinal stenosis is a narrowing of the spinal canal. It can put pressure on the spinal cord and the nerves within the spine, commonly occurs in the neck and lower back, and it is often caused by age-related wear and tear. However, it is uncommon to see in patients until after their forties. It is usually labeled as *mild*, *moderate*, or *severe*. If moderate or severe, the patient may have pain and associated radicular pain. While stenosis can be pre-existing and nonsymptomatic, most everyone will agree that it can become symptomatic due to a crash or traumatic injury. Most people who have stenosis can go their entire life not knowing, and not having any symptoms. This is why when you have a client with stenosis found on an MRI, the clinical picture is everything. When the symptoms started is the best indicator to the cause or the aggravating factor that led to the need for medical intervention.

Impingement means the spinal cord or nerve roots are being pressed down on. This will cause pain and associated radicular pain. If you see this term, even defense experts will agree that a surgery is warranted. But they will likely say your client needed the surgery without the crash ever occurring, and that this impingement existed before the crash happened. This is why it's critical to match up clinical symptoms and apply the methods in the rest of this book.

Herniation & Bulge

When you see *herniation* or *bulge* in the report, you have to look and see how that herniation or bulge is affecting the nerves around it. Disc herniations can be painful by themselves. They don't necessarily have to impinge on nerves to cause pain. Is it impinging or abutting a nerve? How far into the canal is it going? Is it getting worse?

It is imperative that you read the jury instructions in your jurisdiction and tailor your case backwards from there. Key in on the aggravation of pre-existing condition instructions. In some jurisdictions, this is one jury instruction for a "prior infirm condition" (if the condition is nonsymptomatic before the injury) and a second for "aggravation" (if the client had symptoms in that area before the injury). In other states, one instruction covers both concepts. Others may have additional jury instructions for people who are medically fragile or "unusually susceptible" prior to the injury. You need to know the language of each, and how they apply to the specific facts in your cases. Because what the insurer and defense counsel may believe is a good defense can be made into an offense with the right jury instructions.

Perhaps most of your cases will be an aggravation of one or more pre-existing conditions. Like making an asymptomatic spinal stenosis hurt, cause pain, and lead to surgery. Or if a pre-existing disc bulge, which was not causing any issues, suddenly is lit up due to a car crash.

Wear-and-Tear & Trauma

These are just little signals while reading an MRI report that can help guide you. Typically, I have seen in my practice that wear-and-tear degeneration happens most often around C5–6 or C6–7—the lowest part of the neck just before we get to the thoracic spine—and at L4-5 or L5-S1—the lowest part of the back. So, whenever you see a protrusion or herniation at the levels above C5–6 or above L4–5, soon after the crash, it could indicate that the herniation is trauma related. Wear and tear may be present at those lower levels, but they can still be injured or worsened by trauma. If you are looking at an MRI and there are nice white or grayish white discs at every level of the lumbar spine, and just L3–4 is black and herniated, chances are that is traumatic and not degenerative.

Injuries also cause a worsening at areas of spine degeneration. For those people with pre-existing disc injuries, many are nonsymptomatic until they are injured.[6] We see that all the time! However, if the herniation is located at levels above those, it just offers more of a clue.

Again, we are looking for clues. These clues aid your argument. And give those twelve strangers what they need to find in your favor. (Your client must have been a helluva fraud to somehow paint just that one disc black.)

Also, look for how the disc is herniated or protruding. If it's just wear and tear over time it'll just protrude centrally. If it is pressure from gravity, it typically just pushes down. So over time the disc will just squish out in the middle. Knowing that, if your herniation is protruding to either left or to the right that can imply that it may be more indicative of acute trauma. Again, clues people! Juries love clues and so should you.

The defense that everyone has pre-existing disc herniations before trauma is based on an old medical research article from 1984 based on CT studies, when MRI was not yet used.[7] We now know that CTs should not be used to evaluate disc injuries. Later studies using MRIs have shown that the prevalence of asymptomatic disc herniations in the lumbar spine ranges from 4 to 28 percent depending upon age.[8] In the cervical spine, the research shows that the incidence of herniation in people without symptoms is only 4 percent (without a prior history of whiplash) to 8 percent for the general population regardless of whiplash

---

6. N. Bogduk and B. McGuirk, "Management of Acute and Chronic Neck Pain, an Evidence Based Approach," *Elsevier* (2006): 96–97, "no model has been proposed to explain why, or how, a intervertebral disc might become symptomatic in the absence of trauma. Indeed, it is difficult to conceive of such an explanation. There is no reason why an uninjured disc should become painful. There is no reason why age changes should render a disc painful. There is no immediate link between nociception (pain sensation) and a disc drying out or developing osteophytes. Recurrent strain, without injury, has not been demonstrated; nor has it ever been formally postulated as the reason why discs become painful."

7. S. W. Weisel et al., "A Study of Computer Assisted Tomography I. The Incidence of Positive CAT Scans in an Asymptomatic Group of Patients," *Spine* 9, no. 6 (1984): 549–51; *See* also, Arthur C. Croft, *Whiplash and Mild Traumatic Brain Injuries*, (Spine Research of San Diego Press, 2009), 159.

8. D. L. Kent et al., "Diagnosis of Lumbar Spinal Stenosis in Adults: a Meta Analysis of the Accuracy of CT, MR, and Myelography," *American Journal of Roentgenology* 158, no. 5 (1992):1135–44.

history.[9] So, even if these people did have nonsymptomatic disc herniations before (which is unlikely), the case is about a difference in the symptoms after the injury. That is where we rely upon the pattern jury instructions on prior infirm conditions and/or aggravation.

There's another philosophy that the defense bar doesn't really like called *chemical radiculitis*. If you see these words in an MRI report: *annular tear, annular fissure* or *high intensity zone*, it means there is a tear in the fibrous ring containing the disc and that could mean it is related to trauma. If you don't see any nerve impingement or nerve issues with stenosis impingement, but they have this nerve-related pain, then that could be chemical radiculitis. There is good evidence that these issues cause problems with the tiny intradiscal nerves. As a result of trauma, these small nerve fibers grow further into the disc, including all the way into the nucleus material. This results in constant irritation every time the person moves. Annular tears, annular fissures and high intensity zones can also be due to just the aging process. Again, this is why the clinical picture is so important. When did the pain start? When did the radicular pain start? And does it match up with the diagnostic imaging?

Chemical radiculitis is when the chemicals leak out from a little tear and go into the spinal canal, causing pain. There is a distinct possibility that this type of finding will never show up on an MRI. There is no specialized test to see it. Not until one goes under the knife can a surgeon see it. But it explains why the patient feels pain and is a theory that's been proven over and over again.[10] Often when you bring up to the defense experts, they will agree it is "possible" and there is literature on it, but they just do not believe in it. Well, of course they don't, because it would kill their source of insurance company income!

9. V. Giuliano et al., "The Use of Flexion and Extension MR in the Evaluation of Cervical Spine Trauma: Initial Experience in 100 Trauma Patients Compared with 100 Normal Subjects," *Emergency Radiology* 9, no. 5 (2002): 249–53 (4 percent of the population without a history of whiplash.); *See* also: Boden et al., "Abnormal Magnetic-Resonance Scans of the Cervical Spine in Asymptomatic Subjects," *The Journal of bone and Joint Surgery* 72, no. 8 (1990): 1178-84 (8 percent of the general asymptomatic population).

10. For more on chemical radiculitis, *see* Baogan Peng et al., "Chemical Radiculitis," *Pain* 127, no. 1 (January 2007) 11–16.

The only way to really prove a traumatic injury is if somebody has done two MRIs: one before the crash and one after. But that never happens. Some attorneys become afraid when they see a herniation shrink from one MRI to another. But a shrinking herniation actually helps your case, because it helps prove a recent trauma. Discs are made up of a gelatinous material that functions as a shock absorber, kind of like a Dr. Scholl's shoe insert. There is a lot of water in the disc. Over time, the disc material will resorb (remove by gradual breakdown into the surrounding material), and this especially applies to the fluid elements. When the protrusion shrinks over time, it is due to the natural tendency of resorption.

In the following example, when we compare MRI findings pre-accident versus post-accident, it means there is a high probability of a recent trauma with enough force to induce injury at the disc space, causing herniation. These are helpful tips whenever deposing a radiologist or medical doctor because these are clear cut medical matters with which you can extract concessions.

Example: Comparing to Previous Crash

Say your client's crash was in 2022. The client had another crash back in 2015, and had back pain, chiropractic treatment, and an MRI. The MRI showed that at L5–S1, there was a disc herniation that measured 1–2 mm. There is no mention of impingement or anything about the nerves. In the clinical record of the chiropractor, there is no mention of radicular pain. Then after your crash in 2022, your client complains of back pain, but now has pain going down her legs in a radicular fashion. A new MRI is done, and this time it shows a disc herniation that is 3–4 mm, and is impinging the nerve at the L5–S1 level. In this scenario, you should embrace the prior crash, the prior MRI, the prior treatment, as it proves your client had a worsening of her condition due to the 2022 crash.

Radiculopathy & the Dermatome Map

We've talked a little about what to look for in diagnostic studies and how to make sense of your client's subjective pain. In this portion, we shift to a discussion on telling their whole spine injury story. For the most part, the medical field uses these big, pretentious words to describe a very basic principle: if a nerve is irritated, you are going to feel pain, numbness or tingling sensations. That's where the concepts of radiculopathy and dermatome maps come in.

Radicular pain is when there is an irritant on a nerve at one place, which causes anticipated numbness, pain, weakness, or tingling into other parts of the body. Think of the spinal canal as a highway, and each nerve root is an exit ramp. From that exit ramp, nerve sensations follow specific lanes down into the body. As mentioned, this is also referred to as discogenic pain. (See the dermatome map picture on the following page.) So if one has an irritated nerve on the left of the C5 nerve root, you can see where it is expected to travel down the arm and into the hand or fingers. If that exit ramp is blocked either completely or partially, it will cause these feelings on the way down to the hand. Or legs. Or butt. Or feet. If you see an MRI report for a cervical spine (neck) MRI and it shows severe stenosis[11] at C5–6, go back to the clinical records before that and see if your client is complaining about these weird feelings down their arms.

Sometimes clients do not communicate these feelings to their doctors and don't think much of it. I have had many conversations with my clients where I see a report like that, then ask them if they are having these feelings in their arms. They say, "Oh my god, yes, how did you know?!" The same thing can happen with a lumbar spine (lower back) MRI. Look at it when it comes and see if it matches with the clinical records and talk to your client about it.

11. Please note that the client's nerve sensations from stenosis will often be different from the type of radiating pain, tingling or numbness in a specific area caused by a disc herniation. With stenosis the client may complain of sensations that feel like fire or ants crawling on their skin rather than just pain, tingling or numbness.

The concept of *radiculopathy* (radiating pain coming from some sort of nerve impingement in the spine that travels down a specific pathway down the body) is one that the defense bar leans on significantly. You can often hear adjusters try to tell you that there is no injury because the medical reports don't reference corresponding radiculopathy.

For example, if you send a demand letter to an insurer with medical records, you might include a report for a cervical MRI and a recommendation for future pain management or spine surgery. The insurance adjustor might respond with this:

> There is no impingement, nothing traumatic on the MRI report, your patient does not complain of pain in the chiropractic record, so none of this is related to the crash. There should have never been a cervical MRI because the patient didn't complain of pain down their shoulders. Here is your [low] offer.

For the most part, this is not true. Every person experiences spinal injuries differently; every person's body, and every crash, is unique. However, radiculopathy can help your cause if your client is experiencing something (like tingling in their toes) that corresponds clearly to an injury found in the MRI or by doctors during orthopedic and neurological tests (typically through reflexes, sensitivity testing and muscle testing for specific nerve roots).

The important issue here is to talk to your client about every new *sensation* (not just pain) that they are experiencing since the crash and, more importantly, make sure they tell their doctors about it. An early reference to radiating pain can go a long way toward the credibility of your client's complaints.

A dermatome map is the pathway of the territory that the nerve covers. As a lawyer you should see that map, look at the findings on your client's MRI, and their symptoms should somewhat match with that map. As an example, an L5–S1 herniation impinging a nerve should go down their backside, onto their calf and into their toe in the pattern seen on the dermatome map below.

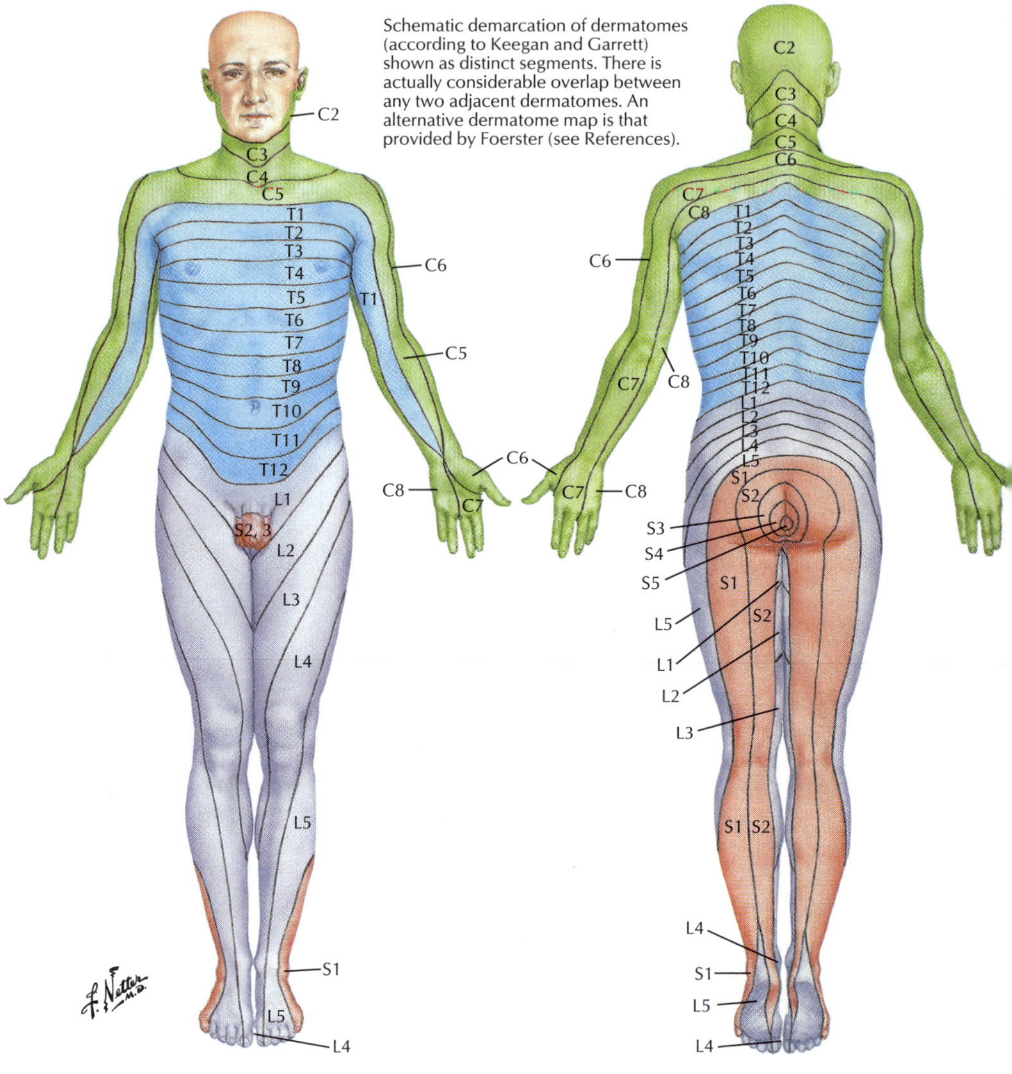

Schematic demarcation of dermatomes (according to Keegan and Garrett) shown as distinct segments. There is actually considerable overlap between any two adjacent dermatomes. An alternative dermatome map is that provided by Foerster (see References).

Levels of principal dermatomes

C5	Clavicles
C5, 6	Lateral sides of upper limbs
C8, T1	Medial sides of upper limbs
C6	Thumb
C6, 7, 8	Hand
C8	Ring and little fingers
T4	Level of nipples
T10	Level of umbilicus
L1	Inguinal or groin regions
L1, 2, 3, 4	Anterior and inner surfaces of lower limbs
L4, 5, S1	Foot
L4	Medial side of great toe
L5, S1, 2	Lateral and posterior surfaces of lower limbs
S1	Lateral margin of foot and little toe
S2, 3, 4	Perineum

Figure 3-1. Adult Dermatomes Dermal Segmentation

(Netter illustration from www.netterimages.com)

Rarely do patients in the real world have this radicular pain down the specific dermatome that matches the textbook. That is because this only addresses the discogenic pain. It is a great indicator, but most patients have dermatomes that cross over. Or the pain varies with movement. Or the pain is "referred pain."

So if your client has an issue in their lower back, at L5–S1, that hits or irritates the nerve, if you follow the highway path of the dermatome map, you will see if goes down the backside, down the hamstrings, wraps around the shin, and into the feet. However, it can be common for a patient to have this feeling wax and wane. It might be worse with activity. It might stop at the hamstrings. Sometimes the feeling will go all the way to the feet. The better you and your client understand the dermatomes, and the pain generator identified by the treating doctors, the better an advocate you will be.

But some defense attorneys will try and trick you by saying your client has to have perfect radiculopathy. They'll say it cannot wax, it cannot wane, it must be down the same dermatome in a fixed manner, and it must be textbook perfect. What they are attempting to do is mislead you and the jury by addressing only one part of the pain (discogenic) while ignoring what is well known as a secondary effect of injury; the referred pain.[12]

Any doctor who is worth their salt knows better—reality doesn't always perfectly fit the textbooks. I get defense doctors to admit this all the time to defeat the defense's entire argument. I ask them during a deposition, "How many times does as a patient actually have perfect radiculopathy?" They'll laugh and say, "Never." It's a way to defeat a defense trap if your client is educated on the dermatome map and if their pain matches up with what is seen on MRI. But also address the referred pain maps in the event the client's pain doesn't match with the dermatome map.

12. For more on referred pain, *see* Ruth Jackson, *The Cervical Syndrome*, 4th ed. (Charles C Thomas Publishers, 1978) 252–253. *See also*, Stephen M. Foreman and Arthur C. Croft, *Whiplash Injuries: the Cervical Acceleration/Deceleration Syndrome* (Lippincott, Williams & Wilkins, 2001).

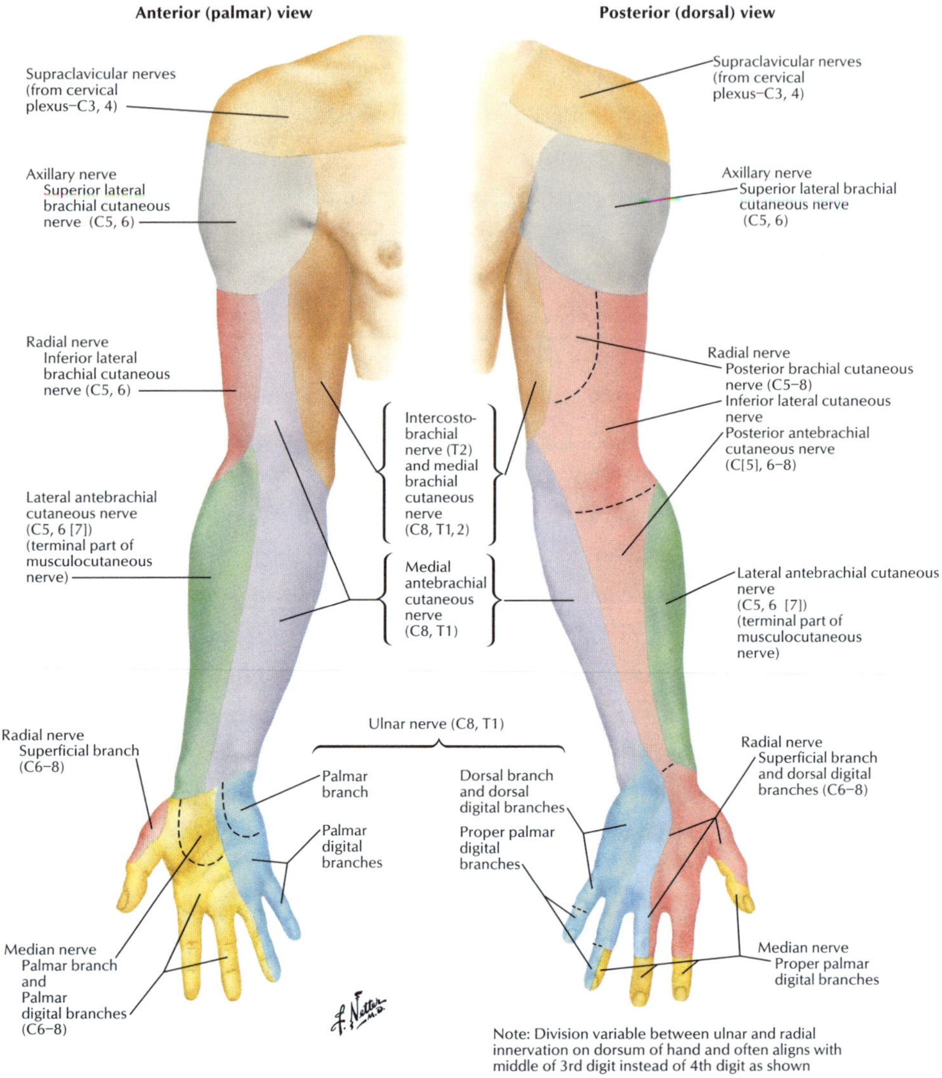

Figure 3-2. Cutaneous Innervation of the Upper Limb
(Netter illustration from www.netterimages.com © Elsevier Inc. All rights reserved.)

Often physicians will perform physical tests in the office to evaluate nerve sensation and muscle function in order to diagnose specific nerve injuries or impingement. These tests are referred to as orthopedic and neurological tests. When looking at disc injuries, these tests usually focus on sensation of the skin, reflexes and muscle strength that corresponds to a specific disc and nerve root. They are clinical validation of a disc or nerve injury that correlate with the MRI findings. Additional diagnostic tests that can be performed in order to prove the location of nerve impingement would be electromyogram (EMG) and nerve conduction studies. In the most serious cases, the patient might show physical signs of nerve injury like muscle atrophy in the region that the nerve supplies.

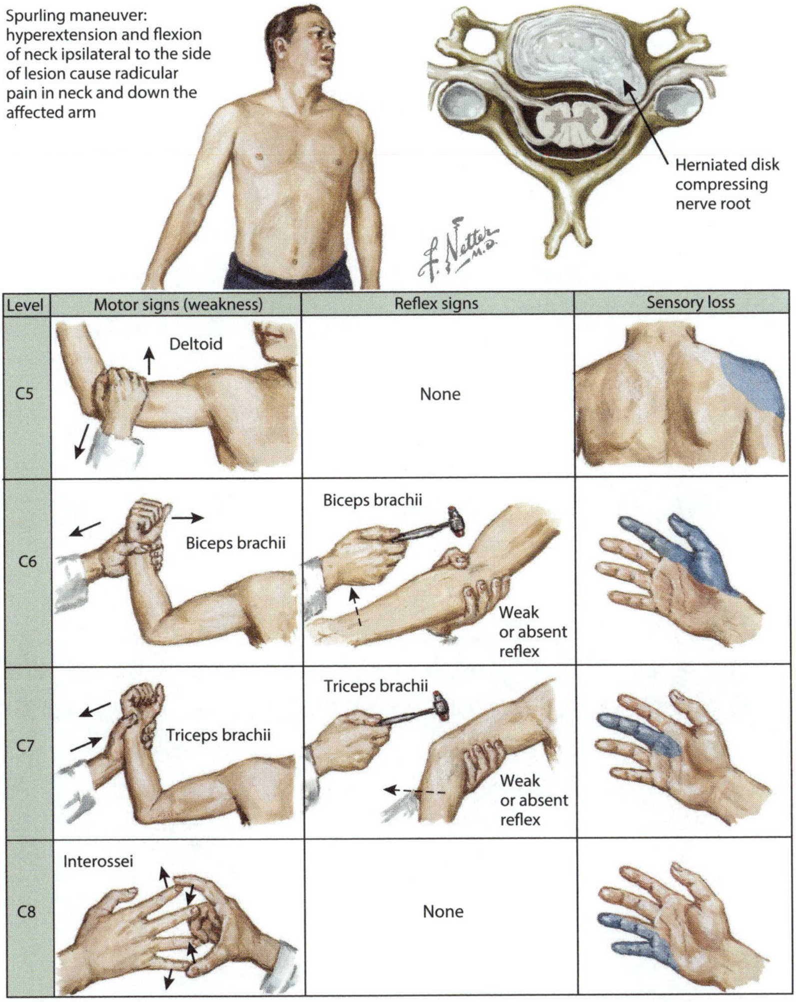

Figure 3-3. Cervical Disc Herniation: Clinical Manifestations

So the important lesson here is to talk to your client about their subjective complaints, then look at the doctor's examination, the imaging, and other diagnostic testing. In the end, who do you trust? The mechanic who just runs a diagnostic on your car and says it is fine, or the mechanic that runs a diagnostic test, gets under the hood of the car, identifies the problem, and fixes it? Sometimes doctors don't get it right. Some look for the easy answer, especially when the insurer pays them to arrive at an answer that favors the defendant.

A Note from Dr. Micheli

Integration of all available information is important and I will go more into detail on this later.[13] *However, the clinical stuff (what the patient says, signs and symptoms present, physician assessment and any available procedural/surgical data) plus the imaging (X-ray, CT, MRI and sometimes but rarely, ultrasound) should combine in such a way that proves or explains what has happened. Furthermore, when applicable, this integrated information should paint a picture of what should come next. In medicine, we call this* diagnosis. *This is a medical term commonly accepted to mean "a recognition of disease from its symptoms." When we examine the Greek etymology we find the stem of the word is:* diagignoskein *"discern, distinguish," literally "to know thoroughly" or "know apart from another." This description, in my opinion, highlights the greater complexity of the task. To make a diagnosis is far more integrative and requires more knowledge than to simply recognize a pattern.*

13. *See* Appendix B, "A Deeper Look into the Radiology Room."

Key Takeaways

- Medical imaging will not always show an injury or the severity of an injury because X-rays, MRIs, and CTs are almost always taken with the client on their back and not moving. As a result, imaging will not show the injury at its worst because it removes the impact of gravity and movement.
- The full clinical picture, before and after the event in question, along with really knowing your client and their story, trumps a lot of stuff put out there by the defense.
- Pre-existing asymptomatic bulges, osteophytes, and degenerative disc disease are very common and will very likely remain asymptomatic unless triggered by an event, like a car crash. However, pre-existing asymptomatic herniations, extrusions, and compressed nerves are not as common as insurance adjusters and defense lawyers claim. Know the science to dispute these claims.
- You need to know the pattern jury instructions in your state on pre-existing conditions or plaintiffs who are medically susceptible. Often your cases will involve asymptomatic or symptomatic conditions that were worsened by injury. Use your state's case law and jury instruction summaries in settlement and trial.
- Pain from a disc injury will not always exactly match with a dermatome due to differences between people. Discogenic pain from a radiculopathy is only one type of pain caused by a spinal injury, also consider referred pain patterns.
- If a doctor's clinical findings and imaging don't support a disc injury, keep looking. Other injuries such as hypermobility and instability can cause permanent spinal pain after an injury and may require surgery.
- Every patient is different. They feel pain differently and have different levels of pain tolerance. They also are unique in some of the medical treatments that will help them. Focus your case specifically on your individual client, and not the grouped generalities the defense tries to throw out there as absolutes.

4

Common Defense Arguments

How does the defense win? It's usually through a combination of BS and confusion. I start telling the juries this in jury selection, and I get them looking to sniff out the BS. I'll give you the defense BS soundbites first:

- "The car is not that badly damaged, so the injury is not that bad."
- "Oh look, there's a gap in treatment."
- "The MRI is not that impressive."
- "The client is a liar."
- "Unimpressive medical record."
- "No structural damage to the spine due to the accident."

The defense's game is as old as time. No matter who the client is, what their MRI shows, or whether the gap in treatment is two days or six months, the defense is going to make these arguments. There are two guarantees in the life of a plaintiff's injury attorney: death and BS defenses.

In the following sections, we will cover these common defenses one by one. We aim to provide some basic strategy for how to respond. However, in a general sense, the best strategy is to remain calm and confident in your case, know your client's injuries inside and out, and develop a storyline that you stick to until the verdict is read. And remember this: *your client is not a statistic.* Your client is an individual human with a story and specific injuries.

The Car Is Not Hurt, So the Person Can't Be Hurt

The defense loves to compare the legitimacy of your client's injuries to the damage to their car. If you have ever presented a claim to an insurance company, you have undoubtedly received this response: it's low property damage, so it was a minor impact, and we are questioning "causation." Insurance companies love this argument. That is, until you have a car with major damage, then the car damage is completely separate and provides zero indication of serious injury.

To support this wild assertion, the defense relies heavily on junk science. Junk science is made up of the crooked accident reconstructionist who manipulates calculations to benefit their position, plus biomechanical "experts" who have never found anyone ever injured in a crash. These so-called "scientists" will create the findings that they need to support their payday and line their coffers.

We will discuss how to crush these junk scientists in more detail later in the book.[1] For now, just remember this: the trick to debunking this myth is to look to and rely on *real* science, while calling out the defense on their junk science. This starts with understanding that a car does not have to be totaled in order for someone to get injured. I've won cases with just a paint scratch.

In most of these cases, the defense wants the jury to believe that had these crashes not occurred, these people would just start spontaneously having all these life-altering symptoms that necessitated serious

1. *See* chapter 11, "Defense Biomechanical Experts."

surgeries. The defense will try and connect the furthest-apart dots, but they won't look at the one right in front of them—the crash.

Defense attorneys might argue there is a direct correlation between chronic whiplash trauma and vehicle damage, or that rear-end crashes that don't result in vehicle damage are unlikely to cause injury. They are wrong, and we have peer-reviewed medical literature to back it up.

A 1999 study in the journal *Spine* determined there is no epidemiologic or scientific basis for saying whiplash is psychological or that rear-impact crashes with no vehicle damage are unlikely to cause injury.[2] Bring up this study to the defense biomechanical experts and they lose their minds. Mostly because this study cites and debunks all the studies on which the defense relies. Oh, and this one is actually peer reviewed and published in the United States.

Gaps in Treatment

When handling a spine injury case, many injury attorneys will treat a gap in treatment like it is the last nail in your coffin. It's not. Not even close. A gap in treatment is not always a bad thing or detrimental to your case. Often, it is founded in practicality, and you can easily explain it.

In addressing a gap in treatment, the trick is to bring everyone back to reality with a little dose of common sense. That is, many injured people hold off on medical attention due to a wide variety of very normal reasons. I mean, after all, very few people love going to the doctor's office. So, in dealing with a gap in treatment, talk to your client about the reason they missed that month (or two) and help make sense of the gap for the defense and, ultimately, the jury. Some common reasons for gaps in treatment include the following.

2. Michael D. Freeman et al., "A Review and Methodologic Critique of the Literature Refuting Whiplash Syndrome," *Spine* 24, no. 1 (January 1999): 86–96, https://doi.org/10.1097/00007632-199901010-00022.

Cost of Treatment

The actual cost to the client is often more concerning to the client than anyone else evaluating the claim or litigating the case. This is especially true with mounting out-of-pocket costs. The client often has to pay co-pays, co-insurance premiums, or satisfy their deductibles when seeking treatment through their personal health insurance. They may have limits on their health care coverage, or their carrier may not cover chiropractors or physical therapists. Their carrier may require that the client go through a lengthy preapproval or specific diagnosis process before getting any substantive treatment at all.

This is also often true even with *lien medical charges* (charges to be paid in the future from a settlement or verdict). After all, the client will be paying for that treatment out of whatever settlement or verdict they will eventually get. Frequently, we deal with cases with long-term or permanent injuries that also have policy limits—where the amount of the insurance available will never fully compensate our clients or even cover their lifetime of medical expenses. Policy limits and treatment caps are an understandable concern for many clients, but this is something that the rigid defense bar doesn't understand—they think that every bit of treatment is attorney-driven.

When it comes to gaps in treatment caused by the client's reasonable concerns over the cost of medical care, it's best to just be honest and relatable. Everyone has been concerned over money at some point in their lives. Unless it is their children or pets, which people tend to put before themselves. These are great voir dire questions for jurors:

Q: Who here would take their kids or pets to the doctor or vet for pretty much anything, but when it comes to you, you have to legit be dragged in or on your deathbed?
Q: Why?
Q: Will you fault my client for doing the same, based on that fact alone?

Fear of a Recommended Procedure

People often fear the unknown. This is even more true when the unknown may cause them more pain or force them to be cut open or stuck with long needles. Many medical procedures can be scary, especially when someone is already in significant pain. People are scared of needles and surgery and they often read (unsubstantiated) horror stories online about procedures. They think that a spinal procedure may cause them even more pain or leave them paralyzed.

There is also the uncertainty that a procedure will be successful. They may be concerned that they may wind up in exactly the same place but with less hope even after going through the surgery, the recovery, and incurring all of those additional medical bills.

Fear over how successful medical procedures may be is a very real thing. Most of our clients want second opinions or to continue with conservative care and wait out the surgery. It happens all the time. Remind the defense, and convey to the jury, that your client is a real person, with real concerns, not simply the sum of their documented medical treatment.

Time

One thing everyone understands is *time*. It is limited and precious to everyone. Your client has a life, kids, a job, and so on. But they are expected to be at the chiropractor every other day? Battling traffic? Missing time from work? Paying for extra childcare? Is that what the average person does? No. They live life. Sometimes they just hope the problem will go away. Most people would take their kids to the pediatrician with even a hint of a sniffle, and even their dogs if they are walking funny to the vet right away, but when it comes to themselves, they put it off. It is a hassle to get places. People are busy.

Unimpressive MRI Findings

When it comes to MRI findings, nothing seems to empower the defense more than what they consider a "lack of objective findings." While we are trying to pull you away from giving so much weight to the herniation measurement, it is what the defense lives for (unless it is significant, then they will just argue it's degeneration, but more on that later).

We constantly hear "unimpressive" MRI findings. An adjuster will read an MRI report and there will be no call outs for acute trauma, and the disc herniations are small in number. But keep in mind that the size of the herniation isn't everything. Look for potential nerve impingement and stenosis. It is not the size that matters, but how it affects the nerves and our body and causes issues. Have your client go to specialists and do other tests, such as matching a dermatome map with their symptoms or dynamic extension X-rays for possible identification of local areas of instability. These additional tests will help bring out the nuances of your client's injuries. I highly suggest sitting in on treating surgeon depositions or expert depositions. Great learning tool. Also Google "dermatome map." This will show you the levels of the spine, and if it's a nerve issue, where it travels down the body.[3]

When it comes down to conveying what your client is going through, you can't rely on MRI findings alone. You have to know your client and listen to them. You have to work to understand what your client is going through, understand the science behind these injuries, and be able to put it all together in a package that makes sense for the jury. MRI findings are not everything and are never the entire picture. And everyone will agree, you cannot see pain on an MRI! No one can see if a disc is hurting. You can even ask the defense experts:

3. *See* Appendix B for more on dermatome maps.

Plaintiff's Lawyer: Looking at this static image here, the MRI, can you tell if my client is in pain?

The answer is always no. You can see an MRI that shows a black dehydrated disc, with it herniating well into the spinal canal, with what looks like compression, and the patient may have no pain whatsoever. One patient may have what looks like a bright white healthy disc, with no herniations, and be in a ton of pain. There are no absolutes in medicine, and every individual is different. Remember, diagnostics are just a tool in the big picture. Doctors treat the entire patient and the entire body. They do not take things in a static picture vacuum like an MRI, and have it be the end all be all. Neither should you. And neither should your jury.

Your Client is a Liar!

So according to the defense, your client is a freeloading parasite using the court system as their personal ATM. They'll claim that all of this was a coordinated effort with your client's doctor and you as their attorney.

It's a really weird narrative if you think about it. Why would a person upend everything in their lives by wasting away three years to the slow grinding hands of the court system, spending thousands of dollars for an uncertain result? And how did they get their doctor to be in on it with them? What's in it for the doctor? Same for the surgeon? And the radiologist? And the hospital? And the people who wrote the jury instructions on aggravation of a pre-existing condition?

What's the obvious answer? They got hurt badly, and they had no choice but to go through hell. I don't know about you, but most people hate hospitals and courtrooms. What would you have to get paid to be poked, cut open, and spend years reorganizing your life to treat your injuries? It simply doesn't make sense. Logic is definitely your friend here.

Set the stage for this theme during jury selection. I usually ask the jurors if they are good BS detectors. I ask if they can look at a witness and see if they are some grand criminal conspirator mastermind. I ask if they can look at an expert, with a bunch of statistics, and call BS if they see it. I also throw down the credibility gauntlet from the beginning with questions like:

Q: If you believe the defense, and my client is a liar, a cheat, a fraud, and the doctors are all in on a conspiracy, can you give my client zero dollars?

Q: Okay, now the inverse, if you believe this isn't some kind of fraud, can you fully compensate them $8 million if we prove our case?[4]

In voir dire, tell the jurors to use their common sense. Then in opening, lay out all the people who need to be in the conspiracy, as alleged by the defense. Show the jury the medical timeline, describe the symptoms, show when your client first had an MRI, the surgery that was performed, and how everything matched clinically. Dare them in opening; they either believe all these simple truths or the defense's conspiracy theory.

I usually put up a graphic of two roads.

4. These are very similar methods that Rick Friedman advocates in his book *Polarizing the Case: Exposing and Defeating the Malingering Myth* (Trial Guides, 2007).

Figure 4-1. The Two Roads.

One road is simple and leads to the number we're asking for. The other is a road filled with a lot of wild assumptions. If you pick the defense's road, give my client zero. I like to show the jurors the extreme faith I have in our case from the beginning. I think it's also important in the beginning to show the villain. Usually it is the defense itself, or their experts. I tell the jury in opening how their experts say all this stuff, how the evidence will show they are just paid advocates, and their science is junk.

I usually end with telling the jury that credibility is not given. It is earned. And we will earn it by proving these simple truths.

That Single Unfavorable Medical Record

Another game the defense plays is to highlight, then point to, then reassert, then argue about that single unfavorable note in your thousands of pages of medical records. You know the one. The one time, a year before the surgery, where the stand-in physical therapist notes a pain level of two out of ten.

This is mostly fuel for the "your client is a liar" argument and is something the defense loves to find and use. It doesn't matter if your client went to two hundred doctor's appointments, each time noting continuous pain. There will be that one time when your client was feeling optimistic and downplayed their pain level. Maybe they just had an injection. Or maybe they had a really helpful chiropractic session. Or maybe they were downplaying the pain to their orthopedic surgeon to try to avoid surgery. Whatever it is, it's all too common. But it's also logical. A simple black-and-white timeline helps put it all in perspective when the defense finds one record that they think is good for them. Then you get to point out all the other records before and after. Think about the big picture here.

As we discussed in this chapter, people don't love going to doctors. They don't love the idea of injections in their spines. They typically don't love the idea of surgery. So, they often do whatever they can to avoid these things.

When responding to this assertion, it's best to just argue logic and empower your client with this indication of optimism. Make it part of their treatment story. You might say something like:

> **Mr. Simon:** For the most part, they were in pain. However, they remained hopeful that they would recover and on July 10th, 2019, they were at the height of their hope.

We prep our clients in deposition, and in trial testimony, to not be whiners and complainers. They are doing the best they can with the pain. Some days, the pain is a one or two. On their worst days, it is a nine or a ten. We talk about the good days. And the dark days. The jurors can tell your client is genuine when they talk about their good days, and their eyes light up, and they talk about living life as they normally did before the crash. And how it suddenly changes when you talk about the dark days.

Find Damages Witnesses

You can also best explain the single unfavorable medical record by using the witnesses around your client. These are called "damages witnesses." They are friends, family, coworkers, and so on. That have observed your client having a really difficult time, trying to suck it up.

- **Your client's coworker** might talk about how your client always says they are feeling great and can work without any issues. But then they see your client lying on the floor in pain, trying to hide it from everyone so their boss doesn't think they are lazy and cannot do the job.
- **Your client's spouse** might talk about how your client tells them and the kids they are fine, but they observe your client unable to sleep, with a short temper, snapping at everyone, and with heavy sighs in the shower.
- **Your client's friend** might talk about all the active stuff your client did before the accident, how happy your client was, and how they are hard to be around now because they are just constantly negative and sad.

I usually ask these witnesses on the stand, unrehearsed, to describe my client in three words as they were before the crash and in three words as they are now. It's powerful stuff. And I have noticed a common word for after: *sad.*

Jurors love a comeback story and generally don't like malingerers. Use this "unfavorable" record to tell the story of how hopeful they remained for so long, before succumbing to the inevitable conclusion that surgery was absolutely necessary. Use the people around them to paint the picture of what your client's life is really like. Jurors are skeptical of the plaintiff because they are asking for money. But if this message is coming from others with no financial interests, that is a different ball game.

Attorney-Referred Care: Your Doctors Aren't Frauds

A *lien* in a personal injury case is when medical treatment is rendered, and the provider, whether it's a surgeon, physical therapist, or hospital, agrees to defer payment without charging interest. These may be called other things in other states, like *letter of protection*, or *IOU*. These are all put in place to help the plaintiff, who might be living paycheck to paycheck. The plaintiff cannot afford out-of-pocket amounts to meet their deductible, or cash for medical care.

Often, the client is referred to these providers by their lawyers. Which makes sense, right? The clients have never been in a crash or seriously injured before, and rely on their lawyers, who have helped many prior clients, to help them find the best specialists. Despite this being a well-intended and standard practice, the defense industry wants to demonize attorneys helping people and make everyone look like a slimeball. And if you are not careful, you can lose cases on this issue.

Anticipate this *attorney-referred care* defense from the beginning. Here are some helpful tips:

- If your client has medical insurance, and the care they need is in-network, use their insurance and not a lien. If they get their treatment on a lien, then the defense can argue that the doctor is trumping up medical charges and treatment for extra money. Do not make this mistake.

- If the provider is out of network, or accepts no insurance, it is perfectly okay and reasonable to do a lien. Your client will be billed for the balance anyway, cannot afford the deductible, and if the provider is out of network, they would need a lot of cash up front for the services.
- Have your client write a letter to the defense and send it to them during discovery. Tell the defense that they are uninsured, or tell the defense the cost of an out-of-network provider for their needed surgery. Ask if the defense is willing to pay 50 percent up front now, so your client can get the cash rate. Imagine pulling that letter up in trial after the defense says the plaintiff and their lawyers inflated the medical care costs!
- Have your client get their Medicare Care notification letter early on. For any injuries caused by third parties, if there is a potential settlement, the claimant is supposed to notify Medicare whether they have it or not. Medicare has a right of reimbursement for anything paid in the past and will do what is called a "Medicare Set Aside" in the future. Medicare will not pay for medical expenses for this incident or issue in the future because the claimant is supposed to set aside funds for future medical care. Think about that. Your client now has another harm. They have a fund they have been paying into their entire life, for Medicare, and now they cannot use it for these medical issues due to the defendant's wrongful conduct. If you have letters outlining Medicare's lien or Medicare's future set aside, you can argue this to the jury. And when the defense hires that billing expert that we will talk about later, who will say your client's medical bills should be limited to the Medicare rates… Ahem. Not after what the defendant did!
- In the deposition, prepare your client to discuss why they had to go on a lien. Know whether providers are in network, out of network,

and so on. Make believe their answer will be read or played to a jury. Does it sound reasonable? Would a reasonable person do this?

Plaintiff: My deducible is $10,000. I cannot afford that. I even asked the defendant to pay it and they refused. So I had to do it on a lien. This was my only choice.

Or,

Plaintiff: I researched the best surgeons. Unfortunately, this neurosurgeon, who is the best, and does the best athletes, does not take insurance. Their cash rate was 50 percent off. I asked the defendant to help. They refused. I had no choice. And I was not going to risk paralysis by having an intern mess with my spine.

- In discovery and in the deposition, you can object to answering whether the lawyer referred the plaintiff to medical care. This information is attorney–client privilege, because it goes to the communications between the attorney and the plaintiff. You can also just own it, and make sure your client is prepared.

Plaintiff: My attorney is a spine injury specialist. I asked them for a referral. They gave me five. I researched and picked one. And thank God I listened because that surgeon saved my life!

Don't be dissuaded from helping your clients get better. Make sure they get the help that they need. Just please pay attention to how your client answers these questions because the defense will turn something genuine into something nefarious. And the messaging starts early.

Takeaways

The important thing to remember is always take a step back, breathe, and think macro and not micro. See the big picture. Our clients are human beings. They have flaws. They are not perfect. Neither is medicine. The defense is there to shoot little micro holes into our client's credibility and their medicine. Arm yourself by always zooming out and showing that you need all of the pieces in order to finish the puzzle. While these "points" by the defense may seem like big issues, in reality, the common person does not really care. Frame it correctly, attack it head on, and use your common sense—macro common sense.

5

Teaching an Old Defense Attorney New Tricks

By Steve Rosen

A Note from Robert Simon:

This chapter is written by Steve Rosen, who practices both in California and in Nevada. Steve is a respected litigator, with great experience on both sides of the table: plaintiff and defense. I choose Steve to write this chapter because of his in-depth knowledge on how the defense litigates disc injury cases. I often like to ask my ex or current defense lawyer buddies to review my cases set for trial and ask them "what I am missing?" Now here's Steve!

When Robert Simon asked me to help give the defense side for his book, my first thought was: "Finally, an opportunity to set the record straight." I started my career at a national insurance defense litigation and trial firm. I worked for some of the largest insurance companies and defended mostly corporations that were being sued for negligent acts that led to catastrophic injuries. I spent my first seven years of practice fighting (mostly) legitimate claims.

When I started at the defense firm, my mentor lawyers at that firm taught me that, for the most part, plaintiffs' personal injury attorneys are just in it for the money and that they don't really care about their clients. The pieces of advice I heard ranged from "send only objections to discovery requests" to "assume every plaintiff is full of shit." Regardless of the actual words that came from the mouths of my early mentors, the tone was very often the same: jaded. The odd thing to me was that they, for the most part, were seemingly great people with a lot of experience. So, I figured that they must be right in their very negative and cynical assertions.

I heard a wide range of various strategies from partners and supervising attorneys. As time went on, I realized that early conditioning of defense attorneys had become a standard, led by insurance company clients feeding their propaganda to those who serve them.

When leaving the dark side and starting off as a plaintiff's attorney, the ideals driven into me from early in my career were honestly some of the most difficult for me to get past—and some of the most shameful to hold onto for so long. The truth is that cynicism is a hard illness to recover from, and old habits die hard.

The takeaway: apart from wrongful death, underaged victims, or catastrophic injuries, the defense isn't going to weep for the plaintiff. And even if they have that human side (which they do), they typically aren't going to share it with you before the check exchanges hands and dismissal is filed. There is just no benefit to empathy in their line of work. It's sad, but it's also a serious opportunity to gain the upper hand early on.

As my own act of repentance, after spending nearly eight years executing the defense attorney playbook covered in this chapter, I've assembled this guide with the intention of outlining what a successful defense attorney does. However, prior to diving into specifics behind long held defense strategies, it's beneficial for you to have a basic background and understanding of the initial defense assignment and evaluation process.

Defense Intake & Initial Evaluation

When an outside counsel defense firm gets assigned a new file, it's usually assigned to a partner to oversee, a senior attorney to manage, and a newer attorney to work up. The firm typically receives a formal assignment and often just the complaint. Sometimes a claim file is sent with the assignment, which will include the prelitigation demand and the medical records.

When we received a new case, we would spend a good deal of time conducting an initial evaluation. This evaluation would lead to an early outline of defense strategies, memorialized in a lengthy initial status report to the carrier. However, as noted previously, the information we initially received was often very limited. The claim file was usually helpful, but we would often get stuck analyzing a case based solely on what was in the complaint and what we could find on the internet. We would search for the client's name on Google and social media and conduct a background check through Lexis or Westlaw. Often, we would contact counsel for the plaintiff and ask for more information to be sent informally to "help properly evaluate" their client's claim.

With this limited information, defense attorneys are expected to evaluate a claim and prepare an initial report to the carrier representative (claims adjuster), usually sent within the first forty-five days, depending on the carrier's policies. The carrier then used this report to set reserves (the amount of money earmarked for the case) and create notes that helped the adjuster track the case until it was resolved. As such, it was imperative to provide the carrier with accurate information related to liability and the plaintiff's injuries, where possible, to avoid a misunderstanding later on (for example, the adjuster thinking it's a soft-tissue case, when it was a catastrophic spine or brain injury case).

For the most part, these initial reports always included the following:

1. Background and incident facts
2. Liability evaluation and potential defenses
3. Alleged injuries and damages
4. Potential exposure
5. Evaluation of the plaintiff and counsel
6. Initial defense handling strategies and a timeline

The protocol for handling cases on the defense side was almost always the same, regardless of the allegations, injuries, or potential damages. These status reports were formulaic, and our greatest challenge was finding a new way to revise what we wrote in the last report related to recommendations for handling. In other words, we kept similar strategies from case to case and just changed some of the wording in the reports to look like it was something new, yet it rarely was.

Despite the repetitiveness of a great deal of the initial status reports, I always found it more beneficial for the plaintiff if I, as the assigned defense attorney, had more information initially. As such, it was usually in the plaintiff's best interest for their counsel to lay out the factual allegations and damages clearly. If it was a brain injury case, they should have made sure I knew it from the get-go. If I were to have to point to the number one reason I think cases proceed to trial unnecessarily, it would be due to an early misunderstanding related to the severity of the injuries or an overestimation of the viability of potential liability defenses, as outlined below.

Common Strategies for Handling the Defense

The roadmap many defense attorneys follow in defending their clients is the following, step by step:

1. Defend liability.
2. Deny causation or doubt the injuries.
3. Find inconsistencies or confuse the issues.

Generally, the best way to respond to these tactics is with confidence. Know your clients well. Know their injuries well. Get them to treat with reputable doctors without checkered pasts, and so on.

While it's unlikely that you can prevent a defense attorney from going this route (it's hard to teach an old, jaded, and overworked dog new tricks), it's incredibly beneficial to be proactive by knowing and anticipating the positions that the defense will likely take from the start. As such, much of this chapter will include advice on how to minimize the defense's strength in these positions by telling a complete story from the start and curtailing any discoveries that can veer your client's case from the complete story.[1]

Spoiler alert: keep your client's story simple and consistent.

---

1. Recently, while representing a plaintiff in a bicycle crash case, I had a defense attorney try to sell me on a trial continuance, sixty days before trial, by saying that my side wasn't ready for trial either. She noted that I hadn't deposed her defendant driver yet and had only issued a very early round of discovery. She asserted that it was my burden of proof to meet and that I, basically, hadn't done my job during discovery—on a case that she slept on for two years. My response was very simple; I asserted that I had all the information I needed to try the case before ever filing the complaint, that I knew what her driver was going to say, and that everything I still hoped to accomplish could easily be completed in a few weeks. After we got off the phone, she called me back a few hours later and paid our demand.

Throughout the rest of this chapter, we'll go through these three steps of how the defense will defend their clients.

1. Defend Liability

Liability is something that the defense rarely concedes, other than in the month before trial. If there is an argument to make, they will make it. It's the position of the typical defense attorney that proving fault is always the plaintiff's burden. Until counsel has presented evidence to establish that they have met this burden, liability isn't established.

They may say things like, "for the sake of the mediation only, we are conceding liability," or "we may, ultimately, agree to liability but I would have to discuss it with my client." No matter what they say, you should assume that they aren't going to concede liability early or easily. To limit the fight over liability where there shouldn't be one, it's important to establish a clear theory of liability from the beginning. You can do this in prelitigation and in the initial pleading stage.

Early Investigation

Plaintiff's counsel has one gigantic advantage over the defense: we get the case a long time before the other side. We usually get an opportunity to investigate the incident and review medical records long before we are ever required to file a complaint. If you want your case to run smoothly through litigation and to limit the defense's positioning related to issues like liability, or even causation, it's imperative that you take advantage of that time to build your client's case. A well-prepared plaintiff's attorney is usually a successful one. This all starts with early investigation into liability.

To ascertain the facts that you need to lay out in your complaint, it is important to investigate a client's claims properly and extensively prior to pleading the same. This often means obtaining the complete police report and investigative file, sending immediate preservation letters, interviewing witnesses, reviewing photos, reviewing Google Maps (historically[2]), inspecting the scene, and requesting any records (including public records) that you are legally entitled to request. It also often means retaining experts early to consult with on liability issues. In premises cases, we often send a civil engineer to the public site prior to filing. In car crash cases, we often retain an expert to pull the electronic data recorder (EDR) data on our own client's car. We will also hire investigators to interview witnesses, go to businesses asking for surveillance videos, run background checks on defendants, and even pull background checks on our own clients. In litigation, surprises can kill a case. So we do everything we can to limit them from popping up.

Many successful injury attorneys do all of this within the first few months of having a case, long before filing a complaint. They use the information they obtain to put together what we refer to as a "road map" of the case. Once we have a clear picture of the facts surrounding an incident and (hopefully) supporting our liability position, we will then lay them out specifically in our complaint.

As a prior "bad guy" from the defense side, I think that overwhelming defense attorneys with the strengths of your case from the onset can reap significant rewards.

Pleading Your Case

Personally, I am a fan of detailed complaints and believe that laying out facts supporting your theory of liability in your initial pleading can go a long way. As noted above, a lot of the tone of the defense is set very early in their representation. Often, they only receive the complaint and cover sheets, so laying out liability clearly in the complaint can be advantageous.

There are several actions you can take, and they start with the initial pleading stage. As noted earlier, it's important to clearly establish a simple liability story that remains consistent throughout litigation.

2. Tip: When using Google Maps, type in the address you want, move the little orange stick figure on the bottom of the map to the exact location of the incident, then "see more dates" in the black box in the top left corner. This allows you to see Google images of the location over time.

The simpler the story the better. Typically, our clients are eager to tell us why a certain crash isn't their fault. Make note of their story early on and work to obtain evidence to support their view before you ever file a complaint. In doing so, you should have plenty of specifics to include in your factual allegations. This will help deflate the typical defense positions from early on and, ultimately, streamline the discovery process.

In our complaints, we lay out specific facts and allegations that help paint a liability picture. When I was a defense attorney, this often sat very well with me. It showed confidence on the other side and even helped fill in some of the analysis in our initial reports. If there are good facts for the plaintiff, that support a particular theory of liability, don't hide them.

Example: Dangerous Condition of Public Property

In premises liability cases, we routinely cover how many times the client has been on the property, what they saw or didn't see in the past, and why we believe that the client acted reasonably at the time of the subject incident. In a recent dangerous condition of public property case, we asserted the following in the initial detailed complaint:

1. In or around September of 1997, Plaintiff moved to his current address in [City].
2. Since early 2003, Plaintiff has been an avid road cyclist.
3. Since early 2003, Plaintiff has regularly and routinely ridden his road bicycle on [Street A], from its intersection with [Street B] through its intersection with [Street C] (the "Subject Location").
4. Plaintiff estimates that in the span of the last approximately twenty (20) years, he has ridden his bicycle though the Subject Location in excess of two hundred (200) times.
5. From approximately March 18, 2021, to June 7, 2021,

Plaintiff was unable to ride his regular routes due to the need for him to rehabilitate his left knee following an unrelated knee injury earlier that year.

6. During that time, [Subcontractor] A began city approved work on the asphalt at the Subject Location.
7. After completing their work at the Subject Location, [Subcontractor A] failed to restore the asphalt to its prior condition which created a dangerous condition within the Class II Bike Lane at the Subject Location (hereinafter "Dangerous Condition").
8. On June 8, 2021, at approximately 1:40 p.m., Plaintiff rode his bicycle over the Dangerous Condition while traveling on his normal route, within the designated Class II Bike Lane, on [Street A].
9. At that time, the Dangerous Condition was covered by a shadow from a nearby electrical box, thereby blending with the roadway.
10. Plaintiff's front wheel traversed over the Dangerous Condition, causing Plaintiff to lose control and to be violently thrown from his bicycle.
11. Upon hitting the asphalt, Plaintiff suffered significant and immediate traumatic injuries to his head, lower back, neck, collarbone, and left arm, along with other substantial injuries.

In the example above, we clearly cover our theory of liability: a dangerous condition in the asphalt was created by the asphalt subcontractor failing to restore the asphalt to its original condition. In this matter, before preparing the complaint, we personally inspected the roadway with an experienced civil engineer and obtained public records (via public record request) from the subject city related to roadwork completed at and around the location. We also went to surrounding businesses and found surveillance video from a local building. In order to rule out potential notice defenses, we spoke to our client about his prior experience riding his bike through the subject location. Only after we felt comfortable with our investigation and theories, did we prepare and file the complaint.

Liability Issues in Early Discovery

A few years ago, I spoke with a good friend and great trial attorney about the actions he takes early in litigation to further cement liability. In addition to some of the strategies covered above, he added that he hammers liability issues very early in litigation to take the wind out of the defense's sails. He told me that, very often, he exploits the time between his filing of a complaint and the defendant's answer to use his subpoena power to obtain information he couldn't acquire in prelitigation. One example he gave was subpoenaing the full investigative file, including bodycam footage, from the investigating officer or authority. He said that he also subpoenas the concurrent and past medical records from his client's physicians. Once the defendant appears in the action and issues initial discovery, he (of course) provides all of the documentation he obtained via subpoena. However, if he times it right, he said that he usually has sixty to ninety days with additional information before ever having to disclose it.

Outside of issuing early subpoenas, we sometimes notice the deposition of a defendant immediately after receiving the defendant's answer, before receiving written discovery. In these instances, we insist that the deposition of the defendant happen expeditiously, and we don't relent until it occurs. While many defense attorneys will insist on the plaintiff's deposition occurring first, there is nothing in the code, that I am aware of, that requires this. We often press for the defendant to be deposed early so that it limits the time for the defendant to work with their own counsel to alter their story in a way that supports their counsel's attempts to confuse the issues.

Being Aggressive on Liability

Knowing that most defense attorneys will rarely recommend agreeing to accept liability early in litigation, I often like to take a firm approach to responding to this position. This method starts with well-written requests for admissions (RFAs). In California, we have Code of Civil Procedure § 2033.420 which allows for recovery of post-trial sanctions for having to prove an unreasonably denied RFAs.[3] Under this section, we can recover attorney's fees, litigation and trial costs, and even expert costs incurred to prove up the issue.

Even in situations where the defense counsel eventually stipulates to liability, as covered below, they rarely stipulate to causation/substantial factor. As such, it can be very advantageous to issue clearly written requests that cover each element of negligence separately. We often send these requests worded a few different ways to help eliminate the argument of ambiguity. For example, we often issue the following requests in a bike versus car crash case:

Example: Requests in a Bike versus Car Crash Case

1. Admit that on DATE of INCIDENT, YOUR VEHICLE collided with Plaintiff's bicycle.
2. Admit that YOU were negligent at the time of the INCIDENT.
3. Admit that YOU caused the incident.
4. Admit that YOU were a contributing cause of the INCIDENT.
5. Admit that YOU were comparatively negligent at the time of the INCIDENT (irrespective of any percentage, i.e. at least 1%).
6. Admit that PLAINTIFF's actions at the time of the INCIDENT were not a contributing factor to the cause of the INCIDENT.

3. Keep in mind that this varies from state to state—please research equivalent rules in your state.

7. Admit that YOU did not see PLAINTIFF ahead of you on the road before making impact with PLAINTIFF's bicycle.
8. Admit YOU operated DEFENDANT VEHICLE at the time of the INCIDENT.[4]

When we issue these requests early in litigation, we are often met with objections related to timeliness. Keeping that in mind, we frequently wait for the depositions of the plaintiff and the defendant to occur before issuing these RFAs. If the other side denies these RFAs based on timeliness after we have completed substantial discovery, we will press the issue until they provide a clear denial. This often means sending a meet and confer letter, then filing a motion to compel.

No matter the timing, we then demand supplementation of all prior discovery responses in the last sixty days of discovery. They often fail or refuse to supplement and rarely will ever change their responses to RFAs. Then, when they attempt to "stipulate to liability" before trial, but refuse to stipulate to causation/substantial factor, you can seek cost of proof sanctions if the jury finds liability on that defendant.

Outside of strategically worded RFAs and other written discovery, we press the issue of liability firmly in the deposition of the defendant and other witnesses. In cases with a defendant driver, I like to hit their witnesses with liability questions during depositions.

I ask the defendant, directly, why it's not their fault and press them on the issue. I ask questions like:

Q: Do you accept *any* responsibility for the subject incident?
Q: Do you take 100 percent responsibility?

---

4. Please note that the California Code of Civil Procedure, like many other state's regulations, requires that the propounding party define terms within each request. In this example, those terms are in all caps. For the sake of brevity, those definitions are not included in these examples.

Q: Taking full responsibility means you are accountable for all the harms and losses you caused, correct?
Q: Do you have any knowledge of the extent [Plaintiff] was injured in the subject incident?
Q: We sent [Plaintiff]'s medical records to your attorneys, have you reviewed any of these records?
Q: [If no] Why not?
Q: Do you have any reason to believe the medical providers are lying about [Plaintiff]'s injuries?
Q: Do you have any reason to believe [Plaintiff] is lying about the injuries?
Q: Do you believe that [Plaintiff] should be compensated for the injuries they sustained because of the subject incident?
Q: Are you aware that [Plaintiff]'s medical damages alone are approximately $XXX?
Q: Do you feel that you are responsible for paying those expenses?
Q: At this time, do you feel you are not responsible to pay for damages that [Plaintiff] is legally allowed to recover?
Q: As you sit here today, is it your opinion that you do not owe anything to [Plaintiff] for hitting them with your vehicle?
Q: Would you like to resolve this case?
Q: Are you aware that a statutory offer to settlement (under CCP 998) was issued and you provided no response?

These are questions that I routinely ask in a defendant's deposition. They are the type of questions that there is no great answer on the defense for. Regardless of the position that the defendant takes, you can often get great soundbites for trial. Now, defense counsel will often object to these questions. Objections vary from calling for expert opinions to improper contention questions.[5]

---

5. If you practice in California, you need to be familiar with *Rifkind v. Superior Court*, 22 Cal.App.4th 1255 (1994).

For the questions that lead to contention objections, savvy defense attorneys will then instruct their client not to answer. However, we rarely have the defense object to every question, and we often get very good soundbites from these. So, just keeping asking the next question, even if counsel seems unrelenting. For the expert opinion objections, we will then change the wording to something like:

> Q: Based on your X years of driving in the state of California, do you personally believe that…

The moral of the story here is that if you keep pressing the subject and rewording the questions based on the objection you received, you will often break through and get the deponent to respond.

On rare occasions, where the defense attorney is being unreasonably obstructive, it's sometimes worth it to toss a Hail Mary pass. On the defense side, I once had a very well-known older plaintiff's attorney ask me, on the record, during my client representative's deposition, if I would stipulate to liability. At the time, I was a young defense attorney and absolutely despised him putting me on the spot. I wasn't supposed to be the deponent and it was obviously "outside the scope" of the deposition. That being said, it was really effective for one reason: it made me realize that he knew what we all knew; liability was never going to be an issue.

I've done this on the plaintiff's side a few times since. While it's not admissible, and is relatively improper, it's always fun to see the other guy's unsuspecting face.

2. Deny Causation & Doubt Injuries

Going back to our list of how the defense handles cases, we're now onto point two: the defense will deny causation and doubt injuries. Knowing that denying liability will ultimately lead to punishment by the jurors, many defense attorneys will likely want to enter into a stipulation or other agreement regarding liability before trial, or they may just plan on not actually contesting it. Either way, it's unlikely that even a clear liability case becomes an accepted liability case before trial. And is likely that you will have to fight the liability fight for a while.

If I am going to agree to stipulate on liability, I typically push for causation to be included in some capacity. As noted in the following section, rarely are they going to agree that the crash caused your client's actual injuries (then 90 percent of the case would be over) but I have been successful in the past in pushing the defense to stipulate to duty, breach, and substantial factor (that is, that the breach led to "some injury"), though that's been a rarity. So, you might as well be prepared for that fight.

In car crash cases, property damage is always going to be perceived as more important to the defense than our side. That jadedness I told you about at the beginning of this chapter really rears its ugly head here. That is, most defense attorneys walk into a new case with some pretty strong skepticism. When the property damage doesn't pass their "eye test," they will likely turn into some wannabe biomechanical hack who is so sure that your client is full of it.

Dealing with Low Property Damage

The common thinking on the defense side is that minimal vehicle damage equals no causation. The amount of damage to your client's vehicle will likely be the second issue the defense attorney reviews. If your client's vehicle does not have a lot of visible damage, then they will push and push and push the narrative covered by Robert Simon in this book: if the vehicle is not hurt, your client can't be either.

Also, when it comes to property damage, you may notice that I said, "your client's vehicle" and not "the vehicles." This is because the amount of damage to the defendant's vehicle often doesn't seem to matter to adjusters and defense attorneys. If *your client's* vehicle isn't crushed, then they will push this narrative—regardless of the state that *either* vehicle was left in. It's rather silly and should be something that we all move past, but we never will.

When thinking of this narrative, one very large insurance company comes to mind. To this particular carrier, your client having a wrecked car is paramount to any hope for recovery. If your client's vehicle damage isn't to their liking, they will send you to the "Special Investigative Unit" (or similar name—it varies by insurer). I've handled multiple cases against this carrier where my client's vehicle damage was minimal, but the defendant's car had significant damage. Each time, the insurer sent the case to this "special" unit.

On one such matter, the insurer had pictures of the defendant's damaged vehicle but the damage to our client's vehicle was minimal. For over eighteen months, the carrier continued to claim that there was no causation; that the crash could not have led to an injury since the damage to our vehicle wasn't major. In discovery, we requested that the defendant disclose all photographs of damage to his vehicle. In the defendant's responses, there were several pictures of the defendant's vehicle damage. They were black and white and grainy. We requested the original copies and, after a short fight, received them. When we reviewed clear copies of the photos, we noticed a flat steel bar bent in one of them. We sent the photograph over to an accident reconstructionist expert we frequently use and were advised that the bent bar's name was the "impact bar." Its purpose was to absorb impact during crashes and, hopefully, limit the passenger's injuries. We enlarged that picture on foam core board with the words "if you can bend steel, you can harm a human" written in bold on the top. We brought that visual to mediation and left it in the hallway outside our door. The case settled (with a good mediator) and the parties moved on.

When it comes to responding to this narrative, just stand by your client's injuries (and common sense). Look at the damage to both vehicles and just keep pushing back.

Explaining Injuries & Causal Connections

If you want to be taken seriously by defense counsel (and you should want to), then you must understand the medical side. Use the resources in your case, especially your client's treating doctor's reports, to educate yourself. If you speak to your client and their doctors, and understand the medical side of their case, then you have a great opportunity to have an immediate advantage over the defense. An advantage that you can carry through litigation, into medical expert depositions, and ultimately into trial.[6]

When I was a defense attorney, I didn't know the medicine. And I wasn't alone, it was kind of the standard. The simple truth is that defense attorneys rarely know much about the medical issues in their cases. They don't really have the time or resources to learn them. Most of them don't attend CLEs put together by orthopedic surgeons, and most of them don't read medical journals. The only way defense attorneys really learn is through experience in other cases, and they rarely get a case with the same exact injuries.

Despite an inherent lack of medical knowledge in the defense bar, defense attorneys will adamantly deny that the crash was enough to cause your client's injuries. They will point to the property damage and use their favorite word, *degeneration*, to blame the pain on gravity instead of accepting that two cars crashing together is enough to cause painful injuries.

In responding to the inevitable causation fight, it is important to make the causal connection between the crash and your client's injuries as simple as possible. I firmly believe that the easiest fought matters are the most consistent ones. So, do proper investigation prior to filing to develop a simple argument related to causation and keep it consistent throughout litigation. The best causation arguments make sense, without the necessity of any background in medicine.

---

6. The opposite is also true: if the defense knows the medical issues in your case better than you, then you have already lost.

For example, in a recent bike versus car crash case, our causation argument was laid out as follows. We wrote this paragraph in a response to a special interrogatory sent by the defendant early in litigation.

Example: Causation Argument in Bicycle versus Car Crash Case

On September 8, 2019, Defendant took a left turn without properly yielding to Plaintiff, causing Plaintiff's bicycle to impact the front, right fender of Defendant's vehicle ("Subject Crash"). Upon impact, Plaintiff was thrown from his bicycle and landed on the hood of Defendant's vehicle before rolling to the ground. The right side of Plaintiff's head and lower back impacted the hood of Defendant's vehicle, prior to Plaintiff rolling to the ground in front of the vehicle. Plaintiff reported temporary loss of consciousness and significant pain to his right side at the scene of the Subject Crash and again at the hospital that day. Prior to the crash on September 8, 2019, Plaintiff, a thirty-five (35) year-old individual, had no history of head injury or limitations on cognitive abilities. Additionally, Plaintiff had no history of lower back pain. We have included ten (10) years of prior medical records which do not include any prior complaints of head or low back injuries, as well as a complete set of Plaintiff's post-crash medical records. Based on the foregoing, it is clear and undisputable that Plaintiff suffered an acute lumbar spine injury and traumatic brain injury as a result of the Subject Crash.

The above response to an interrogatory demonstrates a theory of causation that is both simple to understand and difficult to refute. In our response, we covered mechanism of injury, an immediate onset of symptoms, medical diagnosis, and attempt to rule out the argument that the injury was pre-existing. Concurrent with this response, we served responses to requests for production (RFP) that included all of the plaintiff's medical records for both prior and post-crash. Prior to serving this response, we called the plaintiff's treating neurologist and spoke to them regarding his injuries and the likelihood that they were causally connected to the crash.

Throughout the litigation, we continued to supplement the plaintiff's medical records as we received them. The plaintiff was recommended for a lumbar fusion after receiving epidural injections in his lumbar spine. Along with the initial responses and each time we provided a supplement to our RFP responses, we included a cover letter that offered an early deposition and early defense medical exam of the plaintiff. We continued to show that we had nothing to hide and that there should be little doubt as to causation for the plaintiff's very serious injuries.

Based on my years on the defense, I believed that this action plan would help set the appropriate tone in the defense counsel's early reports to their carrier. I wanted them to relay our confidence in the causal connection between the crash and these serious injuries, so that they would note it as a surgical/traumatic brain injury (TBI) case and set the reserves appropriately. I believe that they did, as the matter settled for seven figures during discovery.

In the same case, we sent clearly written requests for admission (RFAs) that covered causation and substantial factor. Those RFAs included the following:

Example: Requests for Admission in Bicycle versus Car Crash Case

1. Admit that PLAINTIFF suffered pain as a result of the INCIDENT.
2. Admit that PLAINTIFF was INJURED as a result of the INCIDENT.
3. Admit that PLAINTIFF suffered some form of physical injury, no matter how severe, due to the INCIDENT.
4. Admit that YOU saw PLAINTIFF hit YOUR VEHICLE'S hood at the time of the INCIDENT.
5. Admit that PLAINTIFF's body hit YOUR VEHICLE'S hood at the time of the INCIDENT.
6. Admit that PLAINTIFF's body hit the ground after hitting YOUR VEHICLE.
7. Admit that YOU saw PLAINTIFF bleeding at the LOCATION of the INCIDENT.
8. Admit that YOU saw PLAINTIFF holding his right arm at the LOCATION of the INCIDENT.
9. Admit that YOU called EMERGENCY SERVICES to respond to PLAINTIFF's injuries while still at the LOCATION of the INCIDENT.
10. Admit that YOU saw EMERGENCY MEDICAL SERVICES tending to PLAINTIFF at the LOCATION of the INCIDENT.
11. Admit that YOU saw EMERGENCY MEDICAL SERVICES treating PLAINTIFF at the LOCATION of the INCIDENT.

The purpose of the above requests was to establish early in discovery that the plaintiff was injured in this crash. Our goal in this matter was to eliminate arguments related to both fault and substantial factor, so that we would only have to bring damages to a jury if the matter proceeded to trial.

In issuing early RFAs, it is important to include a request to admit that the plaintiff was injured (in the broad sense). A lot of defense attorneys don't understand the nuance between proving substantial factor and proving the plaintiff's damages. That is, they don't necessarily understand that a single injury caused by the defendant establishes substantial factor, and that the plaintiff doesn't have to prove they suffered every alleged injury to meet this burden. Knowing this from my own experience, I continue to press that substantial factor should be accepted and not included in the eventual special verdict form. In making this assertion, I continually point to my client's right to recover the cost to prove the same, under CCP §2033.420, if they refuse.[7]

Dealing with Defense Experts

When the defense comes to you and says that their experts have opined that your client's pain is not causally related to the accident or incident, immediately hit them with reference to evidence of the acute nature of the injury and note early reference to related symptoms.

I recently told a group of attorneys that I have never seen a defense expert physician agree with the extent of the alleged injuries. That's true and was always alarming to me, but it was just a way of life on that side. Defense experts get paid to doubt our client's injuries. There were some that would make it a point to pick up the phone and call defense counsel to verbally convey their concerns and potentially unfavorable opinions. However, for the most part, we would just get an initial report disputing causation and blaming some other factor, like degeneration.

When it comes to the injuries your client alleges were caused by the crash, the best response is also the most effortless: my client says they didn't have the pain before, and they do now. Know your client's injuries, point to evidence that they are acute after the injury, and then

7. Again, research equivalents to this in your state.

just move on. Your fight regarding causation is ultimately going to be with their experts, not counsel, anyway.

Robert Simon happens to be one of the best attorneys when it comes to taking expert depositions and covers strategies for preparing for and taking these depositions. When watching him in action, I often walk away with the thought that the other side must be concerned. Follow the strategies he outlines for expert depositions, and you will be well-prepared to fight the expert fight.

3. Find Inconsistencies & Confuse the Issues

The goal of the defense is to confuse the issues and create doubt in the jurors' minds, even the slightest piece of inconsistent evidence can be valuable. In fact, the more obscure the piece of evidence, the more that MacGyver wannabe on the other side will love it and press it.

When looking for inconsistencies, the defense will often find gems in the medical records—especially the conservative care (chiropractic and physical therapy) notes. While the defense won't put much weight on the hundreds of pages of notes by the therapists each saying that the client is in unbearable pain, they will absolutely hold that one note (that happened on one random good day for your client) of a two out of ten pain rating like it's the Holy Grail.

Another source for finding an inconsistency is with limitation on activities. I listened to a great attorney that I respect very much recently say that in all his years of practice, and there are a lot of those years, he rarely ever met an injury victim that couldn't do something in particular. Think about this for a moment. Our clients often have activity restrictions—they can no longer run as fast or for as long—but how often are they left completely unable to do a certain activity? Almost never. So don't give the other side this gift of a doubt and educate your client on this issue before their deposition.

The most common ways that defense attorneys get evidence to use against your client is through *sub rosa*/surveillance and social media postings. Defense attorneys love checking your client's social media accounts. When I was on the defense side, we found some amazing photos to use against the claimant. For example, very early in my career we found a photograph on an early social media platform of an eighteen-year-old plaintiff smoking a bong. He was claiming very serious respiratory illnesses allegedly due to mold exposure. We reserved the photograph as impeachment evidence and the judge ultimately let it in. The jury later came back with a defense verdict. Jurors hate liars and love photographic evidence that plaintiffs are lying.

Sub rosa is covered at length in this book. For the most part, I agree with what Robert Simon is saying. In big damages cases, the defense attorney is almost always going to hire an investigator to stalk your client and catch them doing something relatively benign, only to make a huge deal out of it. This just further illustrates the importance of advising your client to refrain from saying they "can't" do normal activities. If they say that they "can't run anymore," you'll find yourself dealing with *sub rosa* footage of them running on the beach with their dog.

When it comes to an inconsistency, whether in a medical record or elsewhere, just own it and make it part of your client's story. They had a good day, or the therapist wrote it wrong. Either way, those good days haven't continued and that's why there are hundreds of pages saying they're still in pain.

Robert writes throughout this book that personal injury trials often come down to a contest between confusion and fact (or science). For the most part, I really agree. Coming from the defense side, we are taught to doubt, deny, and pull apart. What does this actually do? It creates confusion.

Defense attorneys often build elaborate theories of defense that pick apart the injuries, pick apart the liability, question the honesty of everyone involved, and try to then hide all of their arguments behind a veil of "common sense."

They will make assertions to the jury like:

- Why would this one record say that?
- Why would the plaintiff say she can't dance when I have a video of her dancing at her daughter's wedding?
- The only practical, sensible explanation is that she's just not that badly hurt.

Then they will throw out a lot of assertions, arguments, records, and they'll bring in hack doctors that make millions testifying only for the defense. All this is simply to create doubt in the jurors' minds by confusing the issues.

When it comes to responding to the many confusion tactics that are found in the common defense playbook, I agree completely with Mr. Simon here: just keep it honest and simple.

Takeaways

The most significant advantage that the plaintiff's side has in any action is the fact that they get the case first. By conducting a thorough investigation before you begin litigation, you can show significant strength when you start your relationship with opposing counsel. To do this, it's imperative to know the medical side of your case. Talk to your client's doctors, get your client's past medical information, and thoroughly investigate the facts surrounding liability and causation.

When the defense gets the case, it's advantageous to you for them to know your positions early. Keeping those positions consistent through discovery will place you in a good position to respond to their standard case handling routines and tactics.

Additionally, it is worthwhile to push back on their arguments or lack of understanding related to liability and causation. It is almost always better to make the case just about damages, so issue early written discovery and take early depositions that will force them to commit to a liability and causation position early. When all else fails, prepare yourself with strong RFAs that will allow you the potential to recover in post-trial motions.

6

Telling Your Client's Story

If recovering a great verdict for your client is your ultimate goal, your case should be founded on building damages. It's that simple. And building damages doesn't start a few months from trial. It starts at the intake. Knowing this is the first step for setting yourself, and your client, up for success.

At my firm, we are as careful as we can be about the clients we accept. We balance that with a strong desire to help everyone out. In the end, we spend time with our clients during intake to better understand what they are going through so we can accurately and effectively tell their story—two to three years later when trial starts. To help bridge this significant gap in time, we work to set a theme early and build on it throughout prelitigation, litigation, and sometimes even trial. A theme may evolve, but it usually stays pretty consistent. The best themes are simple. For example, Ms. Smith was hit from behind, she was injured, and she received the treatment she needed to get better.

Learn to come from a place of empathy. Find the *why* with your client. By immersing yourself with the why of your client, you will find similarities that will make you a better advocate and orator.

Identifying a Theme

Later in the book I will bring you deep into furthering themes at trial.[1] Keeping it simple is the key. Your client was hurt, the injuries make sense, and your client is still suffering. Simple, understandable, straight to the point. Right? Here are some good themes:

- **The simplest explanation is almost always true.** This isn't a conspiracy driven, complicated fact pattern as outlined by the defense. The truth is easy. Here is the truth. No red herrings. No BS. This is life.
- **Responsibility.** The defense is running from responsibility and full accountability for their actions. Full compensation is full responsibility.
- **Freedom of choice.** Your client has the right to choose the best medical providers and handle their medical care the way they choose, on their terms, and not be dictated to by the wrongdoer.
- **Human harms are to be evaluated and compensated.** We appraise everything else in life, and health is the most important. The jury has to weigh it, appraise it, and fully compensate for it.
- **If you cause or aggravate the condition, the law says you must pay.** Key in on the jury instructions, embrace aggravating the preexisting condition from the beginning, and tell the rule-following jury their tasks at hand. I have researched the law in several other states outside where I regularly practice, and there are commonalities in each one. All have laws that compensate for aggravation cases. Think about the "brittle bone" hypothetical we all had in law school. This instruction lays out a great "floor" for your injury causation argument. At worst, it is aggravation. At best, it is acute. But either way, you can impress on the jury how—without this

1. *See* chapter 16, "Opening Statement," chapter 17, "Plaintiff Direct Examination," and chapter 19, "Closing Argument."

crash—your client would have never had the extent of any injuries whatsoever over their lifetime.

- **The client is doing the best they can, they just need the jury's help.** Show the medical records of your client telling the doctors they need to get back to work, asking the doctor to please fix them. Show the client telling their doctors their frustrations at home. Show your client not being the same parent that they were before. Show your client trying to deal with the pain, trying to be upbeat, and doing their best. The doctors can then outline the best future medical care, why your client needs all of it, and how it will help get them back to work, and back to being happy.

Identifying your theme—the story you are going to tell—is the foundation for building damages in your case. Keeping your theme simple will help you win over the jury when it counts, and it will help you repel the cloud of confusion the defense hopes to bring into the courtroom.

When you are building your case early, you need your theme to be malleable. After all, your client most often doesn't even know what their injuries are or what treatment they will need when they first walk through your door. This is why continued communication is key. Speak to your client and their treating doctors throughout the client's treatment. Ask questions of their physicians. The hard, but obvious, questions, like "would this be a likely occurrence following a rear-end collision like Ms. Smith was in?"

Take a look at the themes in the previous list. They can meld into each other. If your client seems to never get better, then concentrate on the pain being real, and your client not being a liar, a cheat, and a fraud. (Rick Friedman's book, *Polarizing the Case*, does a fantastic job with this concept).[2] If your client gets better after surgery, lean into the medicine working; this is *not* a conspiracy theory, and how would your client get better if she were a fraud?

2. Rick Friedman, *Polarizing the Case: Exposing and Defeating the Malingering Myth* (Trial Guides, 2007).

We discuss the treating doctor depositions in chapter 8, "Treating Doctors." In general, remember that during the treating doctors' depositions, you can defeat the normal defenses you know are coming, all while building damages for your client. Following are some sample questions to ask a treating doctor:

Q: Doctor, my client loved to surf. What does that look like now?
Q: Doctor, my client has two toddlers. What restrictions does their injury put on them?
Q: Did they express frustration? Describe.
Q: Doctor, do you think my client was making up their symptoms?
Q: Why not? Please explain.

It is important to establish your theme before filing the complaint and starting discovery. This will help the defense counsel to trust and accept you when you relay how simple the case is during your first call with them. Make them believe it and let them know that their confusion tactics just won't work here.

Identify Jury Instructions Early

It's paramount that you are familiar with jury instructions. In California, we have CACI (Judicial Council of California Civil Jury Instructions)—our judicial council sample jury instructions.[3] Look at your state's jury instructions, and then look at them again. Know what

3. *See* "Sample Jury Instructions (California)" later in this chapter.

you have to prove right away. Then build the theme of your case to support the instructions. Here are the instructions to look into:

1. Medical Care Costs
2. Causation
3. Aggravation of a Pre-existing Condition

Medical Care Costs

How are medical care costs compensated? How are they defined? What language do you have to use to get them into evidence? In California, it is the reasonable and customary cost in the community for your specific client. The amount paid is assumed to be reasonable. So, knowing this, if the bills were paid by cash or insurance, you just need that as proof. You can do it in discovery. If bills are owed in collections or on lien, you need a provider with knowledge of what is reasonable to give testimony. They do not even have to be the doctor that provided the service.

Q: Doctor, what is the reasonable and customary cost in the community for this surgery?
Q: What about the cost for this physical therapy?
Q: MRI?
Q: Medication?
Q: How do you know?

Causation

How is causation defined in your state? What does it say in the jury instructions? In California, causation is a "substantial factor."[4] Mirror the same language from the jury instructions in your questions to the treater or retained expert.

> Q: Doctor, can you say with a reasonable degree of medical probability this injury and the need for all these treatments was caused by the crash?
> Q: Why? Please explain.
> Q: Would the same harm have occurred without the crash?
> Q: Why not? Please explain.

Aggravation of a Pre-existing Condition

Again, find pre-existing conditions in the jury instructions, see how they are defined, and use those exact words in your questions to treaters or retained experts. In some places, like Iowa, it is instruction 200.34, "previous infirm condition." Think about the eggshell plaintiff. This is similar in a lot of states. Mirror the language of your state's jury instruction in both the questioning of your experts and the defense. If your client had prior neck or back pain and sought treatment, do not run from it. Embrace it. Lean into it. They were set up for injury. Their

4. Please note that many states use "but for" causation in single event traumatic injury cases. Please review the state law and pattern jury instructions in your state to ensure your questions are posed correctly, as asking "substantial factor" questions in a "but for" causation state will not be sufficient to meet the burden of proof on causation or survive a motion. Make certain your experts understand the difference as this is a legal concept that they may not understand.

condition was made worse. Or more symptomatic. Press the treaters and the defense experts.

> Q: Had the crash never occurred, *when* would they have needed spine surgery?
> Q: Had the crash never occurred, *when* would they have had this level of pain?

Everyone will agree that is speculation. This is a gift, and it gives you legal causation.

Sample Jury Instructions (California)

Here are the critical jury instructions used in California for your reference. Remember, in every jurisdiction, some form of these instructions exist. Find them. Know them.

CACI 430: Causation: Substantial Factor

This is the "but for" test in many states—we just make it confusing for no reason.

> A substantial factor in causing harm is a factor that a reasonable person would consider to have contributed to the harm. It must be more than a remote or trivial factor. It does not have to be the only cause of the harm. [Conduct is not a substantial factor in causing harm if the same harm would have occurred without that conduct.]

CACI 3927: Aggravation of Pre-existing Condition or Disability

[Name of plaintiff] is not entitled to damages for any physical or emotional condition that [he/she/nonbinary pronoun] had before [name of defendant]'s conduct occurred. However, if [name of plaintiff] had a physical or emotional condition that was made worse by [name of defendant]'s wrongful conduct, you must award damages that will reasonably and fairly compensate [him/her/nonbinary pronoun] for the effect on that condition.

CACI 3928: Unusually Susceptible Plaintiff

You must decide the full amount of money that will reasonably and fairly compensate [name of plaintiff] for all damages caused by the wrongful conduct of [name of defendant], even if [name of plaintiff] was more susceptible to injury than a normally healthy person would have been, and even if a normally healthy person would not have suffered similar injury.

CACI 3903A: Medical Expenses-Past & Future (Economic Damage)

To recover damages for past medical expenses, [name of plaintiff] must prove the reasonable cost of reasonably necessary medical care that [he/she/nonbinary pronoun] has received. To recover damages for future medical expenses, [name of plaintiff] must prove the reasonable cost of reasonably necessary medical care that [he/she/nonbinary pronoun] is reasonably certain to need in the future.

I cannot stress this enough—*aggravation of pre-existing condition* and *substantial factor*, and *but for* are *all* legal causation, and *both* lead you to full compensation.

Here are some examples from other states below. Be sure to request these prior to the start of your trial, and make it a theme from discovery, to depositions, to jury selection, to the trial: the law protects people who have degeneration in their spines!

Iowa Uniform Jury Instructions

Iowa Uniform Jury Instruction 200.34 is titled "Previous Infirm Condition" and reads:

> If plaintiff had [a] condition making [them] more susceptible to injury than a person in normal health, then the defendant is responsible for all injuries and damages which are experienced by plaintiff that are caused by defendant's actions, even though the injuries claimed produce a greater injury than those which might have been experienced by a normal person under the same circumstances.

Arizona Uniform Jury Instructions

Here it is in Arizona, called "RAJI—Personal Injury Damages 2."

> Pre-Existing Condition, Unusually Susceptible Plaintiff
>
> [*Name of plaintiff*] is not entitled to compensation for any physical or emotional condition that pre-existed the fault of [*name of defendant*]. However, if [*name of plaintiff*] had any pre-existing physical or emotional condition that was aggravated or made worse by [*name of defendant*]'s fault, you must decide the full

> amount of money that will reasonably and fairly compensate [*name of plaintiff*] for that aggravation or worsening.
>
> You must decide the full amount of money that will reasonably and fairly compensate [*name of plaintiff*] for all damages caused by the fault of [*name of defendant*], even if [*name of plaintiff*] was more susceptible to injury than a normally healthy person would have been, and even if a normally healthy person would not have suffered similar injury.

In Texas, this is called PJC 28.9, "Personal Injury Damages—Exclusionary Instruction for Pre-existing Condition That Is Aggravated."

Example: Defense Strategy on the *Atlantic* Case

On the Paulina Atlantic case, part of the defense strategy was to try label her injuries as pre-existing. She had a few bouts of lower back pain over her life. In her MRI after the crash, she had abnormalities in her spine that take years to develop. The surgery was done on these conditions.

So how is all this related? Well, embrace the instructions above. Embrace that Paulina Atlantic, like most people in their sixties, had this condition in her spine. Most people will have back pain here and there. But these conditions can become symptomatic due to trauma. Without the crash ever happening, these conditions in Paulina's spine likely would have lain dormant, causing no pain or issues her entire life. It was but for this crash that the pain started. Because of the crash, this pre-existing condition that most everyone her age has, began to hurt. Without this crash, we can say with reasonable probability, she would have never needed any of the treatment. Or she would never have had pain like she was having.

They are legally on the hook for the worsening of the condition. Insurers try this defense on every person with an elevated age. They will try to trick the jury. If you litigate and try these cases, do not fall into the trap in thinking you need to prove an acute new injury. Both paths lead to Pittsburgh! (Or to Rome. Whatever).

Read and include these instructions in every one of your closing arguments if you are in California: CACI 430, 3927, 3928, and 3905A (Physical Pain, Mental Suffering, and Emotional Distress [Noneconomic Damage]). If you're not in California, look for similar instructions in your own state, and include them in your closing arguments. They will educate and empower the jury. Learn these instructions, use them, and build your case around them. Prepare early on to use them as your weapons during trial. In chapter 19, "Closing Argument," I will show you my actual closing with the actual slides, discuss how to effectively use these jury instructions as weapons, and discuss the words that I arm the jury with.

Takeaways

A great client, a great story, or both, can trump anything that the defense can throw at your case. Tell the story of your underdog, that could be in the shoes of any of these jurors, while using building blocks of your evidence to prove your case. Include big picture thoughts on making a compelling motion picture. The more they like their hero (your client), the more the jury will not care about all the minor inconsistencies. Your client should be the hero of your story. You, the facts, the evidence, and the law are the supporting characters to get your clients what they need to become whole. And don't forget, every story needs a villain, which we will discuss in the coming chapters.

7

Gathering the Evidence

I am minimalist when it comes to admitting evidence. I am a big believer in less is more. Keep it simple. Let the defense be responsible for making things long-winded, difficult, and confusing. Remember, confusion is a defense lawyer's best friend. So don't give any confusion to the defense.

Following is a list of exhibits we start to compile in every single case. And we do it early. You need to collate exhibits early, and you need to have a working set. They should be numbered and Bates stamped, so when treating doctors do expert depositions, the numbers match. Here is a list of the exhibits we usually compile:

- Before and after damages photos
- Medical timeline
- Surgery illustrations and animations[1]
- Past medical bill chart
- Diagnostic imaging

1. We have a standing order with a medical animation company called Multus Medical. I recommend that you find a company that you like and form a relationship with them. http://multusmedical.com.

- Police report
- Property damage—photos of both cars (or scene)
- MRI illustrations
- MRI films themselves
- MRI reports
- Surgery reports
- Expert reports
- Any medical reports that help you

In the following sections, we will discuss a few of the items on this list in detail.

Before & After Damages Photos

What are *before and after damages photos*? These photos help illustrate to the jury your client's loss. When it comes to gathering evidence to show the human loss to your client, the pain and suffering, I like to ask the client for everything and then weed through it. Clients will often self-filter what they give you. I tell them right away that they shouldn't. It is *critical* to go to their home. Ask permission to snoop around. You will find what is important to them. And what was taken from them. Dust on their surfboards. Cobwebs on their tools. Pill bottles next to the bed. Family photos galore. A map in their bedroom showing everywhere they traveled before the crash. The backyard full of weeds behind the house instead of a garden. And so on.

If they aren't self-filtering for your sake, many clients hold back personal details because they don't see them as relevant or often feel embarrassed. They will think it's embarrassing, or you will judge them if, for example, they have twelve empty bottles from pain pills in their medicine cabinet or if they have a handwritten note from a friend or family member about how they just aren't the same.

I ask my clients to give me everything. I talk to them regularly and encourage my associates to do the same. The clients tell me stories and I listen. It's pretty simple, actually. They will give you incredibly valuable information if you just seek it. Then, you use the stuff that is most impactful and works best within your storyline. If they tell you about being tired of taking so much medication, ask them if they kept the pill bottles. Or if they are heartbroken over missing that event they used to go to every year, ask for photos from prior years. Did they complain about not being able to work out as much? Ask them if they have an app that tracks their exercise or exercise classes.

Sometimes the most powerful photos are the ones that show what is missing or show your client's absence. An empty basketball court where a father and son used to play ball. Or maybe a family photo of everyone except for your client.

An effective theme will include a detailed account of the real loss your client suffered. It will go beyond physical loss and will include symbolic photos to bring the client's story together for the jury. Photos involving your client's passions (such as painting, running, or dancing) will help the jurors understand what your client has lost.

The second best are real-life photos (not those manufactured for litigation) that show the impact these injuries have had on them. Showing them even just lifting their children (or grandchildren) can be so effective when placed next to the photo of them in a wheelchair or of the family huddled around them sitting on the couch in the recent holiday shot.

Other effective photos include images that show pain, suffering, or significant inconvenience: handicapped toilets, a cane, a medicine cabinet full of medicine, the adjustable hospital bed in their home, and so on.

Damages Storytelling—In Home Visits

It is vital to learn and know the damages story of our clients during discovery. Affirmatively produce damages witnesses for the defense to depose and produce damages photos to tell their stories. Get in the habit of meeting clients in their homes, which allows you to look around and take photos. Many times, your client does not know what makes them relatable to the eventual audience of jurors, judge, or auditor. So cover all the bases. Each photo will be a trigger for a pain point, a story, and someone to resonate with the audience.

Here's an example of a client's photos taken at their home. These photos were taken during a thirty-minute meeting, which in my opinion, makes the cases worth much more. Find the hook for your client's story.

Figure 7-1. Your client's fridge is a good place to look for photos. (The faces in this example have been blurred for privacy.)

Figure 7-2. The client's personal photo of a Tough Mudder race and Tibetan flags shows her past life.

This client had bad fractures and surgeries to her pelvic area and hip. Her ob-gyn said she likely would not be able to carry a child. This will be a trigger to talk about that pain point—such as getting Christmas cards, and seeing other people's kids, which she may now never have. This story can be told either by this client directly or by her husband. This is very powerful and any juror who has struggled having kids will know this pain.

The client's photo and the Tibetan flags are more examples of what she can no longer do. She was very active. She climbed in Tibet for these flags. She won't be able to do it again.

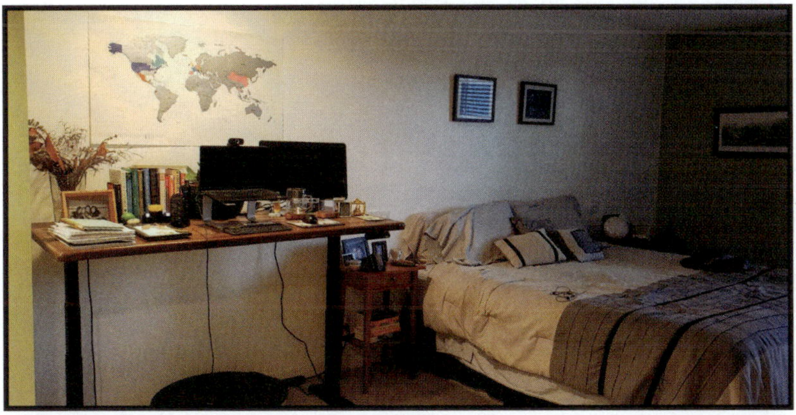

Figure 7-3. The client's home standing desk shows how she is a normal working person, but also where she can no longer travel.

A picture of the workstation in your client's bedroom can show how her life has changed. Jurors can see how she is working from home in her bedroom. She has a standing desk. She has a map of the world showing where she traveled with her husband and won't be able to again.

You must have in-home meetings with every client, before the discovery cutoff, to produce all these details and learn the storytelling hooks for your client. Assume that every case is going to trial. These photos and images will help you use the art of storytelling to re-create your client's life. Not just for you in closing, but for your client on the stand. Or their friends, family, or coworkers. Here are some more ideas.

- Put up a picture of their workstation set up from work and ask the guy in the cubicle next to your client to describe what we are looking at, and to tell some stories about your client before and after the crash.
- Put up a picture of your client and their son before the crash. Asking them to describe that day. Then a picture of a basketball game where

his son was playing, and asking your client where he was that day. How he never missed a game until this crash. And now he misses road games because he has too much pain. Then ask him if he feels like less of a father. All with that image still up.

Medical Timeline

A *medical timeline* puts all the medical events in chronological order. Every juror needs a visual. We are increasingly a visual-based society. This can become glaringly true when talking about the extent of your client's treatment to a jury. That is where medical timelines come in. Here is an example of a medical timeline that I use in every trial:

[redacted]

Medical Summary

DOI: [redacted]

11.02.2015: Admit Date: CT of C-Spine, L-Spine and T-Spine - [redacted]
11.03.2015: ER Visit - [redacted]
12.09.2015: Trigger Point Injection - [redacted]
12.09.2015: Physical therapy evaluation – [redacted]
12.11.2015: Physical therapy visit – [redacted]
12.14.2015: Physical therapy visit – [redacted]
12.16.2015: Physical therapy visit – [redacted]
12.21.2015: Physical therapy visit – [redacted]
12.22.2015: Physical therapy visit – [redacted]
01.06.2016: Physical therapy visit – [redacted]
01.06.2016: MD Visit - Dr. [redacted]
01.08.2016: Physical therapy visit – [redacted]
01.11.2016: Physical therapy visit – [redacted]
01.13.2016: Physical therapy visit – [redacted]
01.15.2016: Physical therapy visit – [redacted]
01.18.2016: Physical therapy visit – [redacted]
01.22.2016: Physical therapy visit – [redacted]
01.25.2016: Physical therapy visit – [redacted]
01.27.2016: Physical therapy visit – [redacted]
01.29.2016: Physical therapy visit – [redacted]
02.01.2016: Physical therapy visit – [redacted]
02.03.2016: Physical therapy visit – [redacted]
02.05.2016: Physical therapy visit – [redacted]
02.08.2016: Physical therapy visit – [redacted]

Plaintiff's Exhi

02.11.2016: Physical therapy visit – [redacted]
02.12.2016: Physical therapy visit – [redacted]
02.15.2016: Physical therapy visit – [redacted]
02.17.2016: Physical therapy visit – [redacted]
02.17.2016: MD Visit - [redacted]
02.18.2016: MRI of L-Spine – [redacted]
02.22.2016: Physical therapy discharge – [redacted]
03.04.2016: Initial Evaluation - [redacted]
03.21.2016: Spine evaluation - [redacted]
03.23.2016: MD Follow-up Visit - [redacted]
03.31.2016: MD Follow-up Visit - [redacted]
04.04.2016: Physical therapy visit - [redacted]
04.14.2016: MD Follow-up Visit - [redacted]
04.06.2016: Physical therapy visit - [redacted]
04.11.2016: Physical therapy visit - [redacted]
04.29.2016: Physical therapy visit - [redacted]
05.13.2016: MD Follow-up Visit - [redacted]
05.20.2016: Physical therapy visit - [redacted]
05.24.2016: Operative procedure: Lumbar epidural steroid injection at right L4-L5 transforaminal - [redacted]
05.26.2016: Physical therapy visit - [redacted]
06.02.2016: Physical therapy visit - [redacted]
06.07.2016: MD Follow-up Visit - [redacted]
07.01.2016: MD Follow-up Visit - [redacted]
07.08.2016: Operative procedure: Lumbar epidural injection at L5-S1 interlaminar - [redacted]
07.18.2016: MD Follow-up Visit - [redacted]
08.17.2016: Neurosurgical eval – Dr. [redacted]
08.17.2016: X-ray of L-Spine, CT of Lumbar, 3D post processing – [redacted]

Plaintiff's Exhibit 59-2

12.14.2016: Neurosurgical Follow-up eval – Dr. [redacted]
04.10.2017: MD follow up visit – Dr. [redacted]
04.10.2017: Pre-op consultation - Dr. [redacted]
04.10.2017: X-ray of frontal and lateral chest – [redacted]
06.23.2017: MD visit - Dr. [redacted]
06.29.2017: Operative Procedures: Transforaminal approach, left L4-5 level with facetectomy and discectomy of intraforaminal disc and far lateral disc herniation - [redacted] Center – Dr. [redacted]
06.29.2017: MD visit - Dr. [redacted]
06.30.2017: PT eval and OT eval – [redacted]
06.30.2017: MD visit - Dr. [redacted]
07.01.2017: PT visit – [redacted]
07.02.2017: PT visit – [redacted]
07.12.2017: Post-op eval – Dr. [redacted]
07.31.2017: IME Report – Dr. [redacted]
11.15.2017: Neurosurgical Follow-up eval – Dr. [redacted]

Plaintiff's Exhibit 59-3

Figure 7-4. This is a sample medical timeline showing all the treatment and events for this client.

These timelines are great for telling the complete story of your client's treatment and injuries. Have on hand a list of every visit to a doctor your client has ever had prior to and after the accident. This shows what kind of life has consumed your client.

Medical timelines are also valuable for showing the client's condition before the accident. If they had a prior back injury years before, show how many doctors they saw for that, then show the gap in time with no treatment.

This can also be valuable to cross over with *activity timelines.* If you are able to show that they were working out regularly, maybe through a workout tracking program, include a couple notes of those workouts with the gap in treatment after the last injury, then how the timeline transitions back to more medical appointments with fewer workouts.

Medical timelines are also handy for explaining gaps in treatment. Fill those gaps in with life events. Or show the procedure that immediately preceded the gap.

Let's go back to Figure 7-4. In this case (which resulted in a $3.8 million verdict), the crash happened in January of 2016, and then my client had a fall in March of 2016. The defense was alluding that this fall caused the need for her treatment, and not the crash. The defense also questioned the large, almost two-year, gap between the crash and her fusion surgery. So I put up this timeline when questioning all medical doctors, even the defense's experts. I got the defense to concede that the MRI was taken after the crash, but *before* her fall, and those findings on the MRI made her a candidate for the fusion surgery. The date of the first MRI, in February of 2016, was within six weeks after the crash and one month before her fall. In February of 2016, she was a surgical candidate. She tried everything after that point to get better and avoid surgery. She tried conservative care, rest, and even prayer. She talked about how scared she was and just hoped it would get better.

Then, using the timeline, we went back to the events before her fall in March of 2016. We showed that at those medical visits before her fall, she was complaining of weakness in her legs. Then we had the doctors explain to the jury that where she was injured, at that level of her lumbar spine, it would cause nerve damage that would affect her legs. That made her a fall risk. Her fall was due to her injury, which was caused by the crash.

These are powerful visuals to bring the jury back to your client's big picture. Doing this verbally just doesn't work—you have to *show* them. You can bring your timeline up for other purposes too.

- Show the jury when the defense doctor examined your client.
- Point out when she hired a lawyer.
- Add in the dates that the defense followed her with a video camera.
- Show the dates when the defense took mountains of depositions.

Then the jury can see all the things the defense was doing to avoid responsibility, while your client was getting medical treatment and suffering from her injuries.

Surgery Illustrations & Reports

Surgery illustrations and reports make it easier for the jury to understand what your client went through while the medical doctors are testifying. They can be for surgeries already performed or ones your client needs in the future. I use surgical animations and have them made before the depositions of the treating surgeon, or before they testify in trial if they are not deposed. The surgery illustration will allow the treater to walk the jury through the surgery, why they did it, and what is going on. Again, visuals are imperative in today's day and age. With animations, however, it is very unlikely they will be admitted into evidence. They will be used as demonstrative only.

Practice Tip: Foundation for Surgical Animations & Models

A quick note on foundation for surgical animations or models. Work with a reputable company that does animations and models, day in and day out. Send them the surgery reports, the MRI files, and put them in touch with the treating surgeon or your expert. The medical doctor will need to provide the foundation that the animation or illustration is medically accurate and demonstrative of what was performed or will be performed. This will aid the jury as well as the physician's testimony. Again, I like to get animations done far in advance. This is the same methodology if you want to create a 3D rendering or a physical model of your client's actual spine.

Here is an example of a medical illustration slide I have used in trial.

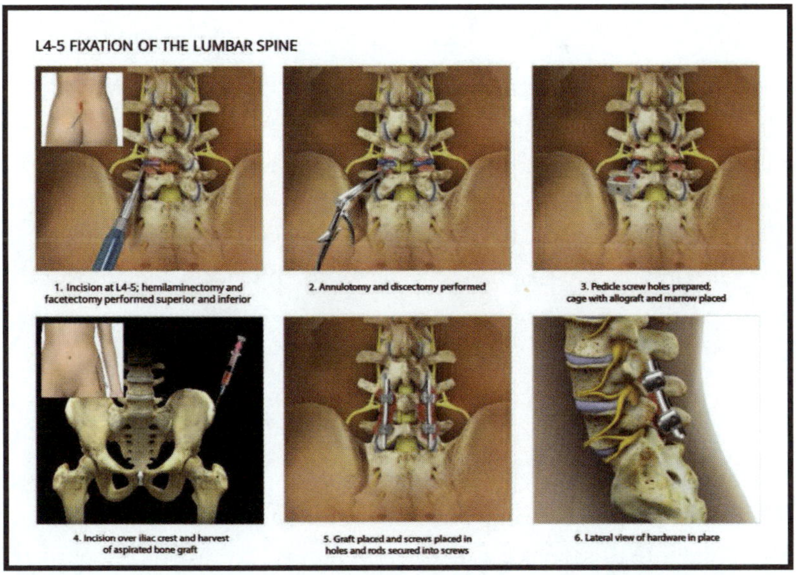

Figure 7-5. This slide shows surgery illustrations created by a medical illustration company and verified by the client's treating doctor.

Use illustrations like this in conjunction with the surgery reports. Definitely read these reports! There can be signs of trauma in a report that could help your case. Then get the surgeon to lay the foundation for a report to admit it into evidence. These reports can also defeat the defense when the defense's expert says, "I saw no indication for surgery based on the MRI report." But if the client's own surgeon saw compression during surgery, wouldn't that be more reliable than the film? If the surgeon saw disc fragment material during surgery, guess what was just proved to be traumatic, or an aggravation? Read the report. Look up terms you do not know. Talk to your client's surgeon well in advance of trial or deposition.

Here is an example of a portion of a surgery report from a trial that I conducted:

Example: Portion of a Surgery Report

Specific Findings: During our dissection, there was an acute disc herniation that was clearly noted on the right side going into the foramen of C5–6. Also, there was a disc fragment that pushed on the spinal cord on the right side. This disc herniation had to be removed to decompress the cord and the nerve. The signals for C6 came back to normal on both sides. The right side was more affected at the beginning of the operation with decreased aptitude, which again came back to normal. There was some osteophyte centrally at C5–6 that had to be removed. The side where the disc herniation was free of osteophytes on the right side.

Look at the gold in this report. The defense in this case was harping on their experts' opinions that they did not see any need for surgery looking at the MRIs. They did not see any nerve compression. They also opined that any need for the surgery was just due to the patient's degenerative condition. Instead, look what we found.

- **"Disc Fragment that pushed on the spinal cord on the right side."** This is not normal. When I asked the treating surgeon about this, he opined that the subject crash broke a part of the disc off, and when it was out, it pushed on the spinal cord. It was on the right side, and he explained how this matched with his patient's complaints of right-side neck pain, and pain going down her right arm.

Practice Tip

See if the surgeon sent anything after surgery to pathology. Many times, the surgeon will send things to pathology, and they will take a photo of anything removed during surgery. Get the full records from the hospital and surgery center. You might get lucky and someone took a photo of a disc fragment when it was sent to pathology. Now that is a powerful exhibit!

- **"...decompress the nerve and the cord."** The surgeon explained that during surgery, he observed the compression and removed the pressure. So much for the defense experts' opinions about no compression now! Your client would have to be a heck of a fraud to pull this off—actually faking compression in her neck while under anesthesia during surgery.
- **Nerve signals "back to normal."** During surgery, surgeons will many times use nerve conduction studies, in real time, to see if there is a delay in the nerve conduction passing through the area where they are doing surgery. In this report, when the surgeon writes that there was "decreased amplitude" before the surgery and that the nerve conduction is "back to normal," he is telling the reader that the nerve function was not normal before the surgery but was normal after the surgery. See the sentence "[t]his disc herniation had to be removed to decompress the cord and the nerve." This means the spinal cord and nerve were compressed and not working correctly

before the disc surgery, but after he pulled that disc material off the nerve, then the nerve was free-flowing again. So pull up this report, have the surgeon read it, verify he wrote it, then ask him what it means. The defense cannot recover from this.

It is imperative that you speak to your client's treating doctors. Show them their records, ask their opinions, and ask what helps prove their opinions. They are a wealth of information, and if they are armed with demonstratives, it makes their testimony all the more powerful.

Past Medical Bill Chart

One of the items of damages for your client is past and future medical expenses. Depending on your jurisdiction there are varying ways to get these expenses into evidence. They are:

- **Stipulation.** The easiest and simplest way to get past and future medical expenses into evidence is to work with the defense and stipulate to the amount of the past medical specials. In my opinion, the real value in these cases are the general/noneconomic damages. So do not think you have to fight for every penny of the medical bills. Think big picture. By agreeing on a lower value and coming to a compromise with the defense, you may save credibility with the jury, and you certainly will save your client money. Needing experts to opine on the cost of medical care is expensive. Take the haircut (with the client's permission), and move on.
- **Medical doctor or expert testimony.** Anyone with knowledge of the cost of medical care and what is reasonable value can opine on this subject. I usually start by asking if they know the reasonable and customary cost for fill-in-the-blank medical procedures and can verify that the procedure was medically necessary. Then I

ask them how they know. Usually, they discuss their experience as a professional in seeing all these bills, setting pricing, and knowing what providers accept. Then just ask them the cost for each item the client had. Then ask them if they reviewed the bills and if they believe them to be reasonable. Sometimes the bills will be higher that what they think is reasonable, and that is okay. I do this while having an exhibit on the screen, to show the jury all the medical care costs, itemized out. Here is an example:

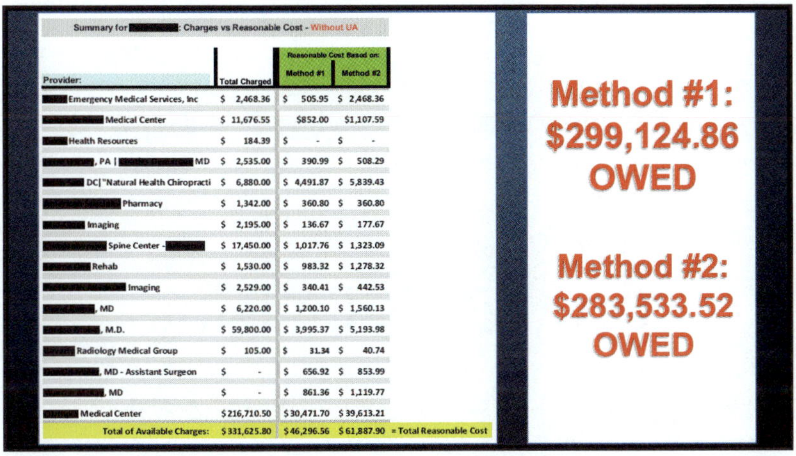

Summary for [redacted]: Charges vs Reasonable Cost - Without UA

Provider:	Total Charged	Reasonable Cost Based on: Method #1	Method #2	
[redacted] Emergency Medical Services, Inc	$ 2,468.36	$ 505.95	$ 2,468.36	
[redacted] Medical Center	$ 11,676.55	$852.00	$1,107.59	
[redacted] Health Resources	$ 184.39	$ -	$ -	
[redacted], PA | [redacted] MD	$ 2,535.00	$ 390.99	$ 508.29	
[redacted] DC|"Natural Health Chiropracti	$ 6,880.00	$ 4,491.87	$ 5,839.43	
[redacted] Pharmacy	$ 1,342.00	$ 360.80	$ 360.80	
[redacted] Imaging	$ 2,195.00	$ 136.67	$ 177.67	
[redacted] Spine Center - [redacted]	$ 17,450.00	$ 1,017.76	$ 1,323.09	
[redacted] Rehab	$ 1,530.00	$ 983.32	$ 1,278.32	
[redacted] Imaging	$ 2,529.00	$ 340.41	$ 442.53	
[redacted], MD	$ 6,220.00	$ 1,200.10	$ 1,560.13	
[redacted], M.D.	$ 59,800.00	$ 3,995.37	$ 5,193.98	
[redacted] Radiology Medical Group	$ 105.00	$ 31.34	$ 40.74	
[redacted], MD - Assistant Surgeon	$ -	$ 656.92	$ 853.99	
[redacted], MD	$ -	$ 861.36	$ 1,119.77	
[redacted] Medical Center	$216,710.50	$30,471.70	$39,613.21	
Total of Available Charges:	$331,625.80	$46,296.56	$61,887.90	= Total Reasonable Cost

Figure 7-6. This chart shows the actual costs, followed by what the defense thinks is reasonable.

On the left are the providers. The next column is the amounts owed. Then the right two columns are the amounts the defense expert said was reasonable. On the far right are the opinions of our expert as to the reasonable amounts. I used this to show the jury how little the defense wanted to give the medical providers who helped our client. The providers all said they expect full payment and would never accept the amounts the defense expert said was reasonable. We got the full amount from the jury. No discounts. It is important to note here that when a defense expert gives you causation for something, you can do a motion for summary judgment on causation, or a directed verdict on that issue during trial.

- **Your client.** In some jurisdictions you can put your client on the stand. You can ask them to testify about the amount of their bills. They owe those bills. The best practice is to subpoena the actual bills to the courtroom for evidentiary purposes, just in case.
- **Defense experts.** Sometimes, but not often, you will get a reasonable expert on the other side, and you may like their opinions on the cost of medical care. So when you take their depositions, just do a direct examination as if you were in trial. Take a video recording of it. Now play it at trial in your case-in-chief and use those numbers.

No matter how you get this information into evidence, or which path you use to do it, have a demonstrative ready to show the jury. They will be expecting it.

Diagnostic Imaging

Diagnostic imaging includes CT scans, MRIs, and X-rays. These are more visuals that will be helpful to the jury.

1. The first thing to do is to order all of these and have them downloaded and ready to go.
2. Then, talk to your treating doctor and/or expert and ask them which images will help prove their opinions and help the jury understand. They are the experts here and are far better at pulling the "smoking gun" image than you ever will be. So ask them.
3. Then mark these images as exhibits and play show-and-tell with the jury.

Here are some examples of diagnostic imaging.

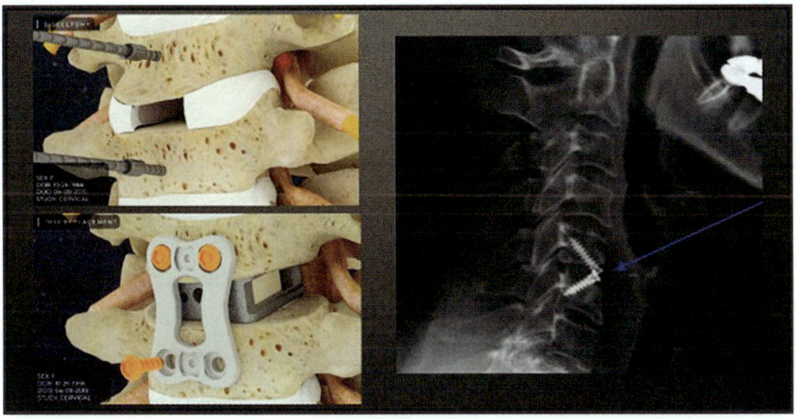

Figure 7-7. This side-by-side image shows our client's neck post-surgery next to a shot from our animation (courtesy of MULTUS medical) of the surgery.

In this image, on the left, is a still shot from an animation we played at trial. On the right, is an X-ray taken after our client's neck surgery showing the screws in place. With this, we were showing the jury not only what she went through, but how the disc above and below where the surgery was performed are starting to degenerate quickly. We then had our expert discuss these images and why he believes she will need another surgery over her lifetime.

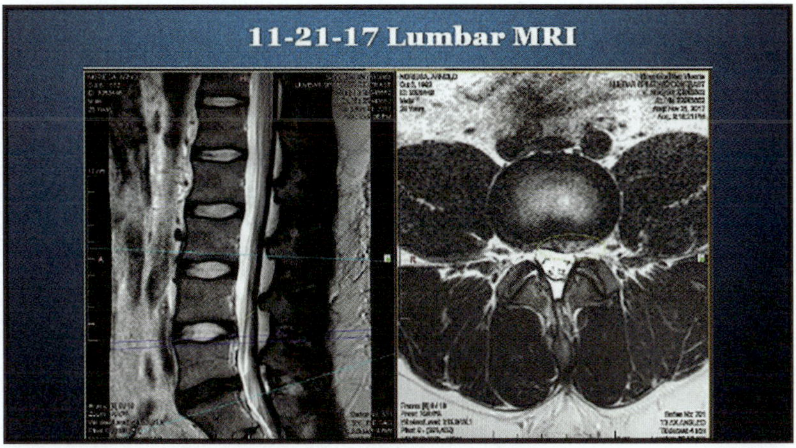

Figure 7-8. Images from the lumbar spine MRI.

The above images are from the same lumbar spine MRI. The image on the left is the side view. The image on the right is looking down. Our treating surgeon used this image to show the jury how there were white healthy discs above an obvious black unhealthy disc on the image on the left. He explained it would be unlikely for this to just be "degeneration" because white means healthy. If someone has a disc that's black at the bottom, and if this were just the aging process, he would expect the discs right above it to be darker as well. He also showed the jury the disc material going into the spinal canal. On the image on the right, he explained how it showed the disc pushing out on one side, and how it correlated with the client's nerve feelings going down one side of her body.

These are very powerful images that win your case. Get them from your medical doctors. And let them explain what they're showing and teach your jury.

Takeaways

Jurors expect visuals. They scroll images and videos all day on their phones. The trial should be no different. Keep your jury engaged, entertained, and educated.

PART II

Witnesses in Deposition & Trial: Why Less Is Always More

When it comes to witnesses in trial, less is more. Confusion is the defense's best friend. Most of the time the jury may believe the experts cancel each other out. The jury mainly listens to the treaters, the plaintiff, and the "damages witnesses" we discussed earlier.[1] That's it. With an effective defense lawyer, your case can be very vulnerable during cross-examination. So limit the opportunity.

Discovery can and should be used in trial. The written discovery, and the depositions taken in discovery, should be done thinking they will be used in trial. They do not have to be. But you should always be planning for trial. When writing a response with your client in discovery, ask yourself, how would this read to a jury in the future? Same goes for depositions. Since the two are so intertwined, and usually I think of them as one and the same, I put both discovery and trial in this next group of chapters.

When putting on cases in my firm, we typically call only half of the witnesses on our list. We put together the list in early litigation, we add to it throughout discovery, then we whittle it down to just the most

1. *See* chapter 4, "Common Defense Arguments."

important witnesses at trial. You only need enough witnesses to support the elements of your theme. Don't overdo it. Jurors will get lost in the weeds if you provide too much information. A single witness can prove a fact. That is in most jury instructions. It does not hurt to tell jurors in jury selection: "Would you hold it against us if we only use one witness to prove a fact, and shorten this trial?" Usually this is full of laughter from the panel.

I call one treating doctor, one retained expert, the plaintiff, and three damages witnesses. I get these seven- to eight-figure verdicts by putting on evidence in a day and a half. Rapid fire. Being efficient appeals to the jury. I've been known to do ten witnesses a day so the defense can't keep up. In basketball parlance, it's a full-court press. The other side better keep up or die trying.

The last thing we really want when our client is on the stand is a sob story. Their testimony should be melancholic, not dramatic. Powerful, but not too emotional. At the end of it, the jury should be ready to help them. Use people who know them well to testify as to how they have changed, and what their daily struggles are. These lay witnesses are essential to your recovery. But also disclose them way in advance so a judge doesn't exclude your lay witnesses for your failure to disclose.

8

Treating Doctors

Deposition as Direct Examination

One thing many spine cases have in common is a lot of treating doctors. Since my firm often acts as trial counsel for other lawyers, I see cases come through our door where the client has seen anywhere from eight to ten different doctors over a year or two. I am all for getting the client the help they need, but things can go awry if there are too many cooks in the kitchen. For instance, when an overly aggressive lawyer sends their client to specialist after specialist, the client follows their lead. The client sees a neurologist, a neurosurgeon, an orthopedic surgeon, a pain management specialist, a psychologist, and their general practitioner. The client is getting second opinions from the same discipline. The doctors are not talking to each other or seeing each other's records. And guess what happens? They all have different opinions. This is a defense attorney's dream. An overly aggressive plaintiff's lawyer can cause the confusion the defense loves. The defense can take the depositions of all these doctors; and unless they have conferred and are prepared, the defense can and will show major inconsistencies with your client's complaints. This also includes the recommendations of each doctor and their findings on both physical exam as well as the diagnostic studies.

Your depositions of treating doctors, in most states, can be used as direct examination to be played at trial. Treat them as such and take them just as seriously.

Recommended Care Team

Your client should have a spine doctor as their care coordinator. That doctor should be the one referring your client for treatment, asking them to seek a second opinion, and most importantly, talking to the other professionals to make sure there is a clear path of recovery for your client. This is how it is in the real world, how it resonates the best with the jury, and it makes your job easier.

Chiropractors & Physical Therapists

Chiropractors and physical therapists are often part of the team, but in my opinion should not be the quarterbacks for your client's care in a disc herniation case. A chiropractor's or physical therapist's positions and opinions should take a supporting role to the medical doctor's (such as an orthopedic surgeon). Detailed reports should come from physicians, not physical therapists or chiropractors. The chiropractor's or physical therapist's chart notes (not detailed reports) are all that you need.

Your Client's Treating Doctor versus an Outside Expert

Don't have your client's *treating doctor* as your expert. (There is absolutely a role for the client's treating doctors as non-retained experts, discussed later in this chapter). Bring in a third party who did not see your client until you retained them as an expert for your own independent medical exam. If you have a treater as your expert, there's always an assumed implicit bias. The defense will say that the doctor is just there just to protect their patients, that doctors are trying to justify the reason for surgery. Or maybe the defense will say we're in court because the treating doctor is owed money for surgery, or the treating doctor wants to get money in the future for another surgery. Make sure that the treating doctor's bill has been paid. In many situations, this may have been through personal injury protection (PIP) insurance, medical payments (MedPay) insurance, or the client's own health insurance.

If you have a neutral third-party doctor saying that your client's treatment was justified, who has no vested interest in the matter, that's different.

Treating doctors can be a secret and lethal weapon if you use them properly. Talk to them. If they are supportive of your position, they have already been paid for their treatment, and they have never worked with you before, that eliminates most of the defense's tactics, doesn't it?

When you're choosing a neutral third-party expert for your client, pick someone who is geographically pleasing to the jury. For example, if I'm in San Bernardino County, I'll pick a professor at Loma Linda University who has ties to the community. Don't choose someone from another state or another metro area if you can avoid it. It not-so-subtly tells the jury, "This place isn't good enough."

Strategic Use of Video Depositions

For purposes of this discussion, we are focusing on medical doctors. There are two categories for labeling these doctors—the retained expert and other doctors (non-retained) that will dictate the timing of taking their depositions and how you use those depositions at trial. A deposition for any witness (whether a medical professional or not) is jurisdiction dependent. Many suggest that if you give proper notice to opposing counsel that you are videotaping for purposes of trial, letting them know that their right to cross-examination is going to be happening during the deposition, then this strategy will work. In some jurisdictions, the other side may want to do a discovery deposition first, and later, a deposition as trial testimony.

You can take doctor depositions during the discovery phase or the expert discovery phase (which is much closer to trial in some states—research your own state). This can also be for any witnesses unavailable for trial.

- **The expert discovery phase.** The retained expert medical doctor (or doctors) usually conducts a medical examination at the direction of either side. This expert is hired specifically for this case. In some states that allow expert discovery, you cannot depose this doctor until after they have given their expert disclosures.
- **The discovery phase.** For all other doctors who are not hired specifically for this case, you can generally take their deposition at any time during the discovery phase. There are very rare exceptions where you can take expert doctor depositions in the discovery phase.

  In some states, such as California, if the defense expert does a physical examination of the plaintiff, they become a percipient witness. Thus you can depose them in the discovery phase. They will likely form more opinions later, so you will end up having to depose them twice. I only use this tactic if I know or strongly suspect the defense doctor will give it up and it will help my case resolve. Another way to get these depositions is if their expert signs a declaration for a motion, like a motion for summary judgment. Then you can, in most states, get their deposition to see the basis for their opinions in the declaration they signed.

Treating Doctors

A huge bullet we all have is our client's treating doctor. In California, any treating doctor is deemed "unavailable" by code. This means that once you take that doctor's deposition, that is your trial testimony if you so choose, and you do not have to bring that doctor into trial, live, to testify. With proper notice you can take the deposition, make a video of it, give notice to your trial judge that you are going to play it, and off you go. A jury will believe the treating doctor over any hired gun for either side, nine times out of ten.

But every jurisdiction is different. However, most mirror the Federal Rules, so I will address it there. First, you have to follow the rules that this is in fact a treating doctor and not a retained expert.

One of the biggest issues surrounding the categorization of a physician as an expert or fact witness is which rules of disclosure to apply.

Under Rule 26(a)(2)(A) of the Federal Rules of Civil Procedure, "a party must disclose to the other parties the identity of any witness it may use at trial to present evidence under Federal Rule of Evidence 702, 703, or 705"[1] (the rules governing expert testimony).

Further, under Rule 26 (a)(2)(B), "if the witness is one retained or specially employed to provide expert testimony in the case or one whose duties as the party's employee regularly involve giving expert testimony," the expert must provide a written report. The report is quite exhaustive, as it provides opposing counsel with a comprehensive summary and basis for the expert's opinion.

Pursuant to the Rule, the report must contain a statement of the expert's opinion and the basis and reasons for them; the facts or data the witness relied upon; any exhibits that will be used; the witness's qualifications (including a list of all publications authored in the past

1. Legal Information Institute for Cornell Law School, "Rule 26. Duty to Disclose; General Provisions Governing Discovery," https://www.law.cornell.edu/rules/frcp/rule_26.

ten years); a list of cases for which the expert testified in the past four years; and the expert's compensation.

In contrast, witnesses who do not fall under Rule 26(a)(2)(B) as "retained or specially employed to provide expert testimony," but are still expected to present evidence under Federal Rule of Evidence 702, 703, or 705, need not provide a written report.[2] Rather in these instances, under Rule 26(a)(2)(C), only the subject matter and a summary of facts and opinions to which such an witness is expected to testify need be disclosed. Non-retained treating physicians fall under this category.

Essentially, this Rule allows treating physicians to present evidence under the Federal Rules of Evidence governing scientific expert testimony but exempt them from the written report requirement because they are not "retained or specially employed to provide expert testimony."[3] Courts have agreed to this interpretation of the Rule as long as the physician will testify solely as a percipient witness, that is, a person who was a direct participant in the events of the case.

While some courts disagree, the majority of courts even allow treating physicians to testify to causation, prognosis, and the permanency and degree of injury without a written report so long as those opinions were reached during the course of treatment. Other courts hold that a treating physician must prepare a written report if the physician reviews materials that were not reviewed during the course of treatment, as this goes beyond the scope and "morphs" the witness into a retained expert.[4]

The treating doctor can give you symptoms they see, the clinical picture, their observations, the causation, why they did procedures, cost of care, and so on. So can a retained expert. But if the treating doctor was paid through insurance, does not have a relationship with the attorney, and "has no skin in the game," then the jury will

---

2. Legal Information Institute for Cornell Law School, "Rule 26. Duty to Disclose; General Provisions Governing Discovery," https://www.law.cornell.edu/rules/frcp/rule_26.

3. *Id.*

4. *Id.*

weigh that heavily. If the treating doctor has seen 10,000 patients for the same attorney, has a huge bill contingent on winning the lawsuit, has an unimpressive MRI, and has low property damage, well, that is why you hire a separate third-party expert to back everything up, because that treating doctor has too much "skin in the game." If you video record your treater depositions early enough, even the overly biased treater may seem like a star with none of this coming out. Often the defense is not prepared for these depositions, or they do not send their seasoned trial lawyers. I even heard from a very prominent jury psychologist that research shows that jurors pay more attention to video depositions, with words scrolling at the bottom, than they do to live testimony.[5] Thank you, smartphone culture! And since it will be evidence given to the jury during trial, you can play it again in closing argument if you want.

Preparing a Treating Doctor for Deposition

1. Communicate with the treating doctor.
2. Give notice of video for trial.
3. Get trial exhibits ready.
4. Prepare trial graphics and animations.
5. Use a reputable deposition company.
6. Trial direct examination by deposition.
7. Designate the transcript for trial.

5. Drew York, "Why Videotaped Deposition Testimony can be More Powerful than Live Witnesses," *Tilting the Scales: Business Issues With a Legal Slant*, June 30, 2017, https://www.tiltingthescales.com/2017/06/30/why-videotaped-deposition-testimony-can-be-more-powerful-than-live-witnesses.

1. Communicate with the Treating Doctor

Before you embark on the plan of preserving the treating doctor's testimony for trial in a deposition, you need to know what they are going say. If they will not get on the phone with you, *send a trial subpoena*, even if your trial is a year in advance. Ask them to sign an on-call agreement rather than show up. And ask them to call you. They will call you, and they will do anything they can *not* to be dragged into court. Trust me. So when you tell them that you can simply take their deposition, at their convenience, from their home, and pay them for their time, rather than ask them to come into trial, they will love it. This is also a good time to discuss with them why you need their help. Explain that the defense is saying their patient's surgery should never have been done, they would have needed it without the crash, their bills are too high, they are in cahoots with the lawyer, and so on. Now you have one ticked off treating doctor ready to help you!

2. Give Notice of Video for Trial

Check your state laws and make sure you give proper notice to all parties indicating that you will be video recording the deposition and using it in trial. This is a critical notice requirement in most venues. If the defense notices the deposition first, that is fine. But you must join the deposition notice and say you are going to video record and play it at trial. In California it is Code of Civil Procedure § 2025.620.

3. Get Trial Exhibits Ready

Start marking your trial exhibits early, so when you play the deposition of this treating doctor, the exhibit numbers match up at the time of trial. If you are asking them to read and comment on exhibit 15, the MRI film from 2022, it should be the same exhibit in trial. Have these all pre-marked, loaded, and ready to go for your deposition. Although this is a deposition, you are about to do a direct exam for trial, and you need to treat it as such.

4. Prepare Trial Graphics & Animations

In chapter 7, "Gathering the Evidence," we discussed many types of graphic and animated evidence. Follow the same plan here. Work with the treating doctor to get an animation done of the surgery they performed. Have them walk the future jury through the surgery. Discuss why they believe the crash was the culprit. Pull up the MRI images and have the treating doctor show the jury why they did the surgery and explain their position (which is also your position) for you.

5. Use a Reputable Deposition Company

Get the right company on board and be comfortable with their platform. Many of these will be remote. The faster you can drag and drop in exhibits, mark them up, and play videos, the better. You also need to order the video and make sure the transcript is synced. This means the spoken words will scroll below as you play the video for the jury. This is just like we see all over social media, and it helps with jurors who might have trouble hearing. It is extremely effective.

6. Trial Direct Examination by Deposition

Make no mistake about it, you are taking this deposition to be played a trial. Treat it as such. Even if the defense lawyer wants to go first with their questions, let them. Stay focused and do your direct when they finish. Here is a general outline for treating doctors that I use.

1. **Introduction.** "Hello, I am Robert Simon, I represent the plaintiff, your patient. Now let's get to know you."
2. **Role.** Let the jury know this is your client's treating doctor, under subpoena, and is not hired to advocate for either side.

They will certainly still advocate for their patient on video, and that is the beauty of it

3. **Background.** Do your research first and get in all their credentials, board certifications, awards, hospital affiliations, charity work, amount of spine surgeries performed, publications, and so on.
4. **Important dates.** Show your medical timeline exhibit, put into perspective when your client saw this doctor, and list the dates. Then start with the first date and pull out the important actions they took, why they did it, what the patient's complaints were, what the doctor thought the issue was in their spine, and why. Then I skip right to the surgery date.
5. **Surgery.** Walk through the animation and ask the doctor to describe what they did and why. Pause during the video and ask them if they formed an opinion on the cause for the need for the surgery. Then ask them why. Let them talk. Make sure you confirm it is to a reasonable degree of medical probability.
6. **MRI Films.** Have them list the films they personally reviewed. Ask them why they like to review it themselves. What was important on the films? Why did they do the surgery? Why do they think this issue was caused by the crash? Ask them to mark up the MRI films to show the jury.
7. **Subjective versus Objective.** Ask the doctor to define these terms. *Subjective* is what a patient tells them hurts. *Objective* is what they see in surgery, on the MRIs, and during their clinical exams. Ask them if the subjective complaints and objective findings are consistent. And ask them to explain. Remember, you are also defeating the known defenses that will be coming months or years later in trial.
8. **Last Appointment.** Ask about the date, their findings, and why the appointment was important.
9. **Recommendations for Future Care.** Make sure to ask what the doctor believes is reasonably certain to occur, to a reasonable degree of medical probability, over the lifetime of your client. It is okay to lead here and ask for specifics on physical therapy

clusters (for example, eighteen sessions over three months, every three years), diagnostics scans, pain management clusters, follow-ups, and any future surgeries. If you do this right, you will not need a life care planner. Or if you do need one, you just made their job a lot easier by laying it all out.

10. **Cost of Medical Care.** In most jurisdictions you have to lay out how the person giving testimony knows the cost of medical care. Lay that foundation. During your pre-deposition meeting, ask the doctor if they can opine on cost of care, and how they know. Educate them on the law in your state, and if they feel comfortable giving estimates. Make sure to ask about the *reasonable and customary* cost in the community for every single item of care that your client had and ask how the doctor knows the cost of these items. This can save your need for a billing expert, or another third-party expert to back up all your bills as well.
11. **Defeating the Usual Defenses.** Make a list of the usual defenses, and the ones you are hearing from the defense lawyer on your case, and ask this treating doctor to address them all. Be sure to ask them *why* as much as possible. Following are some sample questions that you might ask:

    Q: Are all these injuries due to degeneration?
    Q: Is this because of their job?
    Q: Are Medicare rates reasonable value for these procedures?
    Q: Are there any signs of trauma on the scans at the ER?
    Q: Is there delay in neck pain, back pain, or radicular pain?
    Q: What are your thoughts on biomechanics?
    Q: Is my client faking or making it up?
    Q: Are there compression or nerve related issues in the MRI?
    Q: Does this gap in treatment mean anything to you?

12. **Disability.** Does your client require any work restrictions? Do they have any problems with mobility, climbing stairs, carrying objects, and so on?

13. **Catch-all.** Make sure to again have them confirm that all their opinions about the patient's future, to a reasonable degree of medical probability, are reasonably certain to occur.

7. Designate the Transcript for Trial

The last step is to look at the transcript of the deposition you just took. This is trial testimony you know a jury will hear, and you have a chance to read it before the jury hears it. What a gift! Now take the time to designate what specific clips you want played and file it with the court. I usually just designate from my direct on. This means you file a document with the court that says you are giving notice that you will be playing this deposition at time of trial. You give the pages and lines of everything you wish to play. The other side can then object, add their own sections to play, or be lazy and do neither. But there is no need to do their job for them. Just include the story you want to tell.

The Importance of the Treating Doctor's Deposition

At every trial, I have video recorded depositions of the treating doctors. Either side can give notice and depose the treating doctors. I try and affirmatively do it, but if the other side does, it's all good, just join the notice.

The defense will always walk in unprepared and throw a newbie associate at the deposition. They will see it just as a billing exercise. They are not thinking "this is going to trial," nor are they thinking *trial backwards*. Trial backwards means I assume *every* case is going to trial. If I am thinking of proving my case at trial, through discovery, matching it with the jury instructions, and defeating the usual defenses as I go, then I am way ahead of the other side. They think it is a discovery deposition.

The next thing you know, you're playing your deposition of the treating doctor at trial without pushback. At the deposition, hopefully, and often likely, the associate asked no bias questions, did zero cross-examination. Now you have a treating doctor on the stand (via video) who wasn't cross-examined, and they come off to the jury as an unbiased person who is going to disagree with the defense expert.

This is how you win cases. Your preparation laid a massive bear trap, set and snagged in discovery, and you already won your trial.

I try and play as many depositions as I can at trial, depending on how the testimony comes out. Ideally you know you can meet your burden of proof just by playing that deposition. You can also get more bites at the apple if you have two treating doctors and your retained expert giving causation opinions. Also, you have control. You know exactly what the jury is going to hear. You can also use these clips in your opening and to test your case in front of strangers using focus groups. Focus groups are where you test issues, themes, liability, and so on with mock jurors. I find it effective to do focus groups where I play the defense attorney. I will play the treating doctor depositions that I know are coming into trial. Then I will play the deposition of the defense expert that I also video recorded. Then I will do a defense closing and get thoughts from the mock jurors. Even without a plaintiff lawyer telling them, they usually come to the conclusion to trust the treating doctors.

Example: Treating Doctor Deposition

I go into these treater depositions knowing the likely position of the defense attorney and their team.

Mr. Simon: Everyone has degeneration. But does that mean we all need surgery?
Treating Doctor: No.
Q: No? Why not?

Then I wait for the treating doctor's explanation of why everyone doesn't need surgery.

Q: Can people herniate discs in rear-end crashes?
A: They can herniate them sneezing.
Q: Oh, tell me more.

Then I wait for the "more."

Q: Do Medicare or Medicaid pay reasonable value for your services?
A: No, they don't.
A: No? Oh, tell me more.

Then I wait for the "more."

Q: Was the patient faking or lying?
A: No, they absolutely were not.
Q: No? Tell me more.

Then I wait for the "more."

Q: Does the MRI tell the whole picture?
A: No, it does not.
Q: No? Tell me more.

A common explanation from the defense is that the client was hurt while working, not in the crash.

Q: Was your patient hurt while working?
A: I found no evidence of that.
Q: During your treatment of your patient, did you ever find that a new injury happened?
A: No.
Q: Just because my client is a laborer, does that mean they would have needed surgery without the crash?
A: No, that is pure speculation.
Q: I just want to be clear here, doctor, if, hypothetically, one of the parties hires an expert that says it is likely that because my client is a hairdresser, that is the cause of the need for the fusion, and not the crash, what are your thoughts?
A: That is absurd. Who would make such a statement?

Another common defense is that there was not enough force in the crash to cause injury.

Q: You have treated patients who sustained disc herniations in rear-end collisions, right?
A: Yes.
Q: Were those collisions light impacts?
A: Sometimes.
Q: Can you get a disc herniation from sneezing?
A: Yes, I have seen that happen.
Q: Oh, so if the defense had a biomechanical expert who says a disc herniation could not happen in this crash, would you agree?
A: No.

Get these questions and their answers in deposition, then use them in trial.

Example: The *Johnson* Case

In *Johnson*, the treating neurosurgeon (not hired) testified that my client's pain was the likely result of the car accident he experienced.[6] His review of records was consistent with Johnson's pain. The nerve in the neck was pinched and he found diminished reflex in his biceps. Do not forget that the treaters are also a very powerful weapon to defeat the defense theories across the board. But be sure to talk to them before you call them to the stand and know their opinions.

Mr. Simon: And were you able to tell during that examination what caused this rupture that you stated in his C5–6 level of Mr. Johnson?

Defense Counsel: Objection, your honor. Lacks foundation. Calls for speculation.

Judge: Subject to a motion to strike, you may answer.

Treating Neurosurgeon: Based on all the history and the physical examination and the records and imaging studies that I reviewed and received, the accident that he had was the main culprit. Because, basically, he told me he had no neck pain, arm pain, back, or leg pain before the accident. So what I said is, to a reasonable degree of medical probabilities, the accident is the main culprit for his injuries.

Mr. Simon: Alright, and was this caused over a chronic degenerative wear and tear process, or something that was acute due to the car crash?

Defense Counsel: Again, lacks foundation, speculation.

Judge: Again, subject to a motion to strike, you may answer.

Treating Neurosurgeon: To my expert opinion, and treating more than 5,000 patients so far, it is my opinion that this

---

6. For more information about the *Johnson* case, see "About the Cases in This Book" at the beginning of this book, *Michael Johnson v. Jonathan Brown*.

was a piece of disc material traumatically ruptured through the annulus, and it's inside the spinal canal. Given that it was a rear-end motor vehicle accident, it's more than likely the car accident caused this event, as opposed to longstanding degenerative changes. [He is pointing at the actual MRI film projected to the jury.]

Then I kept going with the degeneration question.

Mr. Simon: And you'd agree that every single person probably over thirty or thirty-five has degeneration in their spine?

Treating Neurosurgeon: Yes.

Q: But not everybody has pain due to degeneration?

A: That's correct.

Q: And what is your opinion as it relates to causation in the lumbar spine?

A: Again, based on the fact that he did not have any significant lower-back pain before the accident, and then he has a radicular symptom of pain shooting down the leg, annular, a tear in the lumbar spine with the same type of injury with the disc at the lumbar spine, my opinion is the accident caused his injury.

Best yet, this witness was someone who testified 50/50 for both sides, was not hired as an expert for either side, and was there under subpoena as the treating doctor. The defense had nothing to cross-examine him on as far as being biased or having a financial interest in the outcome of litigation. I also was able to ask about the cost of care, that the light impact was a red herring, and the need for future care. In talking to the jury afterwards, this was the key witness for them. They felt he had no skin in the game, no reason to lie, was not paid as an expert for either side, and was just trying to help.

Other Types of Treating Doctors

There are many more wonderful treating physicians who can help prove your case as non-retained experts, and at the same time discredit all the defenses you know are coming.

General Practitioner

The general practitioner can absolutely crush the defense theory that your client was damaged goods without the crash, and all the injuries were just degenerative. They can also paint the picture of your client's health before the crash: the things they enjoyed and how that changed. They are built-in damages witnesses along with other medical professionals. They likely will stay away from the need for spine surgery, medical care costs, and futures. But that is okay. I like to ask these witnesses questions like:

Q: Before the crash, did it ever occur to you to refer my client for spine surgery?
Q: No?
Q: Why not?
Q: Doctor, you have seen this patient over a decade, correct?
Q: Did they ever seem to you to be a drug seeker?
Q: Have they ever made up their symptoms?
Q: Before the crash, did your patient ever ask to be taken off work due to any pain or disability?
Q: How about after?
Q: Please explain.

These witnesses may also be able to talk about depression and referrals for other care within their discipline.

Radiologist

The radiologists who read the MRI films after the car crash can also be a hidden treasure. But again, you have to *talk* to them. They might not be willing to talk to you, but why not try? The defense will likely hire a radiologist to create confusion, and to make assertions like "there are no acute signs of trauma on the MRI, I see no nerve issue nor compression, there are only signs of degeneration in the spine, and I see no need for surgery."

Call up the radiologist who read your client's film and ask them if they agree. Most radiologists can and should be neutral. They do not have the benefit of the clinical picture and are reading films in a vacuum. Any radiologist worth their salt will admit this and will say that unless you have an MRI taken before the crash, and after the crash, there is no way to know when the herniation occurred, and you have to look at the clinical picture. They will explain that there are many forms of nerve irritation and issues, and they can point to several in the scan that they read. They will defer to the actual spine surgeon on the need for surgery and explain why. You may find after talking to the radiologist that they may think it is actually acute and why. They can be a powerful witness if they feel that way. At the very least, they can explain medical science and neutralize the craziness spouted by the ones the defense hired.

Neurologist

Often, the treating surgeon will refer the patient out to a neurologist who specializes in nerve conduction studies for a needle electromyography (EMG) study. These are painful studies where the neurologist (or their staff) will put needles in your client to see if there is a nerve that has a distorted signal. They send electrical stimulus into a nerve and see if there are issues with nerve function. For instance, if their suspected culprit is at the C6 nerve root, they will test and see if there is a delay in signal down that pattern of your client's arm and hand. This test is not fun. If your client has positive nerve conduction studies that match up with the MRI, what your client is complaining of, and the area of the surgery, well, this is pure gold. It just adds in yet another treating doctor who would have to be in on the grand conspiracy against the defense. I usually take these depositions in about ten minutes. Have the doctor describe who they are, what they did, and how it matched up with everything. And establish with them that there is no way to fake these test results.

Takeaways

Preparation for trial starts the moment your client walks through your door. Making sure the treating doctors are talking to each other is critical. Communication is key in any relationship. So is education. Educate your client and the treating doctors on the law, what the defense is saying, or likely will say, to make sure that your client not only gets the treatment they deserve, but also so that their compensation is not quelled by savvy defense lawyers. Many juries are generally skeptical of hired guns. But a doctor just helping patients? They're truth sayers. Get their testimony early. And use it often.

9

Defense Experts

Deposing to Prepare for Cross-Examination

I host the Justice Team podcast.[1] We once had on a panel of prominent defense lawyers. During the discussion, one of them said, "You know, I wish my carrier would let me rest without putting on any evidence. Because I swear my case gets worse and worse when I start putting up my experts. You guys are just overly prepared and any points I scored when you were putting on your case just get totally lost."

I did not tell him then, but I am telling you now: he is right. It would be pretty powerful to tell the jury that the defense couldn't put on a single witness to support their case. But the defense lawyer still gets credibility and credence because his well-paid hired guns are not exposed. The jury will not hear about nefarious professionals selling out to the defense industry. The jury will never hear about how often these

1. Justice Team Podcast, www.justiceteampodcast.com.

nefarious professionals have the exact same opinions in every single case with this same defense firm.[2]

Yes, obviously I think the defense's case gets worse once they start putting on evidence because they can get destroyed on cross-examination. But if defense lawyers start to get wise, and many have, and *not* call their clown show as witnesses at trial, how can you still expose it all? In most jurisdictions, with proper notice, you are allowed to play the defense expert's deposition in your case-in-chief. Therefore, you can insulate yourself by taking effective depositions of the defense experts and using them during your opening and case-in-chief. Let me show you how.

Earlier in this book, we discussed proper notice to play video depositions of treating doctors in trial. You need to follow the same protocol, and let the other side know that you are going to video record their experts' depositions; and that you will be using them in your opening, during testimony, and during closing. Then after the deposition, get the transcript and edit the video as you need to. Designate the transcript of the portion that you wish to play, file it with the court, and off you go. Now, even if the defense lawyers get wise and choose not to call their defense experts live in front of the jury, you will still show the jury the truth.

Let's talk about the defense's usual circus performers:

- a biomechanical engineer
- a radiologist
- a surgeon
- a billing expert

The next several chapters will discuss how to deal with each of these types of experts after we cover some generalities, specifically:

---

2. See Patrick Malone, *The Fearless Cross-Examiner: Win the Witness, Win the Case* (Trial Guides, 2016). This is a great book with many techniques for exposing paid defense doctors who haven't practiced real medicine in years but make their living completely in the courtroom.

- Chapter 10, "Deposing Defense Doctors"
- Chapter 11, "Defense Biomechanical Experts"
- Chapter 12, "Defense Medical Billing Experts"
- Chapter 13, "Responding to Defense Doctors"

Cross-examination is one of the single most deadly ways to crush your opposition's case. This all starts long before trial. Preparing for the defense experts is like winning any other competition. You have to play to win. Your client's future well-being is at stake. Get to know as much about the subject and the person as possible. Go deep on a search to find that 2011 products liability convention flyer where a biomechanical expert sat on a panel with a defense attorney, or a twenty-five-page Reddit thread to find that one comment by a radiologist hating people who sue for spine injuries. Late at night, some people watch Netflix. I like to Google "defense expert" and "fraud."

Research the Defense Experts

During discovery, the other side will tell you the experts that they have hired when they set the defense medical exam of your client. Or the engineer they asked to inspect your client's vehicle. Or the radiologist they listed in their mediation brief. As soon as you learn who they hired, it is time to start doing your research. You need to look for things that show bias, impeach them, invalidate their credentials, or support your position. Here are some things we look for right away.

Search Social Media

Sometimes you can find social media accounts by searching their name or their email. You can find and screenshot some powerful stuff. They might show bias towards the injured, or show they are a full-on quack. You might be able to impeach them with what they put on the internet versus what they tell juries. Some just love posting photos of themselves at the courthouse. You might find them at conferences, which can lead you to other searches to see if they presented.[3]

Search YouTube

Search the expert's name on YouTube. Sometimes they are doing videos right on point for your case. They can be saying that the surgery done on your client was the right one, and totally contradict themselves. They can be warning about adjacent segment disorder and saying that it is real. They can be saying the surgeon is more credible than the MRI read. Record, save, and get the clip to your favorite court reporting company. In trial, the video is not good enough to introduce into evidence, you will need a certified transcript to use with it.

Search Websites

Many of these defense experts have their own websites. Browse and screenshot them. Sometimes on their own websites, they are not even holding themselves out to be experts in the field they are about to testify on. Several "spine" surgeons hired by the defense in my cases have never done a spine surgery, and their own websites will tell the world that they are in fact specialists in hips and knees. They may also list their publications. See if you find those as well. It might help prove your case if their own research supports your position.

---

3. A really good tool is called Expert Radar, created by the Expert Institute. They can find a lot of this information for you. "Expert Radar: Uncover Critical Intelligence on Opposing Experts," Expert Institute, https://www.expertinstitute.com/expert-iq/expert-radar.

Search Google

Google and other search engines like refined searches. Put the expert's name in quotes: "Daryl B. Payne." Then search, pairing that name with other terms (also in quotes) that may elicit what you are looking for.

- "Daryl B. Payne" and "[defense firm name]"
- "Daryl B. Payne" and "seminar"
- "Daryl B. Payne" and "fraud"
- "Daryl B. Payne" and "attorney" and "golf"
- "Daryl B. Payne" and "defense" and "expert"

You get the gist of it.

Ask Your Community

Use your community of lawyers to build a *box of death* for this witness. What is a box of death? This is a collection of certified transcripts of depositions, cross-examinations, records of speaking engagements with the defense lawyers, and any other information you can get from your community about this witness. Many times, the defense expert is used so often that this witness's box of death may already exist. Reach out to your sisters- and brothers-in-arms and see what they have. Use Listservs like Trial Guides, Trial by Human, your local and state bar organizations, and membership groups like Justice HQ. We are all here to help!

Ask Your Experts

Ask if anyone on your team has come across this expert before and what they know. No one likes an industry sellout. There are players who work for both sides, toe the line, and give concessions when you ask the right questions. Those folks I respect. But there are also folks who go all out for the side that hires them, regardless of which one, and they try to make up medicine and twist the facts.

Research Court Dockets

I usually have an investigator pull anything where the expert is a named party. You might find nothing, but you might find gold. You might find previous medical malpractice lawsuits. Divorce proceedings are wrought with fun stuff as well, such as declarations from the husband and wife talking about their earnings from various entities, and where the money is hidden. You might find out how much they are truly getting from insurance companies. You never know unless you look.

Subpoena the Insurance Company

My firm has had some luck just subpoenaing the insurance company and asking for all 1099s for payments to the experts. You will need to send a "notice to consumer" to the expert along with the request since you are obtaining their records from a third party. You never know what may happen. This is a great tactic in uninsured and underinsured motorist cases, where the insurance company is a party. It doesn't work all the of the time, but even some of the time can be great.

Research Public Filings

You can access portals to see if the defense doctor is licensed within the state, and their specialty. You can see if this doctor has any disciplinary issues. If your doctor is a state employee, at a state-funded hospital affiliated with a university, there are several things you can find with a public record search. You can find their salary. If they are practicing relatively little medicine and are mostly doing insurance defense work, their salary may be quite small. You can find their disclosures to their employer, the state, on their earnings outside the hospital. Many times, they straight-up lie to their own employers. They do this because they know they are not allowed to make over a certain amount outside the hospital. Pull their disclosure and compare it to how much they are making in your case alone. Tsk tsk.

Search Your Internal Database

Search the expert's name in the archives at your own firm. Another person at your firm may have already done your work for you.

Examples from Deposition & Trial

Following are three examples of showing defense experts with dubious activities, proof that they are courtroom-only experts, and fraudulent credentials.

Example: Lies & Bias

Before an expert deposition, I found a picture of one defense lawyer winning a golf tournament with that expert. My wife was wondering why I was laughing, and I told her I was Googling old white dudes and struck gold. She was likely still confused. But whatever. What gold! During the deposition I asked:

Mr. Simon: Doctor, do you know any of the lawyers in this case socially? Go to any functions with them, speak at events, that kind of stuff?
Defense Expert: No.

I didn't show my hand because I knew this one was going to trial. So when we got in front of the jury, the expert denied it on the stand, but I had a photo of them from my late-night internet search. At trial, this was our exchange:

Mr. Simon: Doctor, now you told me in deposition you don't know these guys socially, right?

Defense Expert: That's right.

Q: Like, you guys don't go golfing and come up with plans to wash out plaintiffs, right?

A: Of course not.

Q: Do you remember playing in a charity golf tournament with this lawyer, right here?

A: Oh, well, he does look familiar.

Q: Don't you guys play together all day, go all the time, and are buddies? Just tell the jury.

A: I hardly play golf; I am not that good. [Tries to joke with the jury.]

Q: But you guys got third place. Here's the photo.

Then I show the photo to him and the jury.

A: Um, wait, what?

Example: Courtroom Expert Unmasked

I like to spook the defense by coming out of left field at the start of a cross-examination. One of my favorite cross-examinations is when I start by asking:

Mr. Simon: Where were you on Monday?

Here's the thing: I knew where they were Monday. And where they were Tuesday. And the week before. And even sometimes that morning before they came into testify. I talked to my community of lawyers, and we tracked this expert's schedule. I knew the cases he testified on earlier in that week. I had the transcripts. I knew what he said. But most of these folks do not remember. They forget the plaintiff's name right after they leave the courtroom saying the plaintiff was not hurt. They take their money and move onto their next victim. So if you prove you know their own schedule better than them? Egad.

Mr. Simon: Where were you on Tuesday?

This gets the jury's attention. They'll wonder, where is he going with this?

Defense Expert: I was at the hospital treating patients.
Q: Last Tuesday, you were in [another] court, testifying about another injured person in a car crash case, correct?

It does not matter what their answer is. You got them. They have no credibility. It takes a lot of research, but it is worth it. The jury just laughs at them. I might then point out that they are criticizing my client for not remembering a car crash he was in fifteen years ago, but meanwhile they can't remember where they were a couple days ago. Then, once you refresh their memory of testifying against another injured car crash victim, you can start to get them to concede they are just courtroom experts who give opinions for the defense.

Example: Lack of Credentials

Once I cross-examined a guy who lied on his resume about going to college. We'll call him George Benson, a defense spine surgeon in my *Johnson* case.[4] Johnson, whose life was completely altered by a rear-end collision, leaving him with chronic nerve pain, had never even been examined by Dr. Benson. I knew this case was going to trial, because the offer was in the five figures—way too low—so I set up Benson in the deposition. I knew he had lied about graduating from college. He actually got into medical school because his daddy was a rich lawyer from Beverly Hills. I had his divorce records (they're public record, so I had them pulled), so I knew exactly how much he made doing defense work. I knew he was frequently hired by other defense attorneys. To set up my case, I had my friends take his deposition in other unrelated cases, within the weeks I took his deposition in my case. Then I asked the following questions to set him up:

> Q: Do you know Michael Johnson? [*expecting him to say no*]
> Q: How many spine surgeries have you done as lead? [*my friends' cases were shoulder cases*]
> Q: Who would you refer your patients to for spine surgery?

In the end I had sworn testimony from other cases, taken within weeks of his sworn testimony in my case, affirming he didn't know my client, he was not a spine surgeon, had only been lead in two spine fusion surgeries, which were both in Cambodia, and could not be documented. And oh yeah, all his claimed "specialty training" in biomechanics that could not be documented took place in Germany and he lost the paperwork. I even left a blank exhibit in the deposition and gave him a check for $1,500 for three hours of his time, to search for his

4. *See* "About the Cases in This Book" for a complete description of the *Johnson* case.

actual credentials. As you can imagine, at time of trial, he had nothing. But you better believe he cashed that check. Sigh.

In trial, this courtroom doctor who had never done a spine surgery and never examined Johnson still told the jury that the injury my client sustained was not because of the rear-end collision he was involved in. Meanwhile, I showed the jury the things they weren't being told:

- This so-called expert was a made-to-order witness who collectively made $500,000 a year over twenty years, testifying for one particular defense insurance carrier.
- The studies he relied on, stating his client wouldn't be able to get a disc herniation from his collision, were debunked by a peer-reviewed study.
- He didn't graduate from college before medical school. He was a theater major and didn't graduate.

He tried denying that on the stand too. But I had another certified transcript from ten years ago where he admitted it. By reaching out to my community, another trial lawyer had a certified deposition copy where he got the doctor to admit to all of this. I just emailed a Listserv and asked if anyone knew anything about him. The other trial lawyer called me up and said, "You are not going to believe this. He never graduated from college. He lies about everything. And I can prove it." He gave me his deposition transcript. He let me borrow it for this very special cross-examination. Now I have my own certified trial transcript exposing this expert that I also freely share. That is how powerful the trial lawyer community can be. If you get something great, share freely!

Here's how I broke down the defense's spine "expert," blow by blow. First, I asked him about his time at University of California, Santa Barbara. After getting caught in lies he had to admit it.

Mr. Simon: All right. Dr. Benson, in opening statement, Mr. Jeffries indicated that—he went through your credentials, graduated

UCSB, graduated UCLA, then Director of Spine Trauma and Cedars—oh no, Director of Orthopedics at Cedars.

Spine Expert: Clinical Chief at Cedars.

Q: Okay. That's all correct?

A: That's correct.

Q: Doctor, isn't it true that you never graduated from college?

A: No. I graduated from UCSB. My diploma is on my wall when you were there having the deposition.

Q: Well, you didn't graduate college until a few years ago, not like in the eighties before medical school like you alluded to?

A: I did graduate late because I never took English 1B, so I hadn't finished. I eventually went back and took it in an online class.

Q: When did you graduate from UCSB? When did you go back and take this online class?

A: Three years ago.

Q: So as of 2009—your deposition was taken in 2009—you had not even graduated from college at that point?

A: That's right. I was missing English 1B. I went straight to medical school.

Q: All right. In fact, can you tell the jury what your major was when you were at UCSB?

A: My final major was biology. That's what I got my degree in.

Q: Your degree three years ago, but what was your major when you were at UCSB?

A: I had more than one major. My major I graduated in was biology. My degree is in biology. I have a Bachelor of Science in biology from UCSB. I did do undergraduate work including drama, but my degree is a Bachelor of Science.

Q: Your major when you were at UCSB, actually attending there, not talking when you went back and took an online course to graduate three years ago, your major was theater, correct?

A: No. I have a degree in Bachelor of Science. I did take some drama classes my first two years, and then I went back for three years after that, and I took all science. Do you know what it takes to get to medical school? You have to take every science class there is. Organic chemistry, chemistry, etc. etc. My degree of Bachelor of Science, magna cum laude, out of University of California Santa Barbara, where I got straight almost 4.0 for three years, all in science.

This is a small excerpt of a deposition that I got from the trial lawyer community.

Q: I would like to read from Dr. Benson's deposition, dated February 3, 2009, page 17, line 16 through 19. Sorry, 16 through 21.

The Court: Now that I have a copy, that page again?

Defense Lawyer: You can look at mine, Your Honor.

Mr. Simon: Page 17, 16 through 21.

Defense Lawyer: I don't even think this is actually proper impeachment based on the testimony. So we may want to have a brief sidebar.

A discussion was held at sidebar, which was not reported.

Mr. Simon: [*reading from deposition*]

Question: So you must have a degree from there?

Answer: No. I went straight to medical school. I was a drama major and then a bio major, but I did more than enough units.

Question: Do you have a college degree?

Answer: No.

Immediately after this cross-examination, one of the jurors raised his hand to ask if the jury could deliberate right at that moment. I kid you not. That was so devastating that the witness had no way to recover. For the rest of the cross-examination, he was rambling.

Then I asked him about who he testified for most of the time, which wasn't a surprise, but the jury needed to hear it.

Q: And 85 to 96 percent of the time, it's always testifying against the injured party, true statement?
A: The testifying I do, probably 80 percent or so is.

I also ran through how he disagreed with all of my independent, qualified experts, including a neurosurgeon named Dr. Jacobs, who said my client's injuries were more likely than not caused by the accident.

Jacobs was under subpoena and not an attorney-referred doctor. He was Johnson's treating doctor. He testified that everybody has degeneration, but not everybody has pain because of it. The defense, meanwhile, was basically saying all this came out of nowhere. Dr. Jacobs saw Mr. Johnson once before all the surgeries. He is a well-known neurosurgeon in the community. He was listed as a non-retained expert, the defense never deposed him, he came into trial, and was absolutely devastating to the defense. Just a reminder to subpoena and talk to your client's non-retained treating doctors. It might cost you a $500 consultation fee to get them on the phone, but this is how you win cases.

Mr. Simon: You disagree with Dr. Jacob's opinion about causation in this case?
Defense Spine Expert: To the extent saying it would be caused by the accident, that would be correct.
Q: You disagree with Dr. Harold and his opinions about causation in the case?

A: Yes.
Q: Both board-certified neurosurgeons?
A: Correct.
Q: And you disagree with Dr. Kabani in this case, as well?
A: Correct.
Q: Board-certified orthopedic spine surgeon?
A: Correct.
Q: And you just admitted a little while ago you are not a spine surgeon, are you?
Q: But you are right, and they are wrong, right?
Q: Why do you think they didn't hire a spine surgeon in this case and went with you?

The defense objected to this last question, but it didn't matter.

The expert said Johnson's internal disc disruption was not due to the accident, but just due to being forty years old. He didn't see any diagnostic scans prior to the accident. He didn't recommend any future surgery. He also saw no problem with a screw that was one millimeter away from Johnson's aorta, out of place.

Q: Did you know that [screw] was one millimeter away from his aorta?
A: It probably is a few millimeters away. And, again, it's not going to move. It hasn't done anything now, it's unlikely to do it…but I absolutely agree. It's not in the best position.

The defense radiologist came in next and on cross-examination, said that screw clearly is one millimeter away, is clearly a problem, and definitely would tell the surgeon that Johnson needs to have surgery. Sigh.

Takeaways

I generally believe that the law makes logical sense. So does medicine. So does your client's story. What usually does not make sense, neither in logic nor common sense, are the positions that the defense expert takes. There is a reason it does not make sense. The truth is easy. Distortion is hard, and tough to keep consistent. So teasing out in front of the jury *why* the defense experts are misrepresenting the medicine and facts is important. Usually, they can be the villain that you need in your story.

Next, we'll get into some specifics. Follow this roadmap, and you'll have your opposition madly Googling their own experts.

10

Deposing Defense Doctors

Depositions for Use at Trial

We have learned steps to take in discovery. We also learned how to lay traps for defense experts. Next, let's talk taking their depositions. Setting up a deposition for trial is different than setting up a deposition to settle a case. If you're trying to settle the case, then you want to approach your depositions like they are cross-examinations and get all the dirt. That way, the other side realizes the strength you are wielding and will try to resolve the case. You expose the mistakes in their reports, the money they make for the side that pays them, how everyone disagrees with them, and so on. You will see the other side scribbling furiously—already writing their settlement recommendation to the insurance carrier.

But if you're planning to try the case, you don't want to bring up any of the dirt because it will show your hand. You sort of want to play stupid. You don't want to let them know what you know. Set them up by merely asking for their opinions.[1]

1. This is a method that is similar to James H. McComas's *Dynamic Cross-Examination: A Whole New Way to Create Opportunities to Win* (Trial Guides, 2011).

Q: Doctor, thanks for coming, I don't want to waste anyone's time here, so why don't you just list your opinions and the basis for them, and we can get out of here quickly, okay?

Take a very short deposition, and the defense attorney and expert will think, "These people didn't even ask about all the money you make, or fight you, they must not know what they are doing!" *Au contraire, mon ami.*

I take these depositions with a friendly smile on my face the entire time. I take most of them virtually, from my office. We teach this method at my firm. We walk in, and on the record, ask about all their wonderful credentials, all their charity work, and praise them for them being known to help patients in the community. Tell them it will be a quick deposition. Act like you rarely take depositions. Put the check on the desk for the doctor, already signed, for just an hour of their time. Just ask them, nicely, to list all the records they reviewed. Later in trial cross-examination, this will be killer, because you can point out all the stuff the defense hid from them. You are lulling them to sleep. You are giving them a false sense of security. You will have all the bias and ammunition you need from your research outside the deposition. And yes, defense attorney and defense expert, I know you are reading this book. That is okay. Hopefully by reading this book we all can understand the value of these cases and settle them for a reasonable value, and not have to waste everyone's money and time in trials!

Let's get into taking the actual depositions of the usual cast of defense doctors.

Deposition Outline

I take at least fifty expert depositions a year. Sometimes, I take as many as a hundred. I love it. I'm a junkie for narrowing the issues for trial and laying ironclad traps. I usually need no more than an hour.

Remember, when you, or another member of your team is preparing for trial, nothing is worse than having a three-hundred-page deposition to read over again!

Your expert deposition (usually MDs, but sometimes other experts) has these main purposes:

- Ferret out the bias.
- Put holes in their foundation (the basis for their opinion).
- Get all their actual opinions.
- Get as many concessions as possible.
- Set up the common defenses for exclusion.
- Get to the bottom of their credentials.

Specific Defenses to Anticipate

One crucial thing I make sure to do, and it may change depending on your case, is to write out all the defense positions you have heard throughout litigation and that are imbedded in the other side's mediation brief. Much of this is just lip service from the defense lawyer or the adjuster. These are arguments they wish to make that are not supported by any facts or evidence. So I write down a list, and make sure I cover them with every defense expert. Why? So I can do a pretrial motion to exclude all these silly yet potentially dangerous arguments by the defense in trial. And if that does not work, I can expose the defense lawyer for trying to trick the jury with their big lie. Following are just a few of these ideas that you will come across:

- The plaintiff had full range of motion of their neck and back at the emergency room, so they cannot be hurt.
- The plaintiff did not have neck or back pain reported until a few days after the crash, so it is unrelated.

- Radicular pain has to be immediate after the crash, constant, and down the specific dermatome in order for it to be related to the crash.
- Ownership interest in surgery centers for the treating doctors is unheard of and should not be done.

These are just a few examples of defense excuses. They will be different in each one of your cases. Keep a log of what you hear from the defense. Ask their expert. If their expert cannot commit to a reasonable degree of medical probability of any of the above at their expert deposition, do a motion to exclude these points before the trial, and get these whacky arguments out. Also, their own expert will admit many of these "nefarious" things the defense will argue about plaintiffs, their doctors, and their clients are totally fine.

Following is a nifty outline I use in every expert deposition. This outline was created by Jayme Simpson, a fantastic trial lawyer in San Diego. We were on the same panel at the Dordick Trial College in Cabo, Mexico, speaking on expert depositions. When we showed each other our outlines, they were pretty much the same! My outlines are usually just chicken-scratch on my electronic notepad. Hers were much fancier.

At the beginning of each set of questions, I talk about the questions so you can understand how and why to ask them.

Background

I want to quickly expose how this expert is paid, who hired them, where the majority of their income comes from, and how often they work with the opposing counsel.

These are spine cases. Many times, the defense hires experts on spines who are general orthopedic doctors, do not do spine surgeries, and refer out patients in their clinical practice with spine injuries. The following questions dig out these issues:

Q: Are you board-certified and fellowship-trained on spines?
Q: How many surgeries, like the one Mr. [Plaintiff] had, have you done as lead surgeon?
Q: Who do you refer medical cases to in the community?
Q: Are you published in this field? Can you give examples?
Q: What hospitals are you affiliated with?

This question can help with costing information later, because their hospitals usually have very high rates for the same surgery that the plaintiff had.

Q: Why did you become a medical doctor?
Q: How did you choose your specialty?
Q: Why are you now doing forensic work?

If they say anything other than the money, ask:

Q: Why do you not do it for free?
Q: Can you tell me about your previous medical-legal work?
Q: What testimony have you given in other cases?
Q: Do you typically work for the plaintiff's side or for the defense?
Q: What is your relationship with [opposing counsel]?

Ask them how much money they make, gross, from being a forensic expert. If they claim ignorance, ask if it is more than $1 million. Ask for their accountant so you can subpoena them. If they cannot give you an estimate of their earnings (which every juror can in their own lives), they will look absolutely silly.

Q: How much are you being paid to give your opinion about this case?

Surgery

You want the defense to either commit that the surgery was reasonable to do, and caused by something else, or the surgery was unreasonable to do. If they say it was unreasonable, see if they will commit that it was malpractice. If they won't commit that it was malpractice, by what standard was it unreasonable? Did it harm the patient? If the surgery was reasonable, get them to commit that it was due to something else, but they do not know what it is from.

Q: There is a gap in treatment for Mr. [Plaintiff] from [date] to [date]. What is your explanation for this gap?

Q: What is your clinical experience related to Mr. [Plaintiff]'s injury?

Q: Do you agree that you have not treated the plaintiff?

Radicular Pain

We are asking these questions to see if they buy into what the defense attorney is pushing—that radicular pain must be constant, happen immediately, and be down a specific dermatome. Or do they believe in actual medicine and every patient being different?

Q: Is this a normal MRI with radicular pain?

Q: Does this MRI show a consistency with dermatomes?

Q: Is this a tentative diagnosis?

Bias

Ask for a breakdown of how often they are hired by defendants and plaintiffs. They will pull a percentage breakdown out of thin air.

Q: Have you ever testified in federal court?

If they have, they are required to do a federal rule disclosure and list out every single case they have been hired on, and by whom. Make them pull the information and attach it as an exhibit. Then you can see the breakdown for yourself.

Q: Please list any plaintiff lawyers who have hired you.

Allow them to take a break to pull that information. Usually they cannot find it, which makes them look silly. Or if they do, I contact that lawyer and get the expert's deposition from their case and see how their opinions have changed depending on who hired them.

Ask them if they have ever given any talks to insurance companies or groups of lawyers. You may, again, already know the answer. Either they are truthful, or not. If they fess up to it, ask them for their topic they spoke on and to pull their presentation and attach it as an exhibit. Offer to pay for their time to gather it.

Know Other Experts or Treaters

Ask about any and all social history with the defense attorney, insurance adjusters, and so on. Sometimes they play on the same softball team together. If you have done your homework, you will already know, and will use this impeachment for trial if they lie.

Q: Do you know Dr. _______?
Q: Do you know Mr. _______?
Q: Do you know Ms. _______?

Imaging

You want to see what this expert's own opinions are on the imaging studies, and not just a cut and paste from the radiologist. Then you want to see if they actually read the reports themselves and what their findings were. Did they see any changes over time if there were multiple imaging studies? The defense experts might very well give all kinds of opinions without having actually read the imaging studies.

Q: Have you reviewed both reports and imaging?
Q: Have you taken your own measurements of [_____]?
Q: Can you determine if this is a new or old herniation?
Q: What did you take into consideration?

Records Reviewed

Most of the time, the defense hires experts who already know their opinion before they even review the case. These experts know who is buttering their bread. The knee-jerk reaction by these folks to completely discredit your clients is a valuable sword if you know how to unsheathe it. This is where you do a deep dive into what records the expert received, and when they actually reviewed them.

For example, the defense medical doctor examined your client in March of 2022. He wrote his usual report saying your client suffered no injuries beyond a sprain. The imaging studies only showed degenerative changes. No surgery would help the plaintiff. The bills are too high. Sound familiar? But you may be shocked at how often these experts made all the above opinions without seeing *any* medical records, without seeing *any* of the imaging studies, and without seeing *any* of the bills.

How do you expose this? Before the expert deposition, with your deposition notice, request the expert's entire file, including all correspondence and billing records. You can see in these documents when they received the records, films, and bills. Together with their billing invoices, you can see when they actually reviewed them. Pin them down that, in March of 2022, these were all their opinions to a reasonable degree of medical probability. That they know better than all the treating doctors. Then make them list all the records they received, when they got them, and when they reviewed them. Juries just hate it when they have not reviewed the record, films, and bills before attempting to discredit your client. You may also be surprised how often these defense experts never actually read the diagnostics themselves. Be sure to ask:

Q: You formed your opinion about this case on [date] when you wrote this report?
Q: But you formed this opinion before you received [MRI/medical record/other info] on [date]?
Q: Doctor, you would never do a spine surgery on your patient without seeing the MRI would you?
Q: But you want the jury to buy your opinion in this case when you never saw the MRI?

Problems Can Vary Day to Day

Use common sense and big-picture thinking to show that every patient is different. Everyone is not just data that fits perfectly into a textbook. This patient, and this plaintiff, is real life. Use these questions to see if they will agree.

Q: What are Mr. [Plaintiff]'s ongoing symptoms?
Q: Does Mr. [Plaintiff] sometimes have good days and bad days?
Q: Would you agree that Mr. [Plaintiff]'s improving symptoms could be a good day?

Prognosis

Ask these questions because doctors for the defense do not have a patient–doctor relationship with the plaintiff. The Hippocratic oath does not apply. This is where I try to pin them down—if this was your patient, what would your recommendations be to help this person?

Either they can see that they need future treatment, or they'll take it to an extreme and say the patient is totally fine.

Q: Do you have advice that will help Mr. [Plaintiff] feel better?
Q: Is Mr. [Plaintiff] an unusually susceptible plaintiff?[2]
Q: Is there any sign of adjacent segment disease?[3]

Alternate Causes

In my cases, we have seen the defense try all kinds of alternate explanations for the plaintiff's injury. Maybe she was going through menopause, injured by picking up small children, or needs spine surgery because of her work as a hairdresser. Or the injury is because she has diabetes. Or because she has an autoimmune disease. Get these out in the open with this expert.

Q: Do you think that these injuries were caused by Ms. [Plaintiff]'s work?
Q: Do you think that these injuries were caused by Ms. [Plaintiff] doing laundry?
Q: Do you think that these injuries were caused by Ms. [Plaintiff] lifting children?

---

2. Make sure you differentiate between prior susceptibility (the plaintiff was susceptible to these injuries) and future susceptibility (will be susceptible in future for further injury).

3. This is sometimes called "second level syndrome." When a surgeon fuses one vertebral level it increases the movement above and below the fusion site. This leads to hypermobility at those levels, increases the incidence of osteoarthritis/degenerative joint disease, and substantially increases their risk of having another fusion surgery at the levels above and below the original fusion site in the future. This requires lawyers to get a "probability" determination on those future surgeries and the costs of doing them for the jury.

Q: Do you think that these injuries were caused by Ms. [Plaintiff]'s underlying health condition?
Q: Do you think this plaintiff has a personality disorder like somatic syndrome disorder?

Attorney Referrals

The defense makes it sound like attorney referrals are evil, when most people listen to trusted professionals for referrals in any industry. Most doctors, on both sides, get referrals from lawyers. So ask the defense expert:

Q: Do you treat patients referred by attorneys?
Q: How often do you do this?
Q: Does it impact your treatment?
Q: Do you treat these patients the same as any other patients?

Other Incident

You want to make sure to ferret out if the defense is blaming anything else on your client's injuries, and the medical standard. This is ripe for motions to exclude if they cannot find anything else to blame,[4] and something to overcome with your affirmative evidence if so.

Q: Are you aware of another collision that occurred before or after this collision?
Q: Were you told about this other collision by defense counsel?
Q: Have you seen photographs of property damage from another collision?

4. *See* chapter 14, "Pretrial Motions."

Q: Have you heard about complaints or symptoms from another collision?

Q: Do you have a reasonable degree of medical probability that the other crash affects Mr. [Plaintiff]'s current conditions?

IME Conducted

The medical examination by the defense doctor is full of great information. You can get in all the complaints your client told them during the examination. All their physical findings. And defeat some of the defense lawyer's favorite misdirection defenses.

Q: Have you met with the plaintiff?

Q: Have you taken an oral history and conducted a physical examination with Mr. [Plaintiff]?

Q: Was Mr. [Plaintiff] faking, malingering, or exaggerating?

Q: Have you conducted range of motion tests?[5]

Q: Is Mr. [Plaintiff]'s forward flexion normal?

Medicare Value

A common tactic in trial is for the defense to say that the client's treating doctors charged too much and should only get Medicare rates. However, very few physicians charge Medicare rates because they can't cover their costs to stay in business. Take the time to expose that the defense's own experts don't use Medicare rates either. However, look this up in your state—referring to Medicare rates is not allowed in some states.

5. See *Guides to the Evaluation of Permanent Impairment* 6th ed. (American Medical Association, 2022). This is a great way to discredit defense doctors who say that the plaintiff is not impaired.

Q: Are you familiar with Medicare rates?
Q: Are Medicare rates reasonable?
Q: Do you accept Medicare?

Liens, Letters of Protection, Delay Paid Care

One common defense that comes up is that lien or deferred payment plan treatment by the treating doctors are unethical.

Q: Have you treated patients on a lien before?
Q: Does the price of the care you provide increase if a lien is present?
Q: Do patients typically receive care on a lien if they cannot afford to pay up front?
Q: Do liens allow patients to access medical care?
Q: Do some of your clients pay cash? Is that a discount? That is paid up front?

Video Surveillance of Your Client

You may hear from the defense that video surveillance of your client shows things that no one with this injury can do. If they give it to the defense, there is privilege protection such as work product. They gave it to a third party. So ask and if they saw it, request it.

Q: Have you seen video footage of my client?
Q: Who gave it to you?
Q: Who filmed it?
Q: What is your understanding?

Ownership in Surgery Center

The defense will want to make it seem like doctors who own portions of surgery centers or hospitals are nefarious. In reality, it is commonplace and even defense doctors do this. Most successful physicians do as well.

Q: Do you have any ownership or interest in any medical facilities or hospitals?
Q: Is it customary for physicians to own facilities?
Q: Would you be critical of a physician with ownership in a facility?
Q: Do you partially or fully own large medical devices such as an MRI machine?

Biomechanics

This is just a short outline of potential questions for a biomechanical expert. For more information, see chapter 11, "Defense Biomechanical Experts."

Q: How do you know what biomechanics is?
Q: Have you performed a biomechanical analysis?
Q: Do you agree that biomechanics provide little insight to you?
Q: Do you agree that no studies take into account people with degenerative spines?
Q: Do you have a biomechanical expert on staff to determine the cause of an injury?
Q: Are doctors the best people to determine the cause of an injury?

Is There Anything Else?

Make sure to ask the expert at the close of the deposition if they have now shared all their opinions. In California it is the *Kennemur* case that governs. You do not want any surprise opinions at trial only to learn that you did not "close off" your deposition by asking if they shared all their opinions. In other states it must be contained in their expert reports, especially if they mirror the Federal Rules.

Q: Have you discussed all of your opinions?
Q: Do you plan to review other documents?
Q: Have you been asked to review anything further if your opinions change?

Hopefully now you have a great outline on how to take expert depositions, and how to set the defense up at trial for the ultimate victory.

The Million-Dollar Question

If you get one piece of advice out of this book that is a game changer, this is it. Find the causation jury instruction in your jurisdiction. Blow it up. Put it in every outline to cover in deposition, and every closing to give in trial. I include a slide showing Causation CACI 430. This is an important part of almost every one of my cases. Read the last sentence: "Conduct is not a substantial factor in causing the harm if the same harm would have occurred without that conduct."[6]

So, in all your cases, the defense expert has to commit, to a reasonable degree of medical probability, that your client would have needed *all* this treatment, had *all* this pain, needed the surgery, *all without the crash happening*. They would have to align themselves with the best fortune tellers ever to be able to predict everyone's future. This is how California words it. It is similar in other states with a "but for" test. They could tell the jury when the court reporter would need surgery in the future. Or when the judge will start to need treatment in his neck

6. CACI No. 430. Causation: Substantial Factor.

due to his degenerative condition! Or, they will have to admit that it would be pure speculation when someone would have pain or need treatment if the crash had never happened. So here are the million-dollar questions to ask:

Q: Doctor, with a reasonable degree of medical probability, had this crash never occurred, when would my client have needed any of the treatment that they had after the crash?

I make them commit to an answer.

Q: Doctor, with a reasonable degree of medical probability, had this crash never occurred, when would my client have needed spine surgery?

Q: When would they have had neck pain that required medical treatment?

Q: When would they have had their asymptomatic degenerative condition in their spine start to become symptomatic so they would seek medical care?

And that is it folks. On the stand I straight up tell the defense expert that this is the million-dollar question. And when they concede they do not know, and it would be speculation, I take a gigantic dramatic pause, and thank the doctor. Because they just conceded causation in the case. Then put that doctor's testimony via the court transcript, alongside your jury instruction, and show the jury how you proved your case. Winner, winner four course dinner.

Ask Clear & Usable Questions

When you are taking depositions, you want very clear and usable questions and answers that you can impeach the witness with at trial. Ask the question many times if you have to in deposition to get a clear answer or concession. The clear concession with many of these defense experts in deposition proves an element of your case.

Here is another example of asking a clear question in deposition to use at trial:

Mr. Simon: Doctor, with a reasonable degree of medical certainty, besides the crash, what caused the injury to this man's spine?

Defense Doctor: Well could be a myriad of things. He has degeneration, he is a laborer, he is older, so endless possibilities.

Q: Doctor, I appreciate the possibilities, but as you know, we need more. Just let me ask this question, so we can get out of here, and get home to our families.

Here comes the setup for motions to exclude this defense argument at trial:

Q: Doctor, with a reasonable degree of medical certainty, and without guessing, besides this crash, what caused the injury to this man's spine?

A: I don't know.

The point here is to keep asking the question until you get a clear answer. Ask a question and get an answer that is so easy to follow that you can cut and paste it in a motion to the judge, to show them that the defense cannot meet their burden for alternate cause, and they cannot throw speculation in front of the jury. Ask a question so simple that if you blew it up in a poster in front of the jury, they would understand. Most experts try to be sly and give long-winded answers. Keep pressing!

Do not be phased by the defense counsel's objections in deposition for "asked and answered." You are entitled to your answer. And when you get that clean question and answer, move on quickly so the expert cannot try and explain away their concession.

Defense Radiologists: Turn to the Light

We just talked about the experts who only see bits and pieces of the medical evidence in order to give the jury an opinion. This speaks even truer with defense-hired radiologists. When the defense hires them, they are only looking at images. The defense does not give them anything else. They don't have clinical records; they don't have sworn deposition testimony. That is it. They only get one piece of the puzzle. By the time your trial is over, the jury will have seen and reviewed far more than the radiologists! But I tell you this because when the radiologists only see the films, they are blinded by the defense lawyers.

If you arm the defense radiologist with the full clinical picture of your client, more often than not, they will give you causation. This can be done with hypotheticals. Remember to embrace aggravation of pre-existing conditions when you are dealing with these folks. Later in this chapter, I will show you how to win your case with the radiologist by revealing to them the clinical picture and having them agree that the crash aggravated the previously asymptomatic degenerative condition.

The defense hires radiologists to give these general opinions:

- The scans show no sign of trauma.
- The abnormalities seen on the scans are degenerative in nature, and not due to any acute trauma.
- They do not see any nerve compression or neurological issues in their review of the scans.

Red Herring #1: No Signs of Trauma from ER

The first red herring is films from the ER. It's such a disservice and a trick for radiologists to say, "I see no signs of trauma at the ER and in the diagnostic films." Because when radiologists are in the ER, they are not doing MRIs. MRIs are the only type of imaging that can show disc injuries. At the ER, radiologists just do CT scans or X-rays because they are quick and show the structures most important to life-threatening injuries: bone and blood. Radiologists in the ER want to see if anything is broken or bleeding that could kill the patient or require an immediate surgery. So, the defense attorney goes to the radiologist who doesn't see any signs of trauma in the CT scan done in the ER. But a CT scan isn't going to show anything if there is a disc injury. We're not dealing with fractures in most of these cases. You have to defuse that bomb. Most of the time the radiologist will agree that the emergency room scans are done to rule out acute fracture, or anything life-threatening. They will concede that CTs and X-rays are done in seconds, while MRIs take thirty minutes to an hour. They are difficult for a person with high levels of pain to remain still for, which is required for a viable MRI study. MRIs are far more expensive, and rarely done in the ER setting. They will also agree the MRI is a far better tool to see any disc injuries or abnormalities.

Red Herring #2: No Acute Injuries in MRI

The next red herring is that when the radiologist says they see no acute injuries in the MRI films, they are usually taken weeks, if not months, after the crash. There must be clinical justification for the MRI referral by an examining doctor.

Document *when* the MRI is taken. And that things can disappear within two to eight weeks on an MRI. Remember, MRIs are good for soft fleshy stuff and nerves. CT and X-rays are good for blood and bone. Most people are getting MRIs three or four months later because the symptoms don't go away. People think the symptoms will disappear and then they don't. By the time they get an MRI, those symptoms of trauma are gone. So when the radiologist says they see no signs of trauma on the MRI, well, yeah. Of course. This MRI was taken three months late. They're not going to see evidence of acute trauma. This is a great concession to get from any medical doctor that is deposed.

Red Herring #3: Anything Wrong is Degenerative

Next let's discuss the next reason the defense hired radiologists: to opine that the abnormalities they see on the MRI are a degenerative condition. Abnormalities, referencing the past chapters, are things like disc herniations, protrusions, extrusions, stenosis, and so on. Many times, the defense radiologist will say all of this was degenerative in nature. This can be good for you.

For example, they'll see a disc protrusion and try and play the game of degeneration over time. So walk them through it and talk about how many adults have degeneration. This shows the jury that this is a pre-existing condition that everyone on that jury pool could have. Remember those jury instructions we talked about?

> **Mr. Simon:** Doctor, you would agree that most men in their forties, like my client, would likely have degenerative conditions in their cervical spine, that are similar to what you are seeing in only the films, right?

Now, here comes the setup for them allowing themselves to be willfully blinded by the defense lawyer, and about to give up causation based on the clinical records:

Mr. Simon: Do you treat a patient without pain?
Defense Radiologist: No, I do not.
Q: So with a reasonable degree of medical probability, when did the pain start?
A: Well, I would have to look at the records.

But the defense never gives these radiologists the records. They just give them these films with no context and try to get them to match up what happens. So now you are going to give them context through a hypothetical question. Check your jurisdiction as almost all allow hypothetical questions to an expert. Here is how it plays out:

Q: Doctor, now I know you were not given the records, but let me give you a hypothetical.

Pro tip: write out these assumptions on a whiteboard or easel as you go so the jury can follow along with your assumptions.

Q: Let's assume that:

- The patient has zero prior complaints of neck pain, or pain into their arms and into their fingertips.
- On [date] they were in the subject crash, went to the emergency room, and complained of neck pain.
- On [date] they complained to their doctor of the neck pain continuing, as well has numbness and tingling down their arm and into their fingertips.
- That pain, numbness, and tingling remained until they had cervical fusion surgery on [date], then it went away.

Q: Okay now doctor, given these assumptions, what was the cause of the pain?
Q: What caused this asymptomatic degenerative condition to be lit up?
Q: If they got better after surgery, what does that tell you?

They are pinned down. They have to tell you that there is a causal relationship between the crash and the cause of the pain. You would not do surgery without the pain. The pain complaints match up with the level of abnormality in the cervical spine and the suspected neurological issue. The surgery seems to have cured those issues.

At the end of the day, radiologists don't make the call for surgery. They don't know the clinical symptoms. They don't see the patients. This is important to press to the jury that they hired someone to show you only part of the puzzle, and never show the entire finished product. Their job is to make a determination on causation, yet the defense parades in people who did not see the full picture and cannot help them. So in the deposition, I lay out a hypothetical of what the actual clinical picture is of the patient. The entire picture. And ask them these hypothetical questions.

Red Herring #4: Nerve Impingement

Defense radiologists also like to say that, based on their opinion, they *don't see* any nerve impingement or compression. *Impingement* or *compression* are strong words that have strong connotations to a layperson. So the defense radiologists play with other words that you need to tease out, like "stenosis" or "encroachment." Well, *encroachment* or *stenosis* could mean *compressed*, and that could still affect the nerve. If a nerve is completely compressed it could be severed, it could be paralyzed. But there are different levels of compression. There is stenosis or nerve pain. It could be abutting the nerve. These are all things that could cause nerve pain. MRIs are done static, usually laying down. Your client may feel differently when standing up. If they're standing up, there is gravity pushing down on their forehead and down on their spine. So if the radiologist doesn't see a disc compression or nerve issue when your client is laying down on an MRI, the radiologist might see it when your client is standing up, because the body is dynamic. It moves.

Again, defense radiologists are not given the entire picture. Hand them the surgery report where the surgeon says they decompressed the nerve. Where the surgeon, while in the patient's body, saw nerve compression. And ask the radiologist:

Q: Who would know better, you or the surgeon?

They either say "the surgeon," or give a smug non-answer:

A: Look, this is just my opinion of what I see.

Either way you are good to go.

Show That the Defense Experts Do Not Agree

There is another great tool to implement with defense radiologists: showing the defense experts do not agree with each other. The defense loves to over-designate. In every simple disc injury case, where the defense likely only needs a spine surgeon to opine on everything, they go bananas and hire a neurologist, a neurosurgeon, an orthopedic surgeon, and a radiologist. They are simply trying to outspend the plaintiff. But this over-designation is a gift. The defense attorneys are never organized enough to get their experts all in agreement. Defense attorneys barely talk to their experts. So, many times you can use these defense radiologists to disagree with the other defense doctors by using hypothetical situations based off simple medicine and medical literature.

For example, most radiologists will agree with a diagnosis of *adjacent segment disorder*. Twenty years after a spinal fusion is medically probable, the person will need another spinal fusion at the level above or below where they had the previous surgery. This is due to the added stress on those adjacent levels since one level is fused. The adjacent segment has been doing double or triple the work and having double or triple the stress that that segment would have needed to endure, if the original spinal fusion hadn't been needed. The literature suggests a 1 percent to 3 percent chance per year, compounded, over time.[7] The defense will likely hire a spine doctor who will disagree with that because they are paid by the defense to disagree, but radiologists might agree with it. Many times, I get defense experts to disagree with each other to show what's really going on.

Another example is that radiologists will also agree with a diagnosis of *chemical radiculitis*, the issue when chemicals leak out from a little tear and go into the spinal canal, causing pain. You cannot see these in MRIs. Many physicians subscribe to this theory and will admit it is accepted in the medical community.

Here are some sample questions to throw at the radiologist, because the defense surgeons may not agree:

Q: Doctor, would you agree that the more we age, the more prone we are to disc injuries in our spines due to rear-end car crashes?"

Q: Doctor, you are familiar with adjacent segment disorder, correct?

Q: So you would agree that twenty years after a patient's spine is fused, at any level, it is medically probable that they need an adjacent surgery?

Q: Are you familiar with the AMA Guidelines? What impairment does it have for someone with a fusion surgery?

---

7. Alan S. Hilibrand and Matthew Robbins, "Adjacent Segment Degeneration and Adjacent Segment Disease: The Consequences of Spinal Fusion?," *The Spine Journal* 4, no. 6 (Nov-Dec 2004): 190S-194S, https://doi.org/10.1016/j.spinee.2004.07.007.

Q: Doctor, would you agree that someone with radicular pain due to the condition you see in the MRI, that the pain can come and go and wax and wane?

Q: Would you agree it does not need to fit a specific dermatome?

Q: Doctor, would you agree that there are nerve related abnormalities in your read of the imaging studies?

Q: Doctor, would you agree there is an identifiable issue that can be treated with surgery that you see on the MRI films?

Q: Doctor, would you agree the only way to tell if this is a traumatic injury is to have an MRI taken before the crash and after the crash?

Q: So, anyone that says it is definitely one or the other, just looking at the MRI films, you would not agree with that, right?

The more you impress defense radiologists with your knowledge of the science and get into a philosophical talk about chemical radiculitis, the more they like the mental gymnastics and will give you a carrot. Like, "Thanks for playing! Here's your reward!"

I had one radiologist who loves the game so much. He made $1.5 million a year, over thirty years, as a defense witness. He loves when I take his deposition. I've earned his respect. He'll tell me he is glad to see me and knows it will be a short deposition because I know the questions to ask him. And the defense just looks shook, like, "What's about to happen?"

And here's the hypothetical question for the radiologist:

Mr. Simon: If this person had no pain until after the crash, does that match what you see on the MRI?"

Defense Radiologist: Well, based on the hypothetical, yes it does counselor.

Q: Well, gee, let me ask you another question…

Defense radiologists will also disagree with defense doctors and what they see in the films. Pit them against each other.

> **Q:** When did that herniation occur?
> **A:** Well we have no real way of knowing.
> **Q:** Do you know of anything else other than a car crash that could have caused this?
> **A:** No, I don't.

When it comes to your client's injuries, it's either they have no idea, or it's the car crash.

Example: Defense Radiologist in the *Johnson* Case

In my *Johnson* case, I got one radiologist to disagree with everything the defense doctor said. A fusion had to be redone, and the defense surgeon said a redo wasn't needed. I showed the films to the radiologist, and he said it wasn't fine because the screw fell out and was a millimeter away from Johnson's aorta. Johnson almost died!

Also in my *Johnson* case, I asked the defense's spine expert if he agreed my client had pain down the left side of his body, arm, and leg.

He said yes, and that was even before he had the MRIs.

Then I showed him the pain diagrams my client filled out before any MRIs were taken. A pain diagram is where your client goes into a physical therapist's office, or the first appointment with a new medical doctor, and the doctor asks the client to fill out where they are having pain on a body picture. Sure enough, that pain matched up exactly with what my client said, before he had a surgery recommendation, before he had any MRIs. He drew little X's from the left side of his neck, down his left arm, and into his left hand. He drew little X's from his lower back, down his left butt and leg, and down to his foot. I put my client's diagram next to a *dermatome map* to show those are the nerve patterns for the exact areas where my client had surgeries.[8] Then, I showed the timeline exhibit. This put into perspective when he filled out that pain diagram, when he had that MRI, and when had those surgeries. This is the power of demonstrative exhibits we discussed in chapter 7, "Gathering the Evidence," in the section "Before and After Damages Photos." The jury could see with their own eyes that it all matched up! Of course, the defense next called their hack surgeon who said nothing matched up, the plaintiff never complained of radicular pain, blah blah blah.

It is important to note that with dermatomes and its mapping that rarely, if ever, does a patient have "perfect radiculopathy." Everyone is different and feels pain differently. There are so many variables. But this is a valuable tool to use.

Example: Further Hypothetical Questions with a Radiologist

Here's an example of owning a defense radiologist by going through a series of hypothetical questions. This was a deposition I took in 2017 with a defense radiologist who we will call Dr. Kee, who reviewed imaging studies of my client's lumbar spine. He was a solid witness on paper because he did not accept attorney-referred treatment, and was Ivy League trained. Yale, Yale, Yale. His opinion was that it was possible that my client's injuries were due to his car accident, or they were pre-existing. But he was not able to point to any other factors aside from the car accident. He was hired to only look at the films, but when I confronted him with the clinical picture hypothetical situation we discussed, this is how it played out.

> **Mr. Simon:** Are you able to say that something else caused the protrusion in Mr. [Plaintiff]'s lumbar spine, with a

8. *See* chapter 1 for an example of a dermatome map.

reasonable degree of medical probability, other than the subject car crash?

Defense Radiologist: I'm not sure that anything was necessarily reflected in the clinical records based on my deposition reviews, since I didn't do a primary review of those records. But, you know, I am certainly not aware, based on my limited review, of any specific event that might have caused a protrusion to be there. Often those events may be unnoticed. It doesn't have to be a car accident. It could be. It could be something else, too.

You want to project onto the blank slate that a witness like this provides.

Q: And I just want to know, with a reasonable degree of medical probability, if it's not the car crash, then what caused the protrusion?

A: I really couldn't tell you. In fact, I really can't assign a probability like that, so I just can't tell you.

Q: And based on this hypothetical, if Mr. [Plaintiff] had no prior back pain or radicular pain, he gets in a car crash on November 2nd, 2013. Within two days, he reports lower back pain and radicular pain down his left lower extremity, and then you see the MRI in 2013, a doctor does a neurological exam that also shows loss of neurological sensation at the L5 distribution on the right side, what is your opinion?

A: I think I already answered that question before. You know, assuming that everything you said is true, so we take those assumptions into account, and the onset of symptoms is clearly in an L5 distribution, and the onset of those symptoms is relatively quick after the incident, then I think it's plausible that the incident could've caused the onset of symptoms.

That is your case right there. You just won. He disagreed with the defense's normal hired expert, and the jury believed him.

I also like to ask radiologists who they respect for neurosurgeons. Who treats their patients? Guess what? It is never the defense doctor, because those people are courtroom doctors usually with no actual medical practice. It is always some other doctor in the community. And who knows, you might strike gold! It may be who helped your client in this case.

Deposing or Cross-Examining Radiologists

Defense radiologists are sometimes gifts. Many are asked to give opinions with blinders on. They just get film. You will want to get your laundry list of potential concessions to ask in the expert deposition. If they agree, highlight those concessions again in trial cross-examination. You can get major concessions from radiologists based on general medical science and literature that the defense hired gun surgeon will 100 percent disagree with. Every radiologist will agree with this statement:

> **Mr. Simon:** Does every adult have spinal degeneration?
> **Defense Radiologist:** Yes.

Every single juror has degeneration. Get this concession. The answer to this question (yes) applies to the aggravation of a pre-existing condition—the jury instruction I pointed out earlier in this chapter, also called the "million-dollar question." Then ask the following hypothetical question that is the whole case:

Q: If surgery took away that pain, what happened?
A: If the pain went away, the pain was all caused by the crash.

They'll give it to you. It's almost as if doctors want you to ask that perfect hypothetical question. They couldn't say this person would have had neck or back pain without the crash. The jury instruction is that the defense has to show the injury would have occurred without the harm ever happening.

Defense doctors give concessions all the time. Here's a sample of what I ask defense spine surgeons:

Mr. Simon: Can you say with a reasonable degree of medical probability that this person would have needed spine surgery without the crash?
Defense Spine Surgeon: No, I can't say that.
Q: But you'd agree the surgery was reasonable to do?
A: Yes, it was reasonable to do.
Q: So then you'd agree the trauma was real?
A: Yes.

You'll want to walk radiologists down the same path, so setting up this question is important.

I'll also ask a defense expert what is causing this person's pain.

Q: To a reasonable degree of medical probability, what is causing this human being pain?

You would be shocked at how many times they say:

A: I don't know.

It's a total gift. The defense hired an expert, paid them a lot of money, and the expert just... doesn't know? Some forensic expert we've got here. It is either everything lines up, all the treating doctors are right, or... "I don't know."

An expert doesn't have to agree with you. The point isn't to sway them. In this situation, your goal is to simply point out the absurdity. The defense paid this slick forensic expert all this money to figure out what happened to this person, and why they're hurting, and they don't know. They might as well talk about the weather or give their opinion on the existential dilemma of modern man. Jurors will laugh.

Again, as you can tell with the theme of this book, I love to keep it simple. I almost never affirmatively hire a radiologist as an expert. But if the defense does, I always counter. Fight fire with fire. But do not make your radiologist evaluate your client in a vacuum with blinders on like the defense does. If they are willing, give your radiologist all the records, photographs, and case material, and let them give causation opinions from a clinical radiologist's standpoint.

What do I mean? Many radiologists also do interventional pain management procedures such as epidural injections and the like. They diagnose patients clinically all the time. They treat them. But when the defense hires them as an expert, the defense only asks them to look at one thing. Do not fall for it. Let your experts see it all, and give opinions based on what they see, as if your client were their own patient. Ask your radiologist expert how they would deal with your client in the real world.

Example: Radiologist from Texas

Once, the defense designated a new witness after we rested at trial and flew in this new radiologist from Texas for a shotgun deposition—for a case I was trying in California! Sounds strange I know, but the judge allowed it. This was a brand new expert! In the middle of trial! After I rested! Whatever. Anyway. I had to hit up all my contacts in Texas in order to prepare to depose her that night, after a day of trial, four weeks in. Within hours I had a dozen transcripts. All the dirt was there. My deep-dive Google searches found absolute gold. The deposition that night was just a smiley-face setup. She said she was a professor, but I found out that she only taught ten days a year. She said she has a clinical practice, but in all the depositions and trial cross-examinations I found, she admitted she only saw a handful of patients a year. All her money came from the automotive industry. Two months before, she was speaking at the Defense Research Institute—the defense bar for product manufacturers. She spoke there twice. Better yet, she was on a panel with the defense lawyer!

But when I deposed her, I played it cool.

Here is a sample of that deposition:

Mr. Simon: Hey, sorry, I gotta ask these types of questions, but you never hung out with any of these lawyers, or been to events with them, or anything, right?

Defense Radiologist: No, of course not.

Bear trap set. The defense thinks there is no way you have the information that this expert has been friendly with these lawyers. There was no need to cross her on her opinions of the science. This expert was about to perjure her herself.

Later at trial, my cross-examination went like this:

Mr. Simon: Do you know how many board-certified radiologists there are in Los Angeles County?

Defense Radiologist: Several I would assume.

Q: Tens of thousands likely, you would agree?

A: Yes.

Q: Do you know why they flew you from Texas last night?
A: No.

Then comes the sleeper cell attack. The box of death comes up on the table.[9] Full of certified transcripts and records of speaking engagements with the defense lawyers.

Q: We took your deposition last night, right?
A: Yes.
Q: And it was the first time we met?
A: Yes.
Q: In fact, you said last night, this was the first time you'd met any of these lawyers?
A: That is correct.
Q: Do you know any of these lawyers at this table?
A: No.

Then I whipped out a syllabus showing she was on the same panel as one of the defense lawyers just two months ago. I put I finger over his head and said,

Q: Not even this guy?

The next few minutes were courtroom theatrics: I pulled out the syllabi and passed them to the court, witnesses, and counsel. The judge loved it. Caught in a lie, the witness was red-faced and the jury laughed.

9. The *box of death* is discussed in chapter 9, "Defense Experts," under the heading "Ask Your Community."

A: But it was two months ago.
Q: It was in Columbus, Ohio—you don't remember that?
A: Oh yeah, that's right.

You can find so much gold on these people by Googling terms like *defense* and *seminar* along with the expert's name. You want them to lie and go for extremes. Then show those lies, contradictions, and extremes at trial. After ten minutes of cross-examination, she was destroyed. The defense sat there red-faced. I was reminding *her* what she was doing just a few months ago, testifying where, saying the same thing, and oh yeah, I had her slides from these defense seminars. Stuff where it says she can lighten and darken X-ray images to fit her narrative. I'll bet you can guess the last question in this cross-examination:

Q: Doctor, now do you know why they flew you in from Texas instead of hiring any of the 10,000 board-certified radiologists in the fifteen square miles around this courthouse?
DEFENSE ATTORNEY: Objection.
Q: I withdraw, Your Honor, we all know the answer.

Takeaways

Do not get in the cage with a bear. These experts, while likely making up a lot of stuff to support their position, are still highly educated and crafty. Get any concessions you can, especially the critical ones that help you win your causation case, sprinkle in some bias, then get out.

11

Defense Biomechanical Experts

Depositions for Use at Trial

Biomechanical experts have their place in the legal world. They will tell us how injuries occur from body movements in certain situations. These are situations where the movement of the body is at issue, usually from an alleged trip and fall, or even a gun shooting, and so on. I hire great ones all the time. However, for the biomechanical experts in car crash cases, especially those who only testify for the defense about the lack of injuries that can occur in car crashes, their work is absolute hogwash. There is little to no science behind what these biomechanical experts do. I *never* affirmatively hire a biomechanical expert in a car crash case. If the defense hires one, fine, we will supplement or use for rebuttal to defeat their science. While I truly believe that these experts should be excluded in pretrial motions,[1] you still need to take their depositions and prepare as if the judge will still let it in. The expert deposition of the biomechanical expert can be used as trial testimony. I view the entire biomechanical deposition as a potential part of the trial. Always think "trial backwards." The concessions received in deposition and then

1. *See* chapter 14, "Pretrial Motions."

told in front of the jury are one and the same. The bias pulled out in the expert deposition will then be used in cross-examination. Therefore, it makes sense to do them both at the same time in this book.

How to Exclude a Defense Biomechanical Expert

One tactic to exclude a defense biomechanical expert is to present scientific studies to the judge so you can exclude the expert. Many of these experts talk about the probability of injury based on cadaver studies from the 1980s. They can't say anything about any *specific* injury that our clients sustained in a crash.

Defense biomechanical experts are just there to talk in generalities. They are not medical doctors and they will not be able to talk about your client's injuries specifically. Why some judges let them talk about what other studies show, which have nothing in common with your facts or client, is beyond me. Some states actually allow them to testify on causation. Whether you are setting up to ask for exclusion, or getting the necessary information to make them look ridiculous on cross-examination, the method of your deposition is the same:

- Expose and attack their studies and methodology.
- Attack their lack of credentials in discussing actual injury causation. Ask them if they have a license to practice medicine (they don't). Ask if they have privileges at any hospital (they don't). Ask other defense medical experts if they rely on biomechanists in the ER to tell them if a patient is injured or not (they don't).
- Attack the large amounts of hearsay they will inevitably spew.

The setup is the expert deposition, which you then will cut up into a motion to exclude.

Depose Experts about Studies

The easiest way to get these folks limited or excluded is by showing they have no foundation for their opinions. The data which they claim to rely on is very likely inapplicable to your case. In deposition, ask the biomechanical expert for all the studies they rely on. Make them produce copies of every single study. In deposition, ask them to pull up each study, show you each one that applies to this case, and explain why it applies. It is a great set up for a motion to exclude. When you actually look at these studies, they are so far from your set of facts that a good judge will punt them.

The defense biomechanical experts cannot help themselves. They cannot veer from the party line. They make millions to say the same thing, over and over, no matter what. Many of their studies are funded by insurance companies and are done in their parking lots. I kid you not. It is science created by insurance companies. Many times, the sample size is two people. Or fourteen. Or sometimes just one person. And that one person just may be "Rusty the Superhuman," Rusty Haight. I kid you not.[2] There have been documentaries on him. These "scientists" found him and used him in insurance company funded studies to show that he cannot get hurt. He literally has set the Guinness World Record for amount of human crash tests. Almost one thousand! It is great when you ask them for the sample size for their studies and it is … one.

The set up question is to make their "expert" commit to the fact that they have zero studies at the same crash speed as your client, with the same age and health conditions as your client, under the same conditions, that are done using live subjects, that are peer reviewed, and that are published in the United States. Push them for this concession and it will pay large dividends in your motion before the judge, or the cross-examination during trial.

2. For more information about Rusty Haight, *see* "Crash Tests (Most)," *Guinness World Records*, https://www.guinnessworldrecords.com/world-records/crash-tests-(most); *Stan Lee's Superhumans,* season one, episode 6, "Human Crash Test Dummy," aired September 15, 2010, on the History Channel.

During the deposition, you must also set them up for cross-examination, and get them to lean into their extreme opinions. It will make it seem like they have no common sense. The more they go out on a limb, the harder they will fall. In the pages to follow you will see some extreme positions and my actual cross-examination questions. Common extreme positions are:

- The impact was like getting hit with a pillow.
- You cannot get a disc injury with a rear-end impact, even at eighty miles per hour.
- All plaintiffs in the thousands of cases they investigated were frauds, along with all the doctors treating them.
- Rusty the Superhuman is representative of the community in whole.

It's important that you find their studies, which were most likely not peer reviewed. Then, expose who funds the studies, and expose how much money the expert themselves makes. The fight isn't about how fast the car was going when the crash happened. Even if a car is flooring it at one hundred miles per hour, these experts will say with a straight face that a disc herniation isn't possible. I bet you they most likely won't know about the details of the studies they rely on, making them look silly in front of a jury. If you want to go further, go ahead and subpoena and talk to the authors of the studies they are relying on. Many of them will say that their study is now dated and proven to be wrong! Imagine that rebuttal witness.

Another tactic used by biomechanical experts is saying they have a "database" of articles that say a person cannot succumb to a lumbar injury due to a rear-end collision. But they will only produce a couple of those articles at deposition, allowing them to hide the faulty articles. At trial, point out that this expert only presented two articles and the rest of the "database" remains hidden. This signals to the jury that the expert had something to hide. I also have a database of studies that are peer reviewed, which I can use against them.

Also remember one critical flaw in all their "science." Patients are individual people. Each case is different. Each patient is different. And none of their studies are prepared for those with pre-existing conditions.

Look at the Expert's Own Research

Another fun tactic I use is to look at the expert's own actual research. Their own actual case studies. They may have been hired thousands of times. In many of those cases, a disc herniation is alleged from a rear-end car crash. In almost all of those cases, a medical doctor confirms that the patient had a disc herniation. Real humans, real data. But this expert's opinion, almost every time, is that a disc herniation is not possible. Were *all* these medical doctors committing fraud? What about all these injured patients?

It is important to remember that this is not every biomechanical expert. Most of the honest ones will give you concessions on the limitations of their opinions and their data. They will concede that their studies do not include pre-existing conditions or people who are more prone to injury. They will concede that it is quite possible that the injuries were caused in the crash. Or at the very least were aggravated. But we all have faced the ones that are just another advocate for the defense and go "all in" on everything.

Example: Cross-Examination of a Biomechanical Expert

Here is an actual cross-examination of a biomechanical expert.

MR. SIMON: And you've investigated thousands of cases with rear-end collisions of people who alleged a disc injury in their spine, correct?

DEFENSE BIOMECHANICAL EXPERT: There are many accidents with many claims of injury which—

MR. SIMON: All right.

Defense Biomechanical Expert: —disc injuries are one of those claims.

Mr. Simon: So thousands of cases where people have alleged lumbar disc injuries from rear-end collisions at approximate delta-*v*'s just like the ones we have here today, true?

Defense Biomechanical Expert: I do not know if it is in the thousands or not, but certainly close.

Q: And in all of those cases, the injured victim had a medical doctor back up the disc injury from the crash, right?

A: Well, yes, they did, but there are just so many variables.

Q: Well, sir, in each of those cases you were paid tens of thousands of dollars in each one, to be the forensic expert, to work it up, look into it, and give an opinion, right?

A: Well sometimes a few thousand, but yes.

Q: And you would go in front of juries and tell them there was not enough force to cause injury, right?

A: Well, yeah.

Q: Are you now saying there are just too many variables, and those testimonies, under oath, were misleading or false?

A: No counselor, I am not saying that, stop putting words in my mouth, there was enough for me to give an opinion.

Q: Madame court reporter can you read back my question and his answer just a few minutes ago where I he brought up too many variables?

A: Oh come on.

Q: Well those are your words, not mine, right?

A: Stop it.

Q: Well, let me ask you this: in these thousands of cases, where you say you had enough information to give an opinion on injury causation, and there were thousands of medical doctors who disagreed with you—to be clear with this jury—just tell them why you do not use that data and instead the studies we already talked about?

A: Well, these people want money. These doctors all want money. It is skewed.

Q: Well then, let's talk about your money, sir, $1 million a year, for the past nineteen years, right?

A: Yes.

Q: All for the defense?

A: Yes, we covered this.

Q: Okay, but all these victims and doctors are the ones that want money and skew it, right?

A: Not answering.

Q: But your studies where you have two participants, or fourteen, you are telling this jury—I just want to be crystal clear—is a better sample size, more dependable, than these thousands of cases you worked on, and have been paid $19 million dollars for, right?

DEFENSE COUNSEL: Objection, argumentative and calls for speculation

MR. SIMON: It sure does call for a lot of speculation.

More Points to Ask About

The following are some additional points to bring up with biomechanical experts:

- **Vehicle weight.** One issue these experts fail to talk about during testimony is the weight of vehicles. When a Toyota Prius is struck by a commercial truck that weighs 6,000 pounds, twice the Prius's size, that further increases the risk of a lumbar injury. Many times, the very studies they rely on include this fact, but of course these experts never bring it up.
- **Use of crash test dummies.** Defense experts also love using crash test dummies. That's because dummies don't get hurt like actual humans would. The delta-*v* used is often much lower with human

crash-test subjects, so as to lower the impact of an injury.[3] Due to probability of injury, governing bodies do not allow human crash subjects over five miles per hour delta-*v*'s.

- **Researcher bias.** Ask about researcher bias. There is a reason an expert is retained by one side: they like the result they're getting. They're getting what they want to hear. There have been cases in which partners who did a study were also involved in it as test subjects. The crash test was done at a low velocity to show a person wouldn't have pain after a rear-end crash.

Mr. Simon: Do you know what researcher bias means?
Defense Biomechanical Expert: Sure.
Q: So do you know the researcher in this study authored by your partners?
A: I know of them.
Q: He is a prominent biomechanical engineer, correct?
A: Sure, yes.
Q: And his daughter, [name], also authored this article, along with your partners, correct?
A: I guess so.
Q: So it's true that [name] was also one of the subjects tested, on top of authoring the article?

This is to show how dubious their data is—cross check their sample size, the participants in their studies, and so on.

3. *Delta-v* is change in velocity. They use this term to try and manipulate probability of injury based solely on the change in velocity of the vehicle. Imagine the plaintiff's car at a full stop. When it is hit from behind, it accelerates from zero to five miles per hour. The change in velocity, or *delta-v*, would be 5. Any human testing must be done at velocities slow enough to not cause injury, at zero to five miles per hour. This is in accordance with the Declaration of Helsinki enacted after WWII—any human subject testing must be done at velocities below what is expected to cause any injury.

Outline for Cross-Examining Biomechanical Experts

Here is a general outline for cross-examining these experts.

1. The outrageousness of their extreme opinions.
2. Lack of foundation—how what they say isn't backed up.
3. Records and things done—they likely never even saw the cars, any data from the cars, or talked to the defendant.[4]
4. Point out that they are not a doctor—or at least not qualified to offer certain opinions or diagnoses.

Following is a specific outline for a biomechanical expert cross-examination from one of my trials below. You can see how I match it with specific callouts from the deposition I took, or from other depositions of this expert, so my impeachment material from the *box of death* is ready to rock.

Bias

This section is to reframe for the jury that this is an expert paid by the defense. They are a professional witness who is not a medical doctor. You want to expose their motive. You are also framing the issue as "treating medical doctors versus hired gun non-MD."

Q: Can you confirm that you are *not* a medical doctor?
Q: You have a PhD, you are not an MD?

4. The variability in force estimations solely from picture reconstruction is very high. It's a good idea to contest the admissibility of a biomechanist's testimony that it is not sufficiently accurate enough to be admissible. Wade Bartlett et al., "Evaluating the Uncertainty in Various Measurement Tasks Common to Accident Reconstruction," *SAE Technical Paper Series*, March 4, 2002, https://doi.org/10.4271/2002-01-0546.

Q: You are not here to diagnose the patient? ("Not here to diagnose a single injury."

Q: The video you just showed, it is not published in any journals? ("No.")

Q: The first time that you met the plaintiff is today?

Q: The test dummy from your video is the same weight as the plaintiff? Same height?

Q: You did not review any MRI films?

Q: You cannot say *if* Ms. [Plaintiff] herniated a disc? You are saying it's *just likelihood* based on your studies?

Q: Can't say *what* caused disc protrusions, just that it wasn't this?

Q: Can't say *what* caused Ms. [Plaintiff]'s shoulder tear, it just wasn't this?

Q: 100 percent of what you do for a living is giving opinions to lawyers?

Q: It's been this way since 1994?

Q: And almost 100 percent of the time, your work has been against the injured party?

Q: You have done thousands of depositions?

Q: Other than *one* deposition in 2014 for an injured party, and one trial in 2001, you cannot recall any others?

Q: You earned $950,000 in 2015, the same for the past two years, and close to that in years prior?

Q: So you have spent *twenty years* testifying against the injured almost 100 percent of the time?

Q: [Write on the white board] So *why* do you do this type of work? [$900,000 x 20 = $18 million]

Q: And you say that you are *not biased*?

Q: What is your bill in this case? About $20,000 to $30,000?

Q: Do you have a lab?

Q: Do you do any research?

Q: Do you work out of your home in [city]?

Q: You don't have any employees, just yourself?

Q: You get hired on about 300 new cases, from the defense, *each* year?

Q: You don't have any research conducted?

Q: You don't have any published papers?

Q: You don't have any industry talks?

Q: But you do talk to lawyers, always on the defense side?

Q: In your talks to defense lawyers, do you tell them to be as evasive as possible when on the stand?

Calendar

Bring out recent testimony from your box of death—showing where and when this expert has been testifying lately, for which cases, and for the plaintiff's or defense side. Oftentimes, they will not remember what case they were testifying on the day before.

Ridiculous Opinions

This section highlights the extremes of their opinions. The jury has to be all in on these positions to find against your client. It shows how far the defense's hired gun will go for their client.

Q: In the thousands of cases you have investigated, all being hired by the defense, have you ever come in, regardless of whether the person was hit at eighty miles per hour, ninety miles per hour, or ten miles per hour, have you *ever* said that someone could get a disk injury from a rear-end collision?

Q: You have *never* said in all your testifying that there was enough force to cause a disc injury?

Q: So why do you think the defense always hires you?

Q: Why do you even do the calculation for impact severity if you already know your answer?

Q: Are you using studies funded by the insurance industry or the automotive industry? (Note: be careful saying the word "insurance." By asking the expert on the stand who funded it, they will usually just say it on their own.)

Q: Can I pay you to rear-end you with my car if you are sure you will just get a sprain?

The Million-Dollar Question

I will even call this the "multimillion-dollar question" and sometimes lead with this series of questioning. This tends to be the entire case for the jury. The question they need to answer. Shows how unhelpful this expert is on the most critical question in the case.

Q: You cannot give an opinion on if Mr. [Plaintiff] had a pre-existing condition in his lumbar spine that became aggravated due to the crash? (Note: match it with your state's jury instructions.)

Q: You do not have *any* studies that show if someone has a pre-existing protrusion in their lumbar spine that was not causing problems, at what impact speed will it start to cause problems?

Q: If someone has a pre-existing condition that is *not* symptomatic, such as a protrusion in the lumbar spine, what amount of force is required to make that condition flare up or become symptomatic?

Q: Are you the right person to ask about Mr. [Plaintiff]'s pre-existing condition?

Q: So can you say to a reasonable degree of biomechanical probability where this specific human being, not generally, but specifically this plaintiff, was injured in this crash?

Low Speed

This is always a talking point of the defense. So hit it head on.

Q: Does the US allow testing with human volunteers at the same speeds that Mr. [Plaintiff] was in?[5]

Q: Is your definition of "low speed" when human volunteers are routinely used?

---

5. It is involved and time consuming to get permission through US laws to do crash tests on human subjects legally, and in such a way that the human subjects will not be injured. Tests with human subjects are very slow speed to avoid injury.

Studies

After you get the expert to confirm which specific studies they are relying on in this case, go one by one and show the jury how ridiculous they are. I make a list on white paper (butcher paper) in the courtroom and tear the foundation of their opinions to shreds.

Q: Do you have a single study that is peer reviewed, was done in the US, that says somebody hit at the same speed as Mr. [Plaintiff], with a delta-*v* of 6, *cannot* sustain a disc injury?

Adams & Hutton

A common study that biomechanists rely on is Adams and Hutton from 1983.[6] This is the first one that they love to cite. It is important to actually read this and see that it shows one mechanism for injury but does not rule out all others. And, of course, it has other severe limitations.

Castro Study

The Castro study was published in 1997 for the *European Spine Journal*.[7]

Q: Are you aware of the Castro study, from 1997, with delta-*v*'s up to 8.5?
Q: Are you aware that this study was peer reviewed and accepted in the US?
Q: There were MRIs taken before and after for this study? [Yes.]
Q: Are you aware that this study was done in Germany?
Q: Are you aware that this study was funded by a German insurance company?

6. M.A. Adams and W.C. Hutton, "The Mechanics of Prolapsed Intervertebral Disc," *International Orthopaedics* 6, no. 4 (March 1983), https://doi.org/10.1007/bf00267146.

7. W.H. Castro et al., "Do 'Whiplash Injuries' Occur in Low-Speed Rear Impacts?" *European Spine Journal*, https://pubmed.ncbi.nlm.nih.gov/9455663.

Q: Are you aware that the delta-*v*'s were up to 8.8?

Q: And one person at 8.8 was 30 years old and was vomiting at the scene?

West Study

Q: Are you aware of the West study from 1993, showing the effects of reversing into a barrier, which was not conducted in the USA?[8]

Q: Are you aware that in the West study, there were *two* subjects?

Q: Are you aware that the two subjects in this study were also the *authors of the study*?

Q: Are you aware that this study was done outside the US?

Q: Who funded this study?

Q: Are you aware that the test subjects also being the researchers means that the researchers were biased?

Q: Are you aware that this study was not peer reviewed and accepted?

Q: There were no MRIs taken, just a verbal "I feel fine" from the test subjects who were also the researchers?

Q: Are you aware that this study was not part of any peer review process at all?

Q: Are you aware that it is unethical for these researchers to do crash studies on themselves?

Q: Are you aware that in 1999 a peer-reviewed study from journal *Spine* came out and said both of these studies are absolute junk science?[9]

---

8. D.H. West and J.P. Gough, "Low Speed Rear-end Collision Testing Using Human Subjects," *Accident Reconstruction Journal* 5, no. 6 (May/June 1993): 22-26.

9. Michael D. Freeman et al., "A Review and Methodologic Critique of the Literature Refuting Whiplash Syndrome," *Spine* 24, no. 1 (January 1999): 86–96, https://doi.org/10.1097/00007632-199901010-00022. Another new article has come out since then by Freeman, Croft, and others: Paul S. Nolet et al., "Is Acceleration a Valid Proxy for Injury Risk in Minimal Damage Traffic Crashes? A Comparative Review of Volunteer, ADL and Real-World Studies," *International Journal of Environmental Research and Public Health* 18, no. 6 (March 12, 2021): 2901, https://doi.org/10.3390/ijerph18062901.

[Note: the biomechanist will concede that this 1999 article is peer reviewed.]

Q: Do you ever partake in the peer-review process?

[They do *not* and have only submitted articles for publication.]

Q: Are you saying that the Freeman and Croft studies were peer reviewed and published, but that they are wrong?

Ivancic Studies

It is important to arm yourself with studies that help prove your position—that people can actually get neck and back disc injuries in car crashes. Many are newer studies with new technology, and, lo and behold, show that this phenomenon of folks getting injured in crashes is real! The studies from Ivancic and Panjabi are great sources, and I love to cite them in trial.

Q: Are you familiar with the Ivancic studies conducted at Yale Biomechanical Lab, which are peer reviewed and published?[10] But they are wrong too?

NASS Studies

The defense loves to use the National Automotive Sampling System (NASS) to try and twist their statistics to fit their narrative. Familiarize yourself with their process and what they actually do and how they

10. Manohar M. Panjabi et al., "Cervical Spine Ligament Injury During Simulated Frontal Impact," *Spine* 29, no. 21 (November 2004): 2395–2403, https://doi.org/10.1097/01.brs.0000143173.92241.ab; Paul C. Ivancic, "Mechanisms and Mitigation of Head and Spinal Injuries Due to Motor Vehicle Crashes," *Journal of Orthopaedic & Sports Physical Therapy* 46, no. 10 (September 30, 2016): 826–33, https://doi.org/10.2519/jospt.2016.6716.

get their information. Defense experts love to say that very rarely, if ever, do people get disc injuries in car crashes nationwide, then cite the NASS. But do they even look? What is their process? Getting the failed logic of its use out in deposition is helpful to show the judge that they cannot rely on it. Even if it comes in at trial, you can expose to the jury the illogical use by the defense expert.

Q: Are you familiar with the NASS studies?[11]

Q: Are you aware that these studies are based only on what EMTs say? At the ER?

Q: Are you aware that these EMTs in the study did not follow-up with people later to see if they were injured after an MRI?

Q: Even though my client had a positive neck MRI the day *after* the crash, it would not have shown up on this study because my client's MRI was not done the same day as the crash?

Q: Are you aware that this study is thrown out of court all the time?

Q: Are you aware that this study only tracks statistics if people complain about disc herniation at the scene? Or if an MRI is done the same day?

Q: Are you aware that in the NASS study, there is no follow-up? That we do *not* know if the NASS people would ever follow-up if someone was in a crash, went to the ER, and a month later had an MRI that is positive and got back surgery?

Science

Q: You have been retained on 5,000 to 6,000 cases?

Q: Thousands of the cases that you have been retained on allege a disc injury from a rear-end collision?

Q: And *all* those injured people related their disc injury to the rear-end collision?

Q: All of those people had a doctor agreeing with them?

---

11. "National Automotive Sampling System," NHTSA, https://www.nhtsa.gov/crash-data-systems/national-automotive-sampling-system.

Q: If you are a person of science, why not report this "data"?

Q: Are all these injured people and their doctors part of a conspiracy?

Crash Severity

Q: You have not talked to either party?

Q: Have you personally inspected either vehicle involved in this crash?

Q: Have you personally taken any measurements of either vehicle?

Q: Can you confirm that your last published paper was in 1994?

Q: Can you confirm that was the year you started giving opinions for lawyers?

Concessions

Q: Will you admit that the closing speed was north of fifteen miles per hour?

Q: Will you admit that this crash can cause soft-tissue injuries?

Q: Will you admit it is possible he did herniate the discs in his neck and back?

Q: Will you admit that you could be totally wrong?

Q: Will you admit that *a lot of* people, experts in this field, disagree with you?

Example: Cross-Examination of Biomechanical Expert

For example, my cross-examination of one biomechanical expert during my *Johnson* trial in 2014 is a good guide to follow. This was the defense's expert, who despite not seeing any scans of my client or examining the vehicle, arrogantly assumed that no injury could occur. I began by asking him about the thousands of cases that he investigated over his career.

Mr. Simon: Have you ever said, regardless of whether a person was hit at eighty miles an hour, ninety miles an hour, or ten miles an hour, have you ever said someone could get a disc injury from a rear-end collision?

What followed was a bunch of dodging and long-winded answers.

Defense Biomechanical Expert: That's a different story. If you're asking me about all impact speeds, if you're talking about whether the occupant is contained, which I think I indicated at the time of deposition if they're contained, or there's no breakage of the seat back per se and there's no ejection, it's very difficult to get a disc herniation. That's correct. I would stand behind that.

Q: So zero?

A: If you're talking about something where there's ejection into the back seat, where there's catastrophic failure of a component that is supporting or safety item, I would have to evaluate that on a case-by-case basis, but if you're talking about where the occupant is contained by the seat back, they're lap and shoulder belted, as we have in this case, I would say it's very difficult. I wouldn't just categorically say no, but I haven't in the past because the forces in those particular cases didn't warrant it.

Q: So the short answer is zero?

A: Given the constraints I just gave you, correct.

This expert was retained by the defense 99 percent of the time, and one year he made $900,000 doing it. This was his sole source of income. I showed the jury how the light impact was a red herring. His opinion was the same no matter the speed of the collision.

Then I asked him about the studies he relied on. Here is where I bring up the *Spine Journal* study I mentioned earlier that debunks the views of biomechanical experts.[12]

Q: Doctor, isn't it true that in 1999, a peer-reviewed study came out and said that both of these studies that you just relied on are absolute junk science and need be disregarded?
A: You would have to tell me the author who wrote that.
Q: Sure. It is called *Spine Journal* of 1999 by Freeman and Croft, peer reviewed by *Medical Literature*, and it says that both of those studies are absolutely unreliable; isn't that correct?
A: Let's talk about who the authors are and then we can—we'll go from there.
Q: Well, doctor, is this not a peer-reviewed journal of spine for biomechanics? Yes or no?
A: It is a peer-reviewed journal, yes. And then as I stated at the time of deposition, you need to review each journal on its own—or each article on its own merit—
Q: Do you have any peer-reviewed studies, biomechanical nature, that says somebody in Mr. Johnson's situation, same delta-*v*'s, inactive head restraint vehicle, cannot get a cervical disc injury?
A: Are you asking me is it possible? Is that what your question is?
Q: I'm asking, do you have any peer-reviewed literature? Our expert came up and showed the jury a peer-reviewed study. I want to ask you, are you relying on any peer-reviewed

12. Freeman et al., "A Review and Methodologic Critique of the Literature Refuting Whiplash Syndrome." There are studies done after 2020 that further debunk all the studies that these experts rely on. The 2021 study by Nolet et al., "Is Acceleration a Valid Proxy for Injury Risk in Minimal Damage Traffic Crashes? A Comparative Review of Volunteer, ADL and Real-World Studies," found that biomechanical experts opining lack of injury in low-speed crashes is unscientific and invalid, "...the injury risk of real-world minimal damage rear impact crashes was estimated to be at least 2,000 times greater than for any ADL [Activity of Daily Living.]"

literature for an active head restraint that says somebody the same delta-*v* as Mr. Johnson cannot get a disc herniation?

A: If your question is if there is an article that says it is possible, I've not seen that.

Then I went after his medical credentials.

Q: You can't diagnose an injury as a medical doctor?

A: You're correct. I am not a doctor.

And I got him to admit that he never saw any diagnostic scans of Johnson to show any type of pain before the crash. He couldn't even tell the jury how Johnson's body moved during the car crash.

Q: Can you demonstrate how my client's body moved?

I ask this right there on the stand.

Q: This all happened in a fraction of a second? Show us then.

Other things I learned about this biomechanical expert:

- He doesn't take part in the peer-review process.
- He has not conducted his own research.
- He only talks to lawyers.
- His only source of income is testifying against the injured.

Like I said earlier, in this case study, the expert was making $900,000 a year, all defense, and had been doing it for the past twenty years. I did the math for him behind him, on the stand, on butcher paper. It came out to $18 million. (It's what I would eventually ask for, $15 million for pain and suffering, and about $3 million for medical care costs. And I got it.) Then I walked back to my table and asked what he wanted to be when he was in engineering school. He wanted to be a rocket science engineer. I pointed to the money on the butcher paper behind him, and asked:

Q: Tell the jury why you didn't follow your dreams.

He lost it.

I'll often ask a defense's spine expert point blank:

Q: What do you think about biomechanical experts?

And spine experts will laugh at biomechanical experts. The goal is to pit the defense experts against each other.

Takeaways

Just remember that these experts talk in generalities and not the specifics of your client's case. Juries are very distrustful of willy-nilly data and studies in the present day. They hear and see it all the time on the news and social media. Pick apart their data and make them look foolish. There are so many holes in their "science" that you can get the jury to distrust them on that alone. Tie it in with common sense and the medical doctors that disagree with them completely. Add in the severe bias and you've found yet another villain to your client's hero story. This repeat villain can be dropped into any case against any injured person.

12

Defense Medical Billing Experts

Depositions for Use at Trial

Medical billers, whom the defense brings in to devalue the medical bills your client is on the hook for, can be a hard target. But if you peel some layers back you can start to expose them for what they are: unqualified charlatans. The defense hires these "experts" to come into court and say all the bills should be paid at Medicare rates. It does not matters that no one has Medicare, that the plaintiff already paid more, or that much of it is still owed. It does not matter that the providers sent them to collections, or that the providers want payment in full. The defense has an expert who wants the defendant to only pay a very discounted rate. Discounted justice is not justice at all.

This chapter will help you expose these experts. Again, we will be discussing both their expert deposition and their cross-examination in trial. Both are intrinsically intertwined. If you followed the path laid out in this book, by the time you get to deposing them or cross-examining them in trial, you already have a huge advantage. Because if you did it right, you deposed the treating doctors, video recorded their trial testimony, and they already told you they do not take Medicare. The treating doctors told you they want their full bills and why. You also may have already deposed the defense medical experts who told you that their practices cannot survive on Medicare rates, and they already gave much higher estimates than what the billing expert the defense hired will.

Deposing the Billing Expert

Check the case law for your jurisdiction, and for how the law surrounding the entry of medical bills works. In some states, the full amount of the bill comes in. In some states, it is the lesser of the amounts owed or paid. In some states, is it the reasonable value of the services, and the defense is allowed to put on evidence showing what providers accept as payment-in-full from insurance carriers, Medicare, deferred payment treatment, and so on. Research your jury instructions and the controlling case law. This is important because it will guide how you depose these experts and the issues for cross-examination at trial.

Five Ways to get Medical Bills into Evidence

There are five main ways to get medical bills into evidence, generally, for most jurisdictions (always check your local jurisdiction's laws and rules). They are:

1. **Stipulation with the defense.** Sometimes it is easier to agree on a discounted number rather than spend money on experts and waste days of confusing trial testimony.
2. **Waiving past medical bills.** Depending on the amount sought, it is sometimes best to waive the past medical bills and only seek general damages from the jury, that is, pain and suffering damages. The school of thought is that this provides

a low anchor in a situation where the medical bills are only $50,000 in all for a surgical spine surgery case, including all conservative care, and the ask for general damages is $5 million. It also eliminates issues of attorney-referred care, doctors being owed money, and so on. Since you are not seeking money for that treatment, it is no longer relevant. This will be a judgment call, depending on the case details. It is important to note that some judges may still want past medical bills to come into evidence for other reasons. But I think want you do your best to sanitize your playing field and get the facts that actually matter to the jury.

3. **Expert testimony.** Hire either a medical doctor, a billing expert, or a life care planner to present evidence about the reasonable value of the plaintiff's medical care costs in the past or in the future. Fact-check your hired expert to make sure they have the foundation to know this information. Throughout the rest of this chapter, you will see the pitfalls that the defense experts can fall into. Avoid them with your experts.
4. **Plaintiff's testimony.** Some jurisdictions allow the plaintiff to take the stand, say they received all the bills, what they owe, and the amount. For many of these jurisdictions, the court will require you to subpoena the bills to the department, with a declaration from the custodian of records.
5. **Using the defense expert's numbers.** In some cases, where the numbers are close and it is not worth the fight, you may want to simply agree with the defense billing expert's number, and either call them at trial or play their video recorded deposition in your case-in-chief.

Basic Defense Billing Expert Deposition Outline

When preparing for the defense billing expert's deposition, the first thing to do is fully read their report. See the numbers they give as their opinion. Heck, if you agree with them, or they are not that far off, your job is pretty easy.

Video record the deposition, give notice that you reserve right to use it in trial, and then do a very quick direct examination of their witness. No bias, no making them look bad, no questioning their foundation. Just ask:

Q: State your name.
Q: Can you confirm [defense counsel's name] hired you?
Q: I didn't hire you?
Q: Why did [defense counsel] hire you?
Q: What is the total amount of Mr. [Plaintiff]'s medical bills?
Q: What did you find to be the reasonable amount?
Q: What is the process you use to come up with those numbers?
Q: Thank you for coming.

Now you do not need an expert. You do not need to pay an expert for this opinion. You have preserved this opinion for trial. Designate the transcript to be played in trial. Then play it during your case-in-chief.

Detailed Defense Billing Expert Outline

But we do not always get so lucky, do we? Most of the time the billing experts say 10 percent of the bills is a reasonable value. They say we are trying to unjustly enrich the plaintiff with a windfall and punish the defendant. So here is an outline for a billing expert's deposition that is more complicated:

- Bias
- Foundation
- Documents reviewed
- Methodology and credentials
- Deadly hypothetical question

Bias

When you are discussing bias, you want to ask:

Q: How often are you hired?
Q: How often are you hired for the defense side of cases like these?

And show that in every case, they said the bills were too high. You want to show the jury this is a systematic failure of the defense, and not specific to your client in this case. This expert does this to everyone. It looks very bad when this expert says the total cost for a fusion surgery should be $30,000, and their bill paid by the defense is $45,000. I also love to ask:

Q: What is the hourly rate you are charging for this deposition today?
Q: What is the hourly rate you charge to review records for Mr. [Defense Counsel]?

The rate they are charging you is always higher.

Q: May I pay you the same rate you are charging Mr. [Defense Counsel]?

They always refuse.

Q: Are you aware that [other billing expert] only charges $50 per hour?
Q: Would you be okay accepting that amount?

Foundation

When asking about their foundation, ask to see the resources they use to come up with their numbers. Press them to provide you the specific databases that they use. Find out which hospitals and surgeons they used to compare rates. Ask if they found data on what your specific spine surgeon and the specific hospital in your specific case accepts in these specific instances. The answer is almost always no. Many of the databases they use have disclaimers stating that they should not be used for this purpose. This dovetails into their methodology.

Documents Reviewed

If they are just looking at bills, and then finding out what Medicare would pay for those same procedures, what is scientific about that? Is that even an expert opinion? Most jurisdictions require that the reasonableness of the bills be what the injured party can get the service for.

Q: What would [plaintiff's name] have to pay for these services?
Q: Are the rates different for a person, say, who is uninsured?
Q: Who does not have cash on hand to pay an upfront cash discounted rate?

Get the expert to commit that their methodology is the same regardless of the plaintiff's specific situation.

Methodology & Credentials

Be sure to get into their credentials.

Q: Do you have a degree in hospital finance?
Q: Have you ever run a medical facility?
Q: Have you ever adjusted a medical bill?
Q: Have you ever negotiated a medical bill?

Q: Has your methodology been approved by your peers and published?
Q: Do you have degrees or credentials in this field?

Press them on these things. Get specifics. There is one "expert" I've worked with in previous cases who claims her methodology was signed off on as peer reviewed and approved. After pressing, we found out it was one single person who "approved" it. She paid $5,000 to him to say it was approved. Who was this person? He had written several very inappropriate articles about medical finance. He had also been indicted for fraud and conspiring with an insurance company. Sigh. Bottom line: you need to dig. Make them answer.

Deadly Hypothetical Question

The last and most crucial part of your depositions, and later your trial cross-examination, will be this critical question:

Q: Will any of these providers accept these amounts?
Q: Mr. [Billing Expert], if you are so sure about your methodology, and if the jury accepts the amount you say is reasonable, and then the doctors and hospitals refuse to accept that amount, are you willing to pay the difference?
Q: But I thought you were so sure?

I take it a step further. I ask my client to write an authorization letter for the defense billing expert to negotiate my client's owed bills. I give the letter to the billing expert at deposition. I attach the letter as an exhibit. Then I tell the billing expert that I am happy to pay for their time to call all these providers and get the amounts reduced. I have yet to have an expert take me up on my generous offer. Why do you think that is?

Examples: Working with Defense Billing Experts

Following are several examples from my cases of how I have dealt with defense billing experts.

Example: Questioning a Billing Expert

I walked into a courthouse in 2018 ready to cross-examine Dr. Todd Willoughby, a self-described medical consultant.[1] He used to be a practicing medical doctor—an internist. Then in 1997, he sold his practice and has been working for insurance companies exclusively, making millions of dollars in the process. He had never adjusted a medical bill, yet he somehow determined that my client, Paulina Atlantic, had only $30,000 worth of medical bills when she actually owed $310,000.

For example, I asked him about Ms. Atlantic's $2,500 ambulance bill, which he said was only worth $500.

Mr. Simon: So you're telling this jury that Ms. Atlantic is going to go call up the ambulance company two years past the crash, a bill that's in collections, and they're going to take $505.95?

Defense Billing Specialist: No, Mr. Simon, that's not what I'm saying. My task was to determine what the reasonable cost of care is. And the reasonable cost of care are the numbers that I put up on the board behind me, which actually include this number.

Q: So do you know if they're going to take your $505.95?

1. For more information about Ms. Atlantic's case, *see* "About the Cases in This Book" at the beginning of this book, in the section *Paulina Atlantic v. B&D Transport.*

A: I don't. But the second, method two number is this number, they've said they would take that. That's what they put into collections.

He shorted the value of her emergency room visit, too, which she paid $11,676, in full. He said the reasonable value is $1,107.

Q: So do you think that Ms. Atlantic is going to go ask the emergency room for a refund due to overpayment?
A: I don't think it matters what I think about that, counsel. I'm trying to calculate the reasonable cost of care. The fact that somebody overpaid it, in my estimation, doesn't change the reasonable cost of care. If you went to buy a car and everybody else asked the dealer, "Is that the best you can do," and gets the car for a lower amount and you pay the sticker price, I'm sorry for you. But that doesn't establish the reasonable cost of care that you paid more than everybody else.
Q: So is Ms. Atlantic going to be due a refund based on your methodology?
A: I'm calculating the reasonable cost of care. I don't know whether she'd be due a refund or not.
Q: Did you do any analysis for a person like Ms. Atlantic who has no cash to pay, who has no insurance, and who has already had the value of the services to be rendered, did you do any analysis like that?
A: I only analyzed the marketplace. I didn't analyze it for any specific individual.
Q: So who is going to be responsible for the $310,000 that you left off as being unreasonable? Who's going to pay?
A: I don't know. I don't know that it will be paid.
Q: Well, Ms. Atlantic owes all of that money, true?
A: Technically, she does. But as I have a lot of experience, these amounts are often negotiated to far lower amounts.

Of course he did not take my dare to call and try to negotiate with all the providers on my dime.

Researching the Defense Medical Expert

Dr. Todd Willoughby would be a hard target for a lot of people because he puts himself out as a billing expert as well as a medical doctor. He tried to give opinions about everything. Unless you have background information, it's very difficult to handle witnesses like him.

But leading up to his testimony I had been scouring the internet and various resources for any information on him. And lo and behold, he hadn't seen a medical patient in a clinical setting since 1997. He had been testifying for insurance companies and defendants 99 percent of the time. And now his side hustle was seeing patients at weightlifting gyms and prescribing weird creams to weightlifters—all done pro bono and informally. Those were the only patients he saw in twenty years. I saved all this information for cross-examination because I knew this case was going to trial. On direct examination, when he told the jury that he was a medical doctor, imagine the look on the juror's faces when it came out how he actually used his medical license: prescribing creams to his bodybuilding buddies right there on the mat in the back of a gym.

I also like to dig into experts' pasts. What did they do before they became a "billing expert?" This particular expert was an internist for a couple of decades, not a surgeon. Then he was a consultant for a third-party administrator for health insurance companies. He was the person at an insurer who denies claims. He was the guy, an internist by trade, who would deny our claims through our health insurance when we needed certain medication we were already on, when we needed a shoulder surgery, when we needed a CT scan, and so on. This was the guy who denied our claims and we would get that letter from our health insurance company that enrages all of us. And it enraged the jury in this case when this came out on cross-examination. I made the jury see him for the internist he was, a guy who wanted to play expert, but who hadn't seen a patient in two decades. He made $10 million over the past fifteen years, undervaluing medical bills for the defense. And before that he only worked for insurance companies denying claims.

Example: Revealing an Expert's Credentials

I also went after Dr. Todd Willoughby's actual credentials. Here's how I quickly cut through his credentials, or lack thereof:

Q: Have you ever negotiated a medical bill?
A: No.
Q: Have you ever negotiated a lien?
A: No. I don't do lien work.
Q: Have you ever worked in the finance department of a hospital?
A: No.
Q: Do you have any degrees in billing or healthcare finance?
A: I'm not aware of any degrees in billing. I don't have a degree in healthcare finance.

Dr. Todd Willoughby was retained in almost 3,000 cases by the defense. He made $30,000 in Paulina Atlantic's case alone. Which is about what he said the reasonable value should be for all my client's treatment, in which she owed over $300,000!

Example: Ask Other Experts About the Billing Expert

I also defeat the defense billing experts by asking the other experts about the billing expert. I asked the spine surgeon:

Mr. Simon: Do you think Medicare value is reasonable for service?

Spine Surgeon: No.

Then the billing expert will come in and say it is reasonable.

In Paulina Atlantic's case, where the billing expert said that reasonable value is what Medicare pays, the defense spine expert laughed out loud when I asked him if his practice could survive if it accepted Medicare rates.

Spine Surgeon: Oh it could survive. If I laid off the entire staff and practiced out of a shoe box!

Medicare Rates & the Defense Billing Expert

All these billing experts are the same when you boil it down. They try to use published rates to describe what facilities will accept for Medicare or Medicaid. And that's highly improper, because a lot of our clients don't have health insurance or Medicare, which is the largest medical provider in the world with the largest bargaining power.

The defense hires this billing expert who says Medicare rates are reasonable value. But what they are saying is these doctors who help people and don't even accept insurance should take the lowest rates on the market, from people that they are not even a provider for. And when they start bringing up Medicare and Medicaid, you can frame it as, "You're telling us the responsible party shouldn't pay, but all of us should pay? Taxpayers should pay?"

Most judges should never let in Medicare rates as reasonable value. No one in their right mind thinks these rates are reasonable. It turns the trial into a political debate. But I am already prepared for this Medicare argument to come in, and I turn it into a weapon for our case.

Learn about Medicare Set-Asides

Educate yourself on what a Medicare set-aside is all about. Because with a Medicare set-aside, if your client is injured due to a third party's negligence, Medicare makes them set aside money for their own future care. Medicare will not pay for future medical care for this specific medical issue from this crash, because your client is supposed to put money aside for a third-party settlement. That's really another added damage. If the defense wants to go there and say they want to be entitled to Medicare rates in the future, well guess what? With Dr. Todd Willoughby, I got to expose him and show that our client couldn't even use her Medicare when she's eligible in the future to pay for these costs because of what the defendant did to her. A lot of people don't realize or think about that. And here was their expert, trying to get her physicians who do not take Medicare, to accept Medicare rates in the future. The jury was fuming.

Example: What Happens When Patients Have No Money?

I specifically wanted to dig into what would happen if my client couldn't pay her bills.

Mr. Simon: Let's take this patient here, this human being, her position in the marketplace, her specifically. Did you do any analysis as to what Paulina Atlantic could get the services for now that she owes bills in collections, or that she has paid portions of, since she didn't have insurance and didn't have the cash to pay for them?

Defense Billing Expert: The only analysis that I did has to do with the fact that had she been eligible for charity care, it could have been anywhere between zero and Medicare. Other than that, I did not do any further analysis specific to your client.

Q: So you did no analysis specific to Ms. Atlantic?

A: Other than what I just said, no.

Q: No further questions.

Charity care. He said it. He went there earlier in my cross-examination, and I exposed it. His opinion was that she should have mitigated her damages, not by going to the best neurosurgeon who fixed her, but go to her local county hospital, and have residents learn on her spine. This is how far these people will go. You just have to walk them down the path.

The Dare

I talked about this earlier in this chapter, but I think it is important enough to mention again. Another technique I often use with billing experts is what I call *the dare*. During their depositions, on the record, I offer to their expert and the defense lawyer the ability to have their expert call all my client's providers and get them to reduce my client's medical bills. I have a signed authorization from my client and I attach it to the deposition. I offer to pay for their time, at the same rate they are paid by the defense, to do this noble job for my client. Without fail, they never do it. Why? Because they know their methodology is a fraud. And you better believe I bring this up on cross-examination.

Example: The Dare

MR. SIMON: Do you know if the providers will take these reduced payments?

DEFENSE BILLING EXPERT: No idea.

Q: Remember in deposition a few months back, I gave you the opportunity to call all these providers? I gave you a medical authorization signed by my client and I wrote you a check for two more hours of your time, to see if they would take your reasonable value amounts? Did you do it?

A: No. That isn't my job.

Q: But you cashed the check, didn't you?

I had a copy of the check from our bank. He did cash it.

This is how you beat these people. A lot of times, they are pulling data that has nothing to do with the procedures my client had. They are coming up with made-up formulas. It's just insanity.

Then I go a step further on cross-examination. I write down on an easel pad the total amount that the client owes. Then I write down the total the expert says is reasonable. I ask the expert:

Q: Do you believe in your methodology?

Q: Do you believe it is sound?

Q: Do you expect the jury to only award what you say is reasonable?

Then I write in the difference between those two numbers. And I ask the expert:

Q: If the jury gives your number in the verdict, and the medical professionals and hospitals refuse to reduce their bills, will you pay the difference?

They always flip out. But I remind them how sure they were just five minutes ago on how their analysis is the reasonable cost of medical care. Then I bring up their bill in this case, and ask:

Q: Are you reducing your own bill by the same percentage that you are asking medical professionals and hospitals to reduce their bills? Or will you accept full payment by the defense industry?

The billing experts always begin their careers with an honest profession, such as a nurse or a doctor. Then I ask them about their hopes and dreams, and what they wanted to be when they were young. Dr. Todd Willoughby, the doctor in Paulina Atlantic's case (who was testifying for the defense and selling skin creams in a gym) said he wanted to be the best heart surgeon in the world.

Q: When you were in medical school, was it your goal that whenever you turned forty up until where you are now, that you'd be doing this type of work?
A: No. I was going to be the world's greatest cardiothoracic surgeon.
Q: But you're not doing that now, correct?
A: No.

And you could hear a pin drop and the jury just shook their heads. And now here he was, testifying against injured people for a living. A sellout without having to say he's a sellout.

Show the Billing Expert's Career Path

Show the jury the expert's ultimate betrayal—of themselves. This person was a medical doctor, a nurse, or some kind of medical professional who wanted to help people. Now he's not helping anyone except himself and insurance companies. He's only hurting people by taking lots of money for pro-defense opinions. He likely has not helped a patient in years. And in the past, he actually helped patients find quality care or provided quality care. But then there is always that sellout year. When he gave into the Sith Lord and turned to the dark side. Create a timeline graphic to show the jury how and when this defense expert sold out and how they can never answer the question, "Why?"

Example: Hypothetical Rates for Billing Experts

I also use hypothetical questions, analogizing medical rates to prices at stores. Back to Dr. Todd Willoughby, the gym cream doctor in my *Atlantic* case:

Mr. Simon: Do you ever go buy a candy bar like 3 Musketeers at a store?

Defense Billing Expert: Sure.

Q: Let's use a hypothetical and say you pay a dollar.

A: Okay.

Q: Do you go up to the counter and do you pay that dollar, the amount that they charge, or do you negotiate?

A: No, because that's the reasonable cost. That's pretty much what everybody pays for that service. If they charged $1,000 for it but were willing to accept a dollar, that's more like what we have in healthcare.

Q: Let's use a different example. Let's say you go antiquing and you see a really nice vase, sixty years old, and they charge

$5,000 for that vase. Would you go up and pay $5,000 for that vase or try to negotiate?

A: I probably would.

Q: Let's say you took that vase home and say you got it for $4,000. You had it for a year, maybe two, and the vase broke. And then you saw it at the 99 cent store, and they had a vase that looked similar for a hundred dollars at any other store. Would you take the vase back to the antique store and say, I'm only going to pay a hundred dollars because I saw a comparable one somewhere else, after you had it for two years and it broke?

A: I'm pretty lost in the hypothetical, but I think would be no.

Q: So you want Ms. Atlantic to go back to these health-care providers that have already helped fix her, that she already agreed to pay these rates, and you want her to go and negotiate the Medicare rate?

A: It's not what I want or don't want, Mr. Simon. It is the reasonable cost of care. And you know, [Big Name Hospital] does negotiate their liens. They do negotiate their liens. These are things I know. I run into this all the time.

These billing experts will also say the amount that is owed and what the reasonable value is. It's usually pennies on the dollar. And I'll tell them that if the jury agrees with them, my client can't come back and ask for more.

Q: So if the medical providers do not accept your amount, are you willing to pay the difference?

A: No.

Q: But you're sure that's the reasonable value and the hospital is going to take $20,000, but if you're wrong and telling us you're sure—I'll write out a contract right now saying you'll pay the difference because you're so sure about it.

I do it to them all the time and they always balk at it. When I'm taking the actual expert deposition of these providers, one thing I do is ask about their bill. I'll point out the defense paid out 100 percent.

Q: But you want the doctors to get 20 percent of your bill, is that what you're saying?
A: Well, that's not a reasonable value.
Q: You think you're a very good billing expert, right? And you charge $300 an hour?
A: Yes.
Q: I found an expert who charges $30 an hour. So I'm only going to pay you $30 an hour. How's that sound?

And they get all agitated, but it just shows how crazy it is.

Jurors after trial called Willoughby the "gym doctor." They couldn't believe he wanted the defense to get a discount from the people who helped my client get better. At the end of the day, medical doctors are there to help people. They take a Hippocratic oath. Then they go work for the bad guy. It's all right there, you just have to expose it.

Takeaways

We live in a capitalist democracy. You get what you pay for. Logic will tell you when dealing with a life-threatening medical procedure, you want the best, not discounted medical care. Remember to pull back and think big picture. Defense billing experts, like the biomechanical experts, live in generalities. Live in the specifics for your client in their specific situation. That is the only relevant issue for the jury to determine.

13

Responding to Defense Doctors

Deposition & Cross-Examination

Often, the defense will grasp at straws and blame the client's pain and need for treatment on other issues that the client may have. We already talked about ferreting that point of view out during expert deposition and making a motion to exclude it before trial, due to the defense burden of alternate causation.[1] But what happens if a judge lets that information in, or if the defense expert commits to something else causing the client's medical issues to a reasonable degree of medical probability? What happens if your state law allows the defense to not adhere to alternate causation standards?

This chapter explores several avenues that the defense might explore to explain your client's injuries, and what you can do about them. I call them red herrings and in the case example I use in this chapter, the *Atlantic* case, I show how I pointed them out to the

1. This is discussed in additional detail in chapter 14, "Pretrial Motions," in the section titled "Excluding Alternate Causation Theories."

jury. One of my themes for this case was to not get distracted by red herrings. These include:

- The client must have been hurt in a fall or other incident.
- The client's issues are due to degeneration.
- The client must have been hurt at work.
- The client must have been hurt in a different crash.

In all of these situations, you can turn the defense's own words against them and show that their argument has no merit, sometimes even by using the defense's own experts.

Red Herring #1:
Other Fall at Home

In my *Atlantic* case in 2018, my client was in a crash and had back pain from then up until a fusion surgery she had two years later.[2] But in between the crash and surgery, she had a fall at home and went to the emergency room. The defense's spine expert in *Atlantic* testified that the pain my client was experiencing was due to the fall she experienced, despite the client having the same complaints before the fall, and the defense never seeing her MRIs or CT scans. I always tell all our lawyers to find a way to make your worst fact your best fact. In the previous chapter, we talked about flipping Medicare rates on the defense as an example. So how do we turn the fact that she fell at home, not into a break in our injury causation claim, but into a weapon?

---

2. *See* "About the Cases in This Book" at the beginning of the book, *Paulina Atlantic v. B&D Transport.*

Find the Right Expert

I called an orthopedic spine surgeon who had done thousands of spine surgeries and looked at a wider range of testing than the defense expert. He actually reviewed my client's imaging studies. He actually physically examined my client. He actually reviewed all the of the medical records. He had even testified against me in court in the past. His major takeaway was that the complaints my client was having—radiating numbness and tingling going down her right leg—showed up in records before the reported fall and, of course, after the crash.

Example: Other Fall at Home

My expert also testified that it is common for patients to fall because of neurological problems associated with spine injuries.

MR. SIMON: Do you know whether or not the slippage of the disc existed before the car crash even happened, just with degeneration?

PLAINTIFF'S ORTHOPEDIC SPINE SURGEON: It could have, but in any opinion probably not to this extent.

Q: And why is that?

A: Because if she had the degree of pinching of the nerves seen on the MRI, she would have likely not been living her life as she was without significant neurologic symptoms and problems.

Q: And at this level in the spine, when the nerves are compressed like you see in the MRI that was taken before this fall the defense keeps talking about, what happens to patients?

A: Well, they become fall risks. We see it all the time. The nerves stop working properly down one leg and give out for no reason. This is why this injury is very serious, and surgery is needed.

Q: Is this what happened here?

A: Oh yes. Her damaged nerves from the crash caused her to fall. And she would continue to be a fall risk as long as surgery didn't correct the condition.

Did the fall cause my client's injuries or make them worse? Sorry defense, try again. Science and common sense once again prevail.

Red Herring #2: *Degeneration*

Their next red herring? The good old degeneration theory. The same degeneration theory we see in every case. My expert also rejected the defense's degeneration theory.[3]

Example: Plaintiff's Expert on Degeneration

Mr. Simon: Without the car crash ever happening, can you predict if and when Ms. Atlantic would have ever had her leg give out due to nerve pain?

Plaintiffs' Orthopedic Spine Surgeon: In my opinion, without the crash, it likely would not have.

Q: So degeneration was not the culprit?

3. This degeneration theory is spelled out in some detail in the video *Winning the Unwinnable Case* by David Ball and Gary C. Johnson. DVD or On Demand, (Trial Guides, 2007).

A: Clearly not. Everyone has it, especially people in their sixties like Ms. Atlantic, but people don't go around getting spine surgery just on degeneration.

Need for Future Surgery

My expert spine surgeon also testified as to Ms. Atlantic's future medical costs, stating she would most likely need another spine surgery in sixteen or seventeen years.[4] These are some of the most expensive operations, ranging between $180,000 to $200,000. Further, although these surgeries are good at minimizing pain, they are not good at eliminating it.

Example: Defense Expert on Degeneration

We're going back to the defense spine surgeon they hired in this case. His opinion—as they are most of the time in these cases—is that the injuries were just degeneration, nothing on the imaging studies was acute, and she just had a sprain. Blah blah blah. This is the same opinion we see all the time. This is how I started my cross-examination on their surgeon—with something direct and unexpected.

Mr. Simon: Doctor, where were you last Wednesday?
Defense Counsel: Objection. Relevance. Beyond the scope.

4. This need for future surgery is spelled out in the Hilibrand study. Alan S. Hilibrand and Matthew Robbins. "Adjacent Segment Degeneration and Adjacent Segment Disease: the Consequences of Spinal Fusion?" *The Spine Journal* 4, no.6 (Nov–Dec 2004):190S–194S.

Judge: I'm going to sustain it, Mr. Simon, unless you're getting towards what side he's testifying for. Is that what this is directed towards?

Mr. Simon: Yes.

Judge: All right. Overruled.

Defense Spine Surgeon: Last Wednesday I was in the [city] courthouse.

Mr. Simon: And you were testifying on behalf of a defendant, true?

A: I was.

Q: And how often have you testified on behalf of defendants? 85 to 90 percent of the time?

A: Yes, correct.

Q: And it's true that you've made over $10 million in the past twenty-five years just doing litigation cases like this?

Defense Counsel: Objection. Relevancy. 352.

Judge: That's relevant. Overruled.

A: I have been asked that question, and I—but it was over the last thirty to thirty-five years because I've been doing this a while. And I believe the answer was probably over thirty, thirty-five years, probably billed about $300,000 a year for that type of work. But that, of course, doesn't mean I earned that much. Because I have expenses like everybody else does. But in that—within those parameters, yes.

Q: And Ms. Atlantic, she's not your patient, right?

A: No, she's not.

He saw her for nine minutes and never saw any medical records that predated her crash. I then compared his credentials to my surgeon expert.

Q: Do you think you're more qualified than a board-certified orthopedic surgeon who is fellowship-trained, who does hundreds of spine surgeries a year, to comment on spine cases?

A: Well, sure I don't know how many years ago this doctor was trained. I've been dealing with patients' spine problems for over thirty-five years. So I think my qualifications in offering opinions on spine problems and spine surgeries are as good as anyone's.

Q: All right. Is it true when I took your deposition you didn't see any of the films in this case, none of the CTs, none of the MRIs, none of the experts, true?

A: Right. I just saw the reports here, correct.

Q: You didn't see any of the depositions of either party, correct?

A: Correct.

Q: You didn't see any of the prior employment records of Ms. Atlantic, did you?

A: No.

Q: You didn't see any of the prior physicals of Ms. Atlantic at work, did you?

A: No.

Q: They were not given to you by the defense?

Defense Counsel: Objection. Outside the scope.

Judge: Overruled as phrased.

Defense Spine Surgeon: I didn't see any, like you said, employment records or something. I did not see those, no.

Q: When you told this jury she had a prior chronic condition that was painful, when was she having pain related to her lower back before this crash?

A: She was having it prior to November 2nd, 2015.

Q: Doctor, you never saw her deposition, correct?

A: Right.

Q: You have no medical records that predate this crash, correct?

A: True.

Q: You never saw her employment records, correct?

A: True.

The surgeon went on to say that her slip and fall at home was one of the contributors to her surgery, and that she did not have radiating pain in her right leg prior to the fall. He also testified that she needed surgery due to a degenerative pre-existing condition. So I presented a report from our expert spine surgeon about why she fell. That report said it was because of the crash. But that still wasn't good enough for him.

Q: Doctor, looking at Exhibit 65—looking at the actual report from Dr. Lodestone—do you agree with him that she had right pain going down her leg prior to the slip and fall?
A: No.
Q: So you think he was lying?
A: Again, I've asked that—I've answered that question already. He could have been mistaken. He could be forgetful. He may mix her up with another patient, so I don't know exactly why, but this is not consistent.
Q: Not consistent with your opinion, right, Doctor?
A: No, no, no, not consistent with his earlier note. That has nothing to do with my opinion.

Use Pain Diagrams

Further, the parts of her body where Ms. Atlantic was pointing to her pain were the same before and after her fall. Remember, your client can get their pain diagrams into evidence and they are powerful.

What do I mean by *pain diagrams*? We talked about this in chapter 10, "Deposing Defense Doctors." Your client likely marked up a body diagram their first visit with their chiropractor, or surgeon, which showed where the pain is and where it traveled to. In this case, Ms. Atlantic marked up that diagram with X's all over her lower back and X's all down her leg. Before and after this fall.

Mr. Simon: All right. Doctor, you would agree that the pain diagrams you saw before and after this slip and fall every single time has an X over the top of the neck, the lower back, and over the right ankle, true?

Defense Spine Surgeon: The pain diagrams that I saw, they all had those things.

Q: Both before and after this fall, true?

A: Yes.

Q: And on this visit on [date], where she says she had the fall at home earlier that day, doesn't say anywhere in there that she had radiating pain?

A: No.

One of my themes in this case was "beware the red herrings." This fall was a red herring. I pointed it out in jury selection, opening, during cross-examination, and in closing. And the jury agreed. They gave 100 percent of the medical expenses in the past and future, and almost everything I asked for in pain in suffering, $3 million. This was in a "conservative venue" where no one "has ever gotten a million-dollar verdict on a fusion case."

Red Herring #3: *Hurt at Work*

Another common red herring from the defense is, "They must have been hurt at work." The defense isn't talking about attorneys, doctors, or white-collar workers. Instead, the defense uses this argument against every single laborer or person with a blue-collar job. They try and make it look like the laborer's job in construction, or lifting patients, or gardening caused their spine injuries, and not the crash. But again, make their experts commit to their argument that these people were hurt at work, and this being the cause of the injuries, to a reasonable degree of medical probability.

After they commit to this position—being hurt at work—make them give specifics on how.

- When?
- What are your client's job duties?
- Did they review any employment records?
- Did they talk to your client's employer?
- And my favorite question: why did your client not file a workers' compensation case when this work injury supposedly happened? It is a no-fault system, and everything would have been taken care of.

This "hurt at work" explanation always blows up in the defense's face and comes off looking like what it is: racist and elitist. I love calling in the employer for my hard-working clients. I tell the client's employer beforehand how the defense is trying to insinuate that their employee was hurt at work, and not in the crash. The employer gets fired up, as anyone would. It is not true. The employer is always more than happy to come in, tell the jury there was no injury at work, there is no workers' compensation claim, the injury was all from the crash. Your client's employer is another unbiased witness coming in to destroy the defense's credibility.

Red Herring #4: *Hurt in Another Crash*

Another common alternate cause claim is that the plaintiff was hurt in a prior or subsequent crash. I have been very successful in keeping these out of evidence in trial, but it starts with your depositions of the defense's expert witnesses. If these witnesses cannot commit to a reasonable degree of medical probability what the injuries were from these other crashes, then the theory of alternate cause from another crash is out. The defense cannot talk about these prior or subsequent crashes. What would the relevance of it even be? These defense expert witnesses will not know any of the facts from other crashes, they will not have seen any photos of other crashes, and they will not have seen any medical records from other crashes. They will not be able give a relevant opinion. If they do, they will say it's just a sprain, just like in your case. They have to. It is the party line.

If they did have an exacerbating injury from a subsequent crash, and it does come into evidence, then you can say that the client was in an already weakened condition because of this crash. You're taking your weakest fact and making it your best fact.

Could you imagine these defense expert witnesses saying the surgery was reasonable to do, but the injury was caused by this *other* light-impact crash? Imagine how that would hurt their future business. And that biomechanical expert they hired? He will say that a disc cannot be injured in *any* crash—not the crash at issue in this case, or any that occurred before or after. It is the same thing—this is their story for *every* case.

Takeaways

Do not run away from your bad facts in deposition. Attack them with the defense and find a way for it to be excluded or make the foundation of the defense opinion so silly that it inflames the jury when you are in trial.

PART III

The Trial

We have talked science. We have talked experts. We have talked evidence. We have talked discovery. We have talked direct and cross-examination. Now let's talk about some other areas of trial. If cases are like movies, at this point we have the script, the talent is set up, and we are ready to shoot before turning it over to the audience (the jury).

As discussed at some length, the most important piece of your case (and, ultimately, your show) is your client. They are the star. If you have a nice client with a good story, then that's a great start. If you have a good client, you can win every case. To have a good, believable client, you have to know their injuries well. I think almost every client we represent has the ability to be a good plaintiff for trial. It takes hours of getting to know them. Sometimes it is their story. Sometimes it is just the way they are. But it is up to you to find it.

After that, it's all about telling that story effectively and making the jury want to fight for them. The theme that we talked about in Part 2, "Witnesses in Deposition and Trial," that *is* the story. Unlike a blockbuster, though, we aren't talking about a big, pyrotechnic show. This is one of those Hallmark films that you watch during the holidays and you wind up with happy tears in the end. It's part tragedy and part comeback story; you don't need to overdramatize it, since relatability is the goal.

The next most important thing is jury selection. These twelve people have your case in their hands and you have to win them over with a combination of blunt facts and savvy storytelling. Writer Hunter S. Thompson once described politics as, "the art of controlling your environment."[1] The same can be said of the law and trials. As an attorney, you are the scriptwriter, the casting director, and the director, ushering a script along for an audience of twelve strangers who hold the fate of your client in their hands.

However, before we ever get to voir dire, there are a number of variables to help control the script. But remember, these twelve people are your audience. They are what matters after they are sworn in. You must speak their language.

1. Hunter S. Thompson, *Kingdom of Fear: Loathsome Secrets of a Star-Crossed Child in the Final Days of the American Century* (Simon & Schuster, 2003).

14

Pretrial Motions

Before the Courtroom

Many cases are won or lost before you even enter the courtroom. The entire way you try your case can be shaped by your discovery, expert discovery, and pretrial motions.

In my primary state of practice, California, these are called motions *in limine*. In other jurisdictions they may be called limiting motions, motions to exclude, and so on. For this chapter, they are all one in the same. We are angling to eliminate a lot of the prejudicial or nonsensical BS from coming before the jury. We want the jury to have every ability to make an informed decision on your case, based solely on the specific issues actually in controversy.

This is the crucial time to set the parameters for trial: what will be fair game and what will not. Sometimes if motions *in limine* really go in your favor, your opponent may cave on an important issue, or even the whole case depending on the judge's ruling. I have had dozens and dozens of cases resolve after rulings on these motions.

Here are a few issues commonly fought over during pretrial motions.

Excluding Video Surveillance

For the most part, video surveillance of your client (called *sub rosa* in some jurisdictions) can be super creepy. It's typically video from far away of your client doing normal, daily activities while unsuspectingly being video recorded by some dude hiding in a car (or in the bushes). I'm creeped out just thinking about it.

Defense attorneys and their adjusters seem to love surveillance, and they often put a ton of weight into what they have on video. In particular, they always seem to love to send someone to follow our clients when they have the defense medical exams or depositions. They do this so their MDs or attorneys can set traps in their questioning of your clients, knowing they have video of them that was taken minutes beforehand.[1]

When it comes to video footage of your clients, a lot of it can be excluded in pretrial motions depending on your jurisdictions. Some allow complete trial by ambush. Plan accordingly for either. And it may be benign. "Look at the range of motion in their neck! How can they be hurt?" Or, "Look at them getting up and down out of a car! How dare they!" They are looking for instances of your client doing things they said in their deposition or in their medical exams that they cannot do. Like lifting heavy items. Or hiking. There are ways to deal with this to make it not relevant and get it excluded, or at least take the sting out of it:

- **Admit it.** Have your client say, on direct or in their deposition, that they can do all the things you know are in the video. Own it. Many judges will not allow the defense to play a video of what the plaintiff just said they could do. It is cumulative and wastes the jury's time.
- **Show the video to experts.** Show the video both to your experts and to the defense's experts in deposition. Ask them if this video changes

1. Knowing this, I like to tell my clients to make sure they wear their "I Love My Lawyer" T-shirt those days since they are likely being followed.

their opinions at all. And if your client can have surgery, or needs surgery, and still do these things. And why.

- **Get all the video.** Depose the investigator and get all the video footage and how often they were watching your client, if your jurisdiction permits. Many times, you are just getting the highlight reel. And there may be some good stuff in there for you!
- **Ask for the video footage early and often.** Many jurisdictions say you cannot assert work product privilege for video surveillance if you ask for it in discovery and then later want to use it at trial. Make the defense choose early if they are going to turn it over or throw it out.

In one case, we were able to get three years' worth of video footage excluded from the defense's artillery. We asked for any video of our client multiple times and kept getting the "privileged" objection without any logs or substantive basis. Then, we found out who their investigator was and noticed their deposition. In most jurisdictions, investigators are fact witnesses who need to describe what they did, saw, and how they filmed your client. My research has found that your investigator can carry the work privilege shield as long as you wish it to extend. But if you want to use their findings, they will have to be revealed. They have to lay the foundation. They also have to give up *all* of their video. Unedited. In this case, I sent our own investigator to follow our client to see if anyone was tailing them. Sure enough, someone was tailing our client. By the time my client's deposition was over, we knew the investigator's name and everything about him. We then served the defense's investigator with a deposition subpoena at his car door, by my investigator. Busted!

After this, what did the defense do? They objected, claimed privilege, and did not allow the deposition to go forward. They continued to assert privilege, and then tried including their surveillance video as evidence for trial. They tried using "privilege" as a shield, but then wanted to use the evidence as a sword. This runs afoul of California case law, so we filed a pretrial motion to exclude all video evidence since they refused to produce it in discovery. The defense argued that they should get everything they want, despite the law, but the judge was not having it. We got some potentially damning video excluded, but we had to put in the work and take the right steps.

Another really good way to find out if they have video on your client is ask the defense experts in depositions. Ask if they have heard of any video or reviewed it. If they saw any of it, then you are entitled to it. You can get it in expert discovery. Any potential privilege would be waived because they shared the video with a third party—their expert. I always ask defense experts about defense counsel possessing or showing them any videos or photographs of my clients. I sometimes get good information.

If I do have video footage, I make sure my experts have it as well, so they can verify that people *can* do these things with these injuries. And that these activities are consistent with their injuries and subjective complaints. I love taking up activity restrictions with defense experts who cannot help themselves from saying that our clients are always fine and need no further treatment. I ask them:

Q: Can they walk their dog?
Q: Can they lift a six pack of beer?
Q: Can they drive a car?
Q: In fact, even people who need spine surgery, like the one that the plaintiff had, can do these things, right?

Then I will show them the video and get their exact opinions on it. Many will agree that you cannot see pain on these videos. Or social media photos.

Challenge them during their depositions. It makes a stronger case to exclude it for trial if no experts say this video has anything to do with their opinions. Then it just becomes the defense trying to inflame the jury and speculate.

Excluding Mentions of Attorney-Referred Care & Liens

We also always make motions to exclude disclosing liens or attorney-referred treatment. Why would it matter who helped these victims find care? Just because defense attorneys make it out to be nefarious that attorneys refer patients to doctors—does not mean that it is nefarious. It's important to point out that lawyers know the best doctors.

In the *Johnson* case, the doctor missed a screw one millimeter away from my client's aorta.[2] Be vigilant and thorough. I got him to a specialist, because I know the best specialists, and the specialist did a big operation that genuinely helped Johnson immensely. In this trial, I owned the attorney referrals and liens. I talked about them from jury selection on. Once we got into evidence, the jury could see that it was the attorney's referral (mine) that finally helped this poor guy. At one point, I asked my client on the stand:

> **Mr. Simon:** Who referred you to this surgeon who did this surgery that resulted in a five-day hospital stay and over $300,000 bill?
>
> **Plaintiff:** You did. My lawyer. And thank God. You saved me.

Remember what I said about flipping your worst facts into your best facts?

One way we are often able to get mention of attorney-referred care out of a trial is with case law. There is recent case law in California which says an injured party has the right to choose their best care, and that it should not be bound to the injured party's HMO, Kaiser, or Medi-Cal.

2. See "About the Cases in This Book" at the beginning of this book, *Michael Johnson v. Jonathan Brown.*

The only thing for dispute would be the reasonable cost of that medical care. Most law-savvy judges understand this law and exclude mentioning attorney-referred care. However, defense lawyers want to mention attorney-referred care in an attempt to demonize plaintiffs' lawyers as ambulance chasers trumping up medical bills. So what if the plaintiff's attorney referred the doctor, if the medical costs were not in dispute? If both sides stipulate to the amount, or we agree on the defense expert's number, or waive past medical bills, then the defense cannot make this argument and mention of attorney-referred care should be excluded.

Another way to get the mention of attorney-referred care excluded is with the defense experts. Get the defense experts to confirm that there's nothing wrong with liens, they do it, their peers do it. It offers something to society. Sometimes you get the defense experts who say liens are evil and give the treating doctor a vested interest. This is where is gets fun for me. I ask them:

> **Mr. Simon:** If you were my client's treating doctor, and my client came to you, with no money, no insurance, no means to pay, and needed help, what would you do?

Make them answer. Because there is no good answer. They often will say they will refer them to the local county hospital to be lab rats. Their true colors come out.

If you get these experts to agree that the treatment was all reasonable, and they are just arguing causation, this is another prong to keep out attorney referrals and liens. What would the relevance be? During a pretrial hearing, what if you said:

> **Mr. Simon:** Everyone agrees, Your Honor, that all the treatment was reasonable to do. We agree on the reasonable cost. So what is the relevance of the attorney referral? Or it being

on a lien? We agree the doctor's bill is reasonable, so he is not trumping up charges to "cash in on this lottery ticket."

Again, lay the framework for excluding mention of liens and attorney-referred care.

Review the case law in your state. Read the actual jury instructions for your state. In California they are called CACI instructions. They have helpful notes under the instruction. Use the notes. Most judges will read them and adhere to them. Much of what you want to argue and rely on is right there.

The judge will open their book during this pretrial hearing, and if what you are telling them is accurate and reflected in this reference book, you are good to go!

Excluding Alternate Causation Theories

Always check your state laws as alternate causation varies from state to state. Some states require the defense to *cite to the standard* (reasonable degree of medical probability for causation) if they want to say that something else caused the injury. In other states, the defense can say pretty much anything they want. But jurors still understand that your experts can say things to the standard on causation. And when the defense team cannot show a reasonable degree of medical probability, it is a big selling point. As plaintiffs' lawyers, it is our burden to prove that a car crash was a substantial factor in causing the injuries to our clients. On the flip side of that, the defense can't just go up there and say, "I don't know what's causing the pain, it may be something else." You have to challenge defense experts. These questions are in preparation for filing motions to exclude this kind of testimony.

I ask defense experts:

Q: Can you say with a reasonable degree of medical probability what is causing the pain on this day?
Q: On this day?
Q: Now?

They'll say they don't know. Then you can exclude them from saying anything else about alternate causation. The other thing to do is require them to ask if their alternative cause or excuse is possible or probable. They will usually say *possible*. Then you can move to strike it and exclude it from evidence. I've done this and then moved for directed verdict because they failed to provide any probable evidence on causation.

I see defense lawyers ask:

Q: Could it be diabetes?
Q: Could it be fibromyalgia?

In my cases, they can't do any of that because I took depositions. I have to file a motion on it so it puts a muzzle on the defense from even bringing it up. I take a list of all the stuff the defense lawyer wants to argue into my expert depositions. I know this list because I read it in the expert's mediation brief. I hear it in their questioning to my experts and the treating doctors. And I knock them off one by one. I ask the experts in their depositions:

Q: Was Ms. Smith hurt at work?
Q: She wasn't? Okay.
Q: Was Ms. Smith hurt from a prior crash?
Q: You don't know? Okay.
Q: Was Ms. Smith hurt in a subsequent fall?
Q: You don't know? Okay.

Q: Were Ms. Smith's injuries from an assault by her abusive boyfriend two years prior to this crash?
Q: They were not? Okay.

And yes, this was real. A defense lawyer made the plaintiff's previous assault by her abusive boyfriend his entire case all through discovery. And I destroyed it with that question to his medical expert. This theory was later excluded by the judge.

Q: Can you think of anything else, other than this crash, to a reasonable degree of medical probability, being the cause for all the pain and the need of all these medical treatments?
Q: No?

You better believe I am playing this at trial and putting it in my motions.

That's the big point: you're cross-examining these people, and they don't know the answer to these questions. I'm saying, wait a minute, you're a forensic expert. The defense gave you all the records and they hired you to figure out what's going on, what's causing the pain? But you couldn't do it. You had one job. Maybe it's because the people who hired you didn't want you to give the real answer. Maybe they paid you tens of thousands of dollars, and well, you just don't know.

Takeaways

If you want to get evidence excluded at trial, you have to show that it exists, and that it has no place in front of a jury. Many times, you need the concessions from the defense experts in order to keep it out. So be prepared on what you want excluded from trial and see if you can get those concessions at the expert deposition.

15

Venues, Jury Pools & Voir Dire

Finding the People

I don't think that any venue is a tougher venue than the next one. I just think that in some jurisdictions, the jurors earn more money than others. If you let jurors know the value of things as you go, you're going to be okay. Research your jurors like they are your constituents, and you are running for office. I am "folksy" by nature, and that is my style. I am generally a happy person and always smiling. Even during cross-examination, I like to call out BS when I see it. I talk to the jury like they are my friends at supper. If you travel a lot to try cases, you should be very mindful of juries that don't like outsiders. Getting "hometowned" is very real. I often have co-counsel who is well known in the area to eliminate that fear. If it is apparent that I am an outsider, or from another state, I tell the jury straight up. I prefer honesty.

I relate better to Midwestern jurors or people in rural areas. I feel that they're not looking to punish somebody just because they're not like them. They'll call it like they see it. I do my best to get rid of conspiracy theorists or jaded people. Overly analytical or doubting? Get them off. Other attorneys are also some of my best jurors. They follow the law, the science, and the evidence. People are people. Information is becoming more available at the touch of a cell phone. They are more informed on the value of money and the charlatan tricks of the insurance industry. You just have to ferret out those tort reformers.

Jury Selection

Cases are rarely won during jury selection, but they can be lost. Entire books are written on jury selection. I could go on for days.[1] But for the purpose of this book, I will focus on issues in disc injury cases. Running away from your bad facts, not embracing them, and not getting a gauge from your jurors on these issues is a great way to lose your case. Write down your worst facts beforehand and use jury selection as a focus group for conversations about these topics. You may be able to get jurors off for cause. It important to research your venue and jurisdiction and how to apply various jury selection rules. You will always get good jurors who understand actual science and who will educate the rest of your jurors. You can desensitize the jurors about the defense's entire theme.

The usual issues to flush out in jury selection in the types of cases in this book are:

- The car is not hurt that bad, so the person cannot be hurt that bad.
- The attorney referred the patient to their medical providers.
- Medical providers are holding a lien.
- The patient had degeneration in their spine (pre-existing condition).
- We are asking for millions of dollars.

For the issues above, which you need to address during jury selection, it is all about delivery and the frame. It is about how you ask the question. I will get to this in a second. My first question in almost every trial is this:

1. One of the best resources on voir dire is David Ball, *David Ball on Damages* 3rd ed. (Trial Guides, 2013) Supplement A, "Jury Voir Dire."

Mr. Simon: We just heard from a lot of jurors, who when speaking to the judge, found out they could not serve, or did not want to serve, and some got to go home. So I gotta ask you, who here actually wants to be on this jury and sit with us the next couple of weeks?

This always gets a laugh, but I always get a few hands. Start there. I borrowed this question from my good friend and trial lawyer Gary Dordick. He is one of the best for a reason! If someone is excited to be there, they are usually good jurors for you, are interested, and want to be there and help. They want to do their civic duty. They want to be fair and impartial. The defense knows these are bad jurors for them. And you better believe that when the defense ultimately strikes these jurors, who wanted to be there, the remaining jurors remember. I usually do the disappointed head shake when the defense asks these enthusiastic jurors to leave. The jurors who are left remember, trust me.

The Defense's Themes

Following are several common themes that the defense will use in their case, and how to turn them around and use them for your own case in voir dire.

Light Impact

Okay, so remember, *light impact* will be the defense's entire theme. It is most of their case. Embrace it. Be confident. Ask jurors straight up, and hold up the exhibits you know the defense has ready at their table, and ask:

Mr. Simon: If you see this damage, are you doing to say, "Nah, they can't get hurt. I don't need to hear about science or evidence, that's all I need."

There are always a few who will say they caused minor crashes and people faked being hurt. Challenge them, nicely, and validate their feelings, but they are already thinking in the back of their minds that your client is a liar, a cheat, and a fraud, just like in their situation. Walk them down the path for a "cause challenge." Inform the jury of a favorite line of mine.

Mr. Simon: Now I thank juror number four, Mr. Smith, for his honesty. He talked about his issues and how this wasn't the best case for him to sit in judgment. Maybe a business dispute or criminal trial would be better. But he talked about it. And a famous judge once told a jury, if you talk, you get the chance to walk. So who else feels like Mr. Smith and wants to talk?

All those defense jurors perked up and raised their hands. They saw Mr. Smith, how he answered questions, and how he is going to get to walk out the door and go home. All your bad jurors are now finding a way to get off your jury. After this exercise, ask the rest of the panel:

Mr. Simon: Were you, or anyone close to you, injured in a low property damage crash?

There are always a few. This is just a set-up for a trial theme. Ask them if they or their loved one was really in pain, or if they were just making it up. Of course their friend's or loved one's pain was real. It lays the framework for the "liar, cheat, and fraud" dare, which is a theme in most my cases. There is an entire book on this, and I encourage you to read it.[2] For simplicity, and for the purpose of this book, simply dare the jury:

> **Mr. Simon:** If my client is a fraud, and making it up, give them zero. But if my client is not a fraud, and if they are telling the truth, and everything matches up, then find in their favor.

Asking for Millions

Talk to your jury pool: if the defense is worried about you *asking for millions*, then talk to them about *$10 million*. Another buzzword to use to get rid of your bad jurors is *big-dollar damages*. If jurors stayed quiet during the low property damage questions, there is no way they are going to stay quiet after seeing the low property damage and hearing you talk about asking for millions. Again, the purpose of this exercise is to find and get rid of the bad jurors. And hopefully to get them off for cause so you are not wasting a peremptory challenge.

Often, I will single out a juror I know is good for us. For example, if a juror exposes herself during the judge's questions, and I know the defense is salivating to remove her for cause, I will ask her about sympathy. How, from what I heard during the judge's questions, that they may feel sympathy for our client.

2. Rick Friedman, *Polarizing the Case: Exposing and Defeating the Malingering Myth* (Trial Guides, 2007).

Mr. Simon: Do you feel sympathy due to the back surgery and chronic pain this man is experiencing?

Q: I have to ask you, Mrs. Smith, if the evidence shows that this man is simply a fraud, making it all up, and we do not prove our case, can you give us zero?

Q: Even though you feel sympathy, can you give them zero if it is proven in this court that this man is lying and just making it all up?

If the juror cannot put that aside, I assure them it is fine, because both sides want a fair jury. Then I go up to a bad juror and ask the flip side.

Q: If we do prove our case, and it is found on a more probable or not standard that not only do we win, but the amount of compensation due is $10 million, can you do it?

Then I start to walk them down the path for exclusion. Maybe they need to be convinced of a higher standard. Maybe they have a ceiling of $100,000 and will not go over it. Maybe they do not believe in pain and suffering, no matter what the law says. Again, get these facts out there, and identify and get rid of the bad jurors.

A little aside on sympathy: make sure it applies to the defense as well. Many times, the defendant is an individual. And a nice one. Not a corporation.

So discuss this with the jury. They cannot think about where the money comes from. They cannot think about how any judgment will be paid. It will simply be based on the harms and losses to the injured victim. Ask:

Q: Who will have a hard time putting sympathy aside for the defendant, because you are worried that you are going to bankrupt them?

You must flush this out in jury selection. Impress on the jurors the law, and how it is there for a very good reason; and, for all the jury knows, there is a large amount of money already set and ready to be paid immediately after they render their verdict. Wise jurors know there is insurance. Some will bring it up. You must wisely and with a smile say that you cannot tell them one way or another, and the judge has an instruction on that. You cannot consider insurance—whether the defendant has millions and millions in coverage, or none. The jury will never know. But really, it will be obvious.

The defense loves to ask about sympathy and pretend like we are just trying to win our cases on sympathy. The dare I laid out takes the wind out of their sails. They also talk about how we are asking for too much money and we are trying to win the lottery. Again, we go first. Take away their entire jury selection. They cannot go off script either. They will get up and ask the same questions you just did. After a few questions, and it will be obvious the jury is annoyed because you just talked about the same things, a nice protective objection will go a long way.

Q: Your Honor, objection, asked and answered. We don't want to waste the jury's valuable time.

Attorney-Referred Care & Liens

These go hand in hand. But remember, it is all about the frame. While the defense demonizes, I ask the question like this—and remember—we go first.

> **Mr. Simon:** Does anyone here work in an industry where they know neurosurgeons, their credentials, see their work, and refer their friends and family to the best ones?

Rarely do you get a hand up. Call on anyone and ask:

> Q: Would you consult a referral from an attorney who specializes in these types of injuries, to get a referral to the best doctor?
>
> Q: Would you trust a top of the webpage Google search, or would you seek counsel from your trusted advisor on their personal experiences with these specialists?

Then own it.

> Q: Does anyone have a problem if I referred my client to specialists to get better?

You may find a few who say they wouldn't take a recommendation from an attorney, but trust me, after this framing, you will have others agreeing with you. You will find jurors who went through their HMO, Kaiser, or the workers' comp system, who wished they'd had access to the best doctors right away. You will have others who have been injured, and their attorneys helped them get to the best doctors. It is all about the framing. Do not run from it. Do not believe in the insurance company's poisoned mantra that an attorney-referred doctor must be corrupt. It is not evil. It is a very good thing. We are the specialists. We know the best. We can get our clients into the best doctors without waiting months for referrals and approvals. We are the light.

This is then a good pivot into these fine medical doctors holding a lien. Next ask:

> Q: Does anyone know what a mechanic's lien is?

Someone will explain this to the jury.

> Q: How would you feel if a doctor or hospital does the same and puts a lien on the lawsuit for their payment, rather than send the patient to collections, charge interest, or have them pay large co-pays?

See the reframe? A lien is now a good thing.

> Q: Has anyone here, or anyone you know, ever been put into bankruptcy or put in severe financial peril due to medical bills?

You are also setting the stage for these billing experts coming up and their BS.

> Q: Has anyone here tried to call up any medical provider and try and get them to take 10 percent of their bill as full and final payment?
>
> Q: How did that go for you?

Not only are you flipping what you think is a bad fact into a great fact, but you are also setting the stage for the jurors to hate the defense's billing experts. See, isn't this fun?

Degeneration (Pre-existing Condition)

Every expert will concede that many adults have degeneration in their spine. As we age, it gets worse. But a very low percentage of us will actually need pain management or spine surgery without something causing that pre-existing condition to become symptomatic. So start laying the groundwork in jury selection. What the defense is doing to your client is something they do to anyone over the age of twenty. It will be exposed as the trial goes on, but start getting this out there. First ask the jury:

> Mr. Simon: Does anyone know what "degeneration" is and how it applies to the spine?

Someone usually knows. If not, apply it to knees, shoulders, and so on. Then ask them this:

> Q: Does the law allow for someone who has this degenerative condition in their spine, knees, shoulders, and so on, to be compensated if that pre-existing condition is made worse or symptomatic?

You are telegraphing the ultimate jury instruction that proves you win, even if what the defense says is true about degeneration. You are empowering the jury, during jury selection, to logically follow and get there. During the trial, they will start to realize that they need to protect your client because they are protecting themselves. Here are a few more examples:

> **Q:** Do you think that since we get older, and have more degeneration, that since this is a pre-existing condition that my client had when the defendant hit them, that the defendant should be able to use my client's ordinary degeneration as a free pass to not compensate the injured?
>
> **Q:** Should we be less subject to compensation because we grow older and more frail?
>
> **Q:** If someone has brittle bone disease, and a driver hits that person with their car while they are legally in a crosswalk, and they break a bone when most of the population would have zero injuries, should that person who broke the law be held accountable for all the injuries, or just the injuries a normally healthy person would have suffered?

See it now? We are educating the jury to debunk that biomechanical expert coming later who just uses studies with sample sizes of healthy normal people, and not ones like your specific client. This is all proper questioning because you are trying to find out if jurors can follow the law and compensate those with pre-existing conditions.

Science versus Confusion

I usually think we win on the science and on being very straightforward. Confusion is the defense's best friend, and I try to get people who are as educated as possible and as liberal as possible. I like people who understand the value of money and can see through bullshit. I believe in the quickest and most expedited trial possible. Jurors hate it when we waste their time or when anyone tries to confuse them. I know the defense cannot help but be long winded and to invite confusion. And I bring that up in jury selection.

Q: Who here thinks they have a good BS detector?
Q: Who here thinks experts can be bought?
Q: Do you know what a red herring is?
Q: Has anyone heard of Occam's razor?

You are empowering the jury to think for themselves and look for these things, like a game of CSI. A person who comes to a conclusion on their own is a very good weapon for you in the jury box. They do not need you to tell them, they like to figure it out for themselves first. If you ask them to look out for red herrings, they will. And they will be vindicated and on your side when they find them. If they are the juror who knew what Occam's razor meant, they are empowered to see the simplest explanation and hold it to be true. I use this theory in every case.

- Our story is simple.
- Theirs is complicated.
- Our client was hurt.
- Everything matches up.
- Everyone is being truthful.
- Truth is easy.

The defense theories go down a laundry list of conspiracy theories, people lying, and many people in on a huge fraud. The lawyers, the doctors, the plaintiff, the witnesses around them, the MRI scan, the hospital, and so on. Empower these jurors from the beginning and you will be rewarded many times over in the end.

Gaps in Treatment

Most reasonable people do not rush into surgery. They take time off to heal. They hope it gets better on its own. They go to work, because they need to.

A liar, cheat, and fraud does the opposite. They never return to work, they're at the doctor every day, they rush into surgery, they never get better, and they wait to collect a check.

A reasonable person has large gaps in treatment. Medical care is expensive. And most jurors know this. Ask for a show of hands:

Q: Who has been recommended for a surgery, but put it off?
Q: Who takes their dogs and cats to the vet for any ailment, but never goes themselves?
Q: Why?

The answers are pretty much the same reasons your clients put off care. Jurors like people who act as they would have themselves. If you find the jurors who would have handled this situation like your client did, guess who those jurors are fighting for? The defense loves to use gaps in treatment; but I love to flip it on them, starting in jury selection. In my medical treatment timeline, by the time we get to closing, I sprinkle in all the stuff the defense was doing while my client had these gaps in treatment.

- Denying liability.
- Having their doctors write reports saying, "They're not hurt, needs no treatment."
- Denying.
- Delaying.

Q: What would a reasonable person do when faced with high medical bills with a potential surgery when the other side is denying everything?

They would do what any reasonable person would do. Gaps in treatment are relatable. They are reasonable. And a juror told you that in jury selection before you explained it during trial.

I never bring out all of our good facts in jury selection because I don't want show the defense my good jurors. Instead, get all of your bad facts out. Talk to your jury about every one of your bad facts, like the following:

- Gaps in treatment.
- High medical bills.
- Light impact.
- Attorney-referred care.

Here are just a few examples of how bad facts might play out in trial:

- Imagine I have a case tangentially related to a Hollywood actor. I won't bring him up because there might be a huge fan of that actor in the jury pool. Adverse evidence the jury is anticipating or familiar with degrades the power of such evidence.
- Is my client a veteran? I am not bringing that up if the defense does not.
- What about my client's powerful story of caring for their sick father during this so called "gap in treatment"? I am not bringing that up until opening.

In my *Atlantic* case, the defendant crashed into a car containing two women and left them trapped in their car on the side of the road.[3] He was eventually caught by the police and charged with a hit-and-run, but the defense didn't bring it up during jury selection. If the defense had brought the hit-and-run up in jury selection, the people who want to punish others for crimes would have been off this jury so fast. The

3. See "About the Cases in This Book" at the beginning of the book, *Paulina Atlantic v. B&D Transport.*

first time the jury heard about the hit-and-run was in my opening statement. They all had this expression on their faces like they wanted to kill this defendant.

In that case, which drew a $3.8 million verdict, I represented an older lady with prior back issues. The other passenger in her car got $3 million, solely for her PTSD claim. The defendant tractor trailer driver hit these two ladies at sixty miles per hour in the middle of a desert, then fled the scene. Of course, his attorneys disputed liability. Sigh. I picked a conservative jury in that case, because the truck driver committed a crime (he was convicted of a hit-and-run), and conservative jurisdictions hate crime. So I picked a jury that would punish somebody for a crime. They gave me 100 percent of what I asked for.

Takeaways

Know your facts in jury selection. Study how jury selection works in your venue and apply the methods in this chapter. Get the "bad" facts out, reframe them, and get the poison off your jury. Do not let the good jurors expose themselves too much. And keep your good facts to yourself to use later.

16

Opening Statement

The jury is empaneled. You set your themes in voir dire. The jury is ready to hear the truth. Keep in mind that they would rather be doing something else. It's easy for them to be super bored since they had to show up. Their attention span is short. As a guide, after an hour, a jury's attention starts to fade. My opening statements are usually not more than thirty minutes. Sometimes much less.

Win your case in opening. Expose the defense experts' lies. Unveil their entire theme. Show the jury the property damage photographs and remind them it is their entire case. However, you have to do it carefully, don't be argumentative and annoy the judge. Play by the rules of any court that you're in.

Make it easy for the jury. Tell a simple story. Distill the essence of your case into one sentence. Pretend you're drafting the perfect Instagram caption. I tell the jury the simple story of how this all matches up. All the treaters agree. Everything matches up. So why are we here? Then I show photographs of the defense experts. I tell the jury what they are going to say. I cross-examine them in opening (without them saying a word), showing the jury their bias and lies before they take the stand. I talk about how they do this to everyone.

I present the convoluted theory many defense attorneys deploy, by saying it was a medical conspiracy which everyone was in on. Then I contrast it with the simple, real story: There was a crash. This person got hurt because of it. I put up a slide of two roads. I call it two paths. One path, the simple one, is ours. It leads to full compensation of $X million. The second path, the one of mass distortion and confusion, is the defense's path. It leads to zero dollars. The jury gets to follow the evidence. Follow the clues. And pick a path. There is no path in the middle.

Figure 16-1. "Two Roads."

I use vivid imagery and verbs that give my story a sense of motion. I arrange the facts so they advance my conclusion.

I often tell the jury what the defense and its witnesses are going to say. I'll say that the first thing the defense will talk about is the damage to the car. This has happened more than once during my openings. When it is the defense attorney's turn, the attorney just starts holding up pictures of the car right away, like it was scripted. The jurors just smile and shake their heads. And I know that the defense knows I have a lot of strong dirt on their experts. But I won't tell them the good stuff.

It's like poker: don't show your hand too early. I didn't tell the jury about one defense witness who I found out did not go to medical school. I saved that for the cross-examination to use for maximum effect. But I do give the jury a taste of the defense's bias. The stuff the defense knows I know about. Like how often the experts testify for the defense, how much they are paid, and so on.

The exact opposite is true with bad facts in your case. As I've said before, reveal bad facts right away to minimize their impact. Yup, there is barely any damage to my client's bumper, but that doesn't mean a person can't get hurt.[1] Whiplash is a real thing. Or, yes, the impact only happened at twenty-five miles per hour, but they'll have experts who say people can't get hurt at eighty miles per hour. Light impact is a big red herring because a biomechanical expert's opinion is the same no matter what the situation is. I tell the juries this is their same defense.

It will win points with the jury when they see you are comfortable enough to expose information or a point of view not favorable to your case. This will also potentially make the defense skip mention of it when it comes their time to speak.

Keep your case simple. Show the jury we are here because of them. Show the jury the defense does this to everyone, all the time. We will win

1. Michael D. Freeman, et al., "A Review and Methodologic Critique of the Literature Refuting Whiplash Syndrome," *Spine* 24, no. 1 (January 1999): 86–96, https://doi.org/10.1097/00007632-199901010-00022.

on being efficient and getting to the point—we will not try to confuse them. We will show them actual facts, evidence, and science from this case.

Don't just read your opening argument. Write out some key notes to riff on. I use a PowerPoint of my key talking points. I only talk specific numbers when I know the evidence is very likely to come in clean. Sometimes I am given a case to try and issues were not ferreted out in discovery or expert discovery. There may be video of my client laying around, or some impeachment I do not see coming. In that case, I do not give specific numbers up front. Remember to smile and look people in the eye! Normal human stuff.

Checklist for Opening Statement

- State your theme in a sentence or two.
- Tell the story of the case without arguing it.
- Decide how to deal with bad facts.
- Strategically order your facts.
- Tell the jury what they should do.

The *Atlantic* Case

My client Paulina Atlantic was sixty years old when a tractor trailer hit her from behind.[2] She was in the process of moving from California to Oklahoma to live with her son and grandson. Instead of calling 911, the driver fled and called his brother, who owned the trucking company. Paulina Atlantic and another woman remained trapped in the car until the jaws of life extricated them.

The defense sought to blame my client, arguing that she was idle on the shoulder and merged back onto the slow lane, from right to left.

2. See "About the Cases in This Book" at the beginning of the book, *Paulina Atlantic v. B&D Transport.*

But that's not what the truck driver said in his deposition, or what he said to the officer at the scene. And the passenger was asleep in the car until the car was hit by the truck driver, who didn't even try to swerve. The reason why that is important is because there were rumble strips all up and down that highway. She easily would have woken up. I really thought the defense was joking when they were disputing liability. But hey, our successful practices were not built on the wise decisions of insurance adjusters and defense lawyers, am I right?

The driver was also criminally convicted of a hit-and-run, something I definitely told the jury about for the first time in opening:

> **Mr. Simon:** So you're going to hear—the evidence is going to show—that at the scene of the crash, Mr. Preston actually fled. He hit these two ladies, rear-ended them, pushed them off into the desert and left them there. He drove five miles down the road to a truck stop and tried to sleep in the cab of his truck, until the cops found him some two and a half hours later. His property damage fit with the collision. He was convicted of a hit-and-run. You're going to hear all about this.

The driver said my client pulled out in front of him. But the story the driver told during his deposition was wildly different from what he told officers.

> You're going to find that Mr. Preston really doesn't know what happened that day. That's what the evidence will show. What we'll show is that this was the vehicle alignment, that Mr. Preston rear-ended this vehicle at a high rate of speed, dead on in the number two lane, in the slow lane, and pushed the vehicle off the side of the road. He went out, saw the two women trapped in the car screaming; he says he heard them screaming they're okay and to call 911. So then he just left.

The fire department only came because a passerby had apparently called. The truck driver, meanwhile, drove five miles down the road, waited for his brother and the mechanic, and slept until the police found him.

> And I think the other side's experts will agree. The impact was solely within the slow lane, the number two lane. Mr. Preston's truck was going anywhere from forty to sixty-five, maybe even seventy-five miles an hour at the time of the impact. The speed limit for trucks there is fifty-five. The truck never slowed. It never broke [speed] prior to impact. Any cars or anything on the roadway would have been easily visible within half a mile, that's thirty seconds away—ahead to see anything ahead of you.

The defense also wrongly said my client didn't have her lights on. Her lights were on. The car's *black box*, or event data recorder, said so. The defense also hired an eye doctor who never met Ms. Atlantic or looked at her medical records. The best they could do is say maybe she had cataracts in one eye.

My client stopped working after the accident. Her discs slipped backwards into her spinal canal nerve. She had numbing back pain that caused her right leg to go numb. This resulted in her getting a spinal fusion. But she kept having constant debilitating back pain.

The defense hired a doctor—a non-practicing internist, not a surgeon, who had a side-hustle selling skin creams to weightlifters—who said Ms. Atlantic should only pay 10 percent of her bills, even though she owed a lot more.

> So you ask yourselves, why are we here? The reason we are here is because the defendants do not accept full responsibility for this crash.

The defendants' position was that Ms. Atlantic hovered around the shoulder for half a mile for some reason, and then veered in front of the truck driver, who never saw her, so it was her fault. They called up a truck accident expert who did a simulation to show all of this. Our position was that she was in the second lane, the slow lane, which matched the physical evidence and what witnesses saw that night. But like anyone who passes a driver's test, especially truckers, they are taught to move into the passing lane if someone is driving on the shoulder or slower.

When there is a liability dispute like this, I front-load my opening statement, talking about all the bad things the defense did, all the rules they broke, and show we are here because the defendant is being super unreasonable. This is a great tool to master, and Rick Friedman and Patrick Malone's *Rules of the Road* is the best.[3]

Then I went into her injuries. She had intermittent back pain over her thirty-five years as a nurse. She worked continuously, with no workers' compensation claims, no problems working whatsoever, until the day of the crash. Since then, she has not worked as a nurse. I waived any specific earnings claims, and instead decided to use the loss of her nursing career as a general damage. She lost her own pride in being able to care for her patients. She felt useless. Not once did I bring up in jury selection that she was a nurse. Neither did the defense. This was to their peril.

> You'll find out within the first few months after the crash, it got so bad it would cause her to have numbness and tingling down her right leg, cause her to fall until she got to the surgeons that did a spinal fusion surgery, which you'll hear from the doctors to explain what they did. They cut her open from the back. They put in hardware, screws, and plates in her spine to elevate this position of her lumbar spine, so it would stop slipping and to stabilize it.

---

3. Rick Friedman and Patrick Malone, *Rules of the Road: A Plaintiff Lawyer's Guide to Proving Liability*, 2nd ed. (Trial Guides, 2010).

And I made it very clear that she will continue to have nerve damage down her leg as well as debilitating back pain. All the experts agreed, including ones from the defense, that she will never be cleared to do what she was doing before. She was working at a home, where one of the people she took care of was an eighteen-year-old with cerebral palsy. She will never be a nurse again. I asked all the jurors in this case their passions and goals in life. I made clear in opening that my client's passions and goals were taken from her that very night.

Both the car and the truck were examined for black box data. Inside Atlantic's car, the black box showed her likely speed, that she was not braking, and that her lights were on. However, no black box data from the truck was ever found. By the time our experts reviewed the truck, it was already repaired, and no repair records were ever turned over to us.

The black box from Atlantic's car recorded a frontal impact. To be certain about speed, there has to be frontal impact. So if we had the black box from the truck, we could know exactly how fast the car was going. With *Atlantic,* we had to rely on her bouncing off the road and rolling into the desert to calculate—backwards—how fast her car was going. That's why we have a speed range. Because the speed censors were off and because she was spinning, there was a wide range of how fast she was going. We only know there was a speed differential, like thirty to forty miles an hour between the vehicles. This means that if Ms. Atlantic was going thirty miles per hour; the truck driver was going sixty to seventy-five miles per hour. She was going forty miles per hour or slower.

> We believe this is a very, very simple case. Ms. Atlantic and her passenger were rear-ended by a tractor trailer at a high rate of speed and pushed out in the desert. She has serious debilitating injuries. That's the simple story. We don't want to bring any conspiracy theories to detract you from the truth. That's it.

Both her parents were alive at the time, and she was supposed to be taking care of them. They died in the interim. She never got to take care of them because of what happened to her.

Why is this important? Because the defendants are also denying most, if not all, of the injuries and the cost of the treatment. They say that she should maybe just have a sprain, and other than that, she's fine. And her medical bills that are owed, paid, or in collections are too high, and that the defense should be given a discount on the medical bills as well.

They hired doctors to tell you this. They hired a Dr. Willoughby, who is an internist that will take the stand. He'll tell you the defendants should only pay 10 percent of the medical bills.

So then we had to hire experts. Dr. Samuel, who is not a treating doctor, saw Ms. Atlantic, to tell you, yes, in fact, there was this big car crash that caused her to need back surgery. She didn't have this numbness or tingling before. Her back was fine before. She'll need a lot of future care to be able to stabilize her pain and to hold off from having another surgery.

We also had to hire a counterpart to Dr. Willoughby to tell you that her medical bills are owed in full, they are reasonable, and she's priced out what her care will be in the future.

The only thing we ask of you, ladies and gentlemen, is just to follow the law and the evidence. That's it. We don't want to go off on wild goose chases and speculate about stuff. We just want you to follow the law and the evidence.

Then came the ask. Here's how I ended my opening statement in the case:

Your goal in this case is you have to compensate Ms. Atlantic for the last 800 days, the date of the crash up until today, all the way for the next 8,500 days, the next 23.6 years of her life. The things, her passions and goals, the things that were taken away from her, that she be compensated for.

This is your job in this case. You have to determine who's telling the truth. Is it the truck driver or Ms. Atlantic? Is the truck at fault? What are the past and future medical expenses and the past and future human harm? And I'll tell you, if you believe the truck driver and their defense experts, that you can say, Ms. Atlantic, you're exaggerating, you're making it up, you caused the crash, you can give her zero. If you believe Ms. Atlantic, her story, the facts, the evidence, our evidence will show she's due at least $4 to 8 million for what she's gone through and all her medical bills.

Ladies and gentlemen, that is all that I have for you. I look forward to presenting this case to you as efficiently as we can. We do have the burden of proof as the plaintiff, so we'll have—the lion's share of the evidence should be coming in through us. We'll be calling the officers. We'll be calling doctors, those types of things, to present the evidence to you, to meet our burden of more likely true than not true.

Can you just see the themes? The PowerPoint images of two roads? The conspiracy theory slides of the convoluted facts that the defense is banking on? We are showing we are here because of the defense. We had to hire experts to counter the defense's experts because they cannot accept a simple truth. The die was cast. The case was won by the end of opening statement. We had credibility on our side. They were already rooting for us.

Takeaways

Usually the die is cast after opening statements. The graphics are nothing more than cue cards to give you talking points, and make sure you do not forget anything. The more confident you are in your case, and know your case cold, the more jurors are going to believe you. Slow down. Control your diction. Be confident.

17

Plaintiff Direct Examination

Think of approaching your job as something akin to method acting. You want to *become* your client. Go to their home, see how they live, see who they love. Most of all, see what is missing. Look for the things they struggle with because you can find absolute gold. Once when I was at a client's house, I used the restroom. I looked inside one of his cabinets (creeper, I know) and it was filled with all sorts of medicine. I snapped a photo and used that during trial (with his permission). He wasn't in that photo, but it still resonated with the jury. As we discussed in chapter 7, "Gathering the Evidence," the most effective photos to bring before a jury show the absence of the injured. That case resulted in a $15 million verdict.

During direct, you will usually have to get testimony via non-leading questions that suggest their own answers, such as:

Q: Then what happened?

Or

Q: How does that make you feel?

Use "looping" techniques, where you use the end of your witness's answer, or a portion of it, as part of your next question. For example:

A: It makes me feel sad, because I can't play with my grandkids on the lawn like I used to.
Q: What kinds of games did you play with your grandkids?
A: We used to play tag, but I can't run any more, I just sit in a chair and watch them play.

Rehearse with your witness, but don't make it seem that way when they are on the stand. Make it seem like you are hearing responses to your questions for the first time. Successful direct examinations happen when you don't stick out, and the attention is all on the witness.

You definitely don't want your witness to whine. Help them show their struggle by simply stating the facts. Have them tell the jury how their life is different. In my opinion, this is the hardest part of the trial. Do not be afraid to bring in specialists solely to prepare your client to testify. There are some very gifted people who do this very well.

Basic Direct Exam Outline

Make your direct exam real and relatable to the jury.[1] Following are the details you want to show. There is no need to dress it up any further. Remember your audience. Your client should be someone they are rooting for. The jurors' likes should be your client's likes. Your client's passions should be similar to theirs. Your client's family traditions? Like theirs. Let those details speak for themselves. I usually block it into a few categories:

- **Background.** Take a step back and ask about your client and their history. Show before photos of things that were important to them and their family.
- **Day of Crash.** Ask about the day of the crash until your client's first medical care. Cover the high notes.
- **Medical Care.** Use broad strokes because this has already been covered in detail by physicians. Have your client talk about learning to walk after surgery. Ask them about their relative having to fly in to take care of them after surgery. This is the place for stories, not yes-or-no answers.
- **Bad Stuff.** Bring out things you know the defense will want to cross-examine on. Take the wind out of the defense's sails. This can be gaps in treatment, attorney-referred care, and so on.
- **General Damages.** Usually end here by showing things that this event has taken from your client, such as relationships with kids, grandkids, or a significant other.
- **Last Question.** I ask something like, *Do you feel like less of a father?*

This will be the only time I ask a gut-wrenching question. Right at the end. Then I turn it over to the defense.

1. A full direct examination set of questions is included in Appendix A, "Outline of Plaintiff's Direct Examination."

Pointers for Plaintiff's Direct Exam

My plaintiff direct examination usually goes toward the end of my case-in-chief. I want the jury to hear from all the experts, treaters, family, and friends first. By the time the plaintiff takes the stand, the jury knows everything they have gone through. This leads to a quicker and more pointed direct examination.

Think Ahead about Possible Video of Plaintiffs

If defense lawyers have covert video of your client, they cannot help themselves and bring it up with prior witnesses. For instance, I called my client's sister in a trial before I called my client. I suspected the defense had video. I had her talk about all the things she observed my client do. I warned her that they may have video of him, so when the defense asks questions, be very careful. I tell other witnesses, if you did not see something yourself, say you do not know. Sure enough, the defense lawyer asked her, "Does your brother climb ladders? Can he use a saw?" She said she had no idea. But when my client took the stand, on direct, I brought up how he can still climb ladders. He can still use tools. He has to work. He showed the jury how he does these things. The defense then wanted to play a video of him doing those exact things, but the judge didn't allow it. It was not impeachment. The plaintiff just said he can do all those things. We are not going to waste hours of a juror's time on these things! The dejected defense attorney asked me later, who leaked to me that they had video? Wild guess, I told him.

Preparing My Client for Cross-Examination

I also prepare my clients for their eventual cross-examination, and I give them the three big things to watch out for:

- The defense may have video of you, so never say never! You can do everything.
- If the defense shows you a document or medical record, they are trying to get it into evidence through you. Do not fall for it. If you do not know the document, it is not yours. Just say you have no idea. Do not assume something is true just because they tell you so.
- Do not be combative. Be nice, yet somber. Do not lose your temper. Do not overplay it.

I also prefer *not* to have my clients at the counsel table with me during trial, or there very much at all. Jurors will just stare at them and find reasons to find that they are not hurt that bad. Or not like their shoes, their hair, or their clothes.

Example: The *Johnson* Case

The rear-end collision Johnson suffered resulted in neck and back pain, with it radiating down his upper and lower extremities.[2] His neck injury leaned more traumatic, because the later taken MRI showed a disc extrusion. But his lower back MRI was not conclusive about this crash. It showed long standing signs of degeneration. However, his

2. See "About the Cases in This Book" at the beginning of the book, *Michael Johnson v. Jonathan Brown.*

symptoms showed up with nerve impingement on one side. To make matters worse, medical doctors made him worse. He had to go through three spine surgeries. And the defense tried to argue that he was given unnecessary surgeries.

He had a hard time swallowing, and he had shooting pain down his fingertips that caused him to drop items. Even routine activities such as laying down on a pillow proved to be a logistical nightmare for him. Aside from chronic pain, all of these injuries resulted in a deterioration of his sex life that ultimately saw a relationship dissolve. The defense didn't even ask him about that, despite it being in the medical records. Now he's a disabled single father trying to care for his kid. On top of that, he could no longer coach or play basketball with his son.

Day of Crash

For the day of the crash, I first asked about the pain he had the day after the crash:

Mr. Simon: Can you tell me about the pain you had the first day after the crash?

Mr. Johnson: I was nauseous. I had complaints of vision issues. Left neck—left side of my neck, my shoulder, my collar bone. My left hip was bothering me, and my left leg was bothering me.

Q: All right. Could you show the jury, just describe the best you can, the pain that you had from your neck into your left shoulder and arm?

A: It's coming from behind my ear, and it shoots down to my shoulder blade. It comes down through my elbow and comes down through my hands.

Q: Same thing with your left leg? The best you can, just describe it.

A: It comes from my lumbar. It shoots down my left buttocks, down my thigh, on the left side of my left, left side of my foot, down to my toes.
Q: Have you ever had that pain before?
A: No.

Remember that dermatome map?[3] Well these symptoms at the scene and in days thereafter match perfectly with the issues found in the patient's MRI that was taken much later. The plaintiff would have to be the best criminal in the world to come up with this crazy story.

Surgeries & Medical Issues

Then I asked him about going through with the first of three spinal surgeries, and the complications that came with the surgeries.

Q: What problems do you have today with your neck?
A: It's extremely stiff. I get a lot of radiating pain. I have nerve pain shooting down my left side to my fingertips. I get stabbing pains. It gets numb. It gets weak. I drop things all the time. It shoots down to my shoulder blades. I feel a lot of pressure. It hurts a great deal, and it's hard for me to rest my head down on a pillow and sleep.

And also, I have a difficult time swallowing. The hardware is pressing against my esophagus, and I often cough up water or pills or food that gets clogged in there, and it's very scary at times when that happens.

I also asked about his neck surgery and 'subsequent epidurals.

3. This is first discussed in chapter 4, "Common Defense Arguments."

Q: You went through how many epidurals after that for your lower back?
A: I went through two.
Q: All right. Did they help you in your lower back?
A: They did not.

But he ultimately decided to get lumbar surgery.

Q: And why did you decide to have that surgery?
A: Because I was in so much pain. I tried to hold it off and go through other procedures, and I just couldn't get around the nerve pain and the weakness and everything.

He still experienced pain from the surgery. We then went through the recovery time from the second surgery, which was much quicker.

Q: And how does this recovery time compare to the first lumbar surgery that you had?
A: Oh, it's like night and day. The recovery time has been much shorter. I've noticed a huge difference in the type of pain I was experiencing from the first lumbar fusion compared to the second one. I had to learn how to walk two times. I couldn't walk for a week after the first lumbar surgery. Someone had to teach me to walk. The second time was a little bit shorter than the time I had to learn how to walk the first time.

Family Life Before & After Injury

I contrasted all of this with the things he used to do when he led a normal, uninjured life. Again, I showed what was missing.

A: I was a typical parent like anybody else. I vacuumed, did the dishes, cooked, cleaned—I could be with my son. We could go on the beach and play Wiffle Ball or frisbee. I could coach his basketball team. We used to have a hoop that we would play on all the time together. I would show him how to dunk or how to cross over. Maybe he could get a scholarship one day like I had. But I can't play basketball with him anymore. I'll never run again. I'll never be able to jump again. I can't shoot a jump shot because of my left side. I can't show him how to shoot.

Johnson then went into a good story about how he viewed his son like a little brother, something he never had growing up. I don't know about you, but I am tearing up as I read his testimony over again! Because of this, he felt especially closer to him.

Q: Do you feel like you're losing out with your son because of your injuries?

A: I have two older brothers, and because there was such an age difference between myself and the first child, I felt like I was a single child within a family. And so I always wanted a younger brother to teach the game to and spend time with, and my son is that younger brother to me. He's my best friend. Part of the bonding between us is me teaching him the game. I absolutely miss out on it. I miss every second I spend with that little kid.

Q: Do you feel that you are less of a dad because of this?
A: I not only think I am less of a dad, I feel like I'm less of a man.

Sleep

Q: What's your sleep regimen?
A: I don't sleep at night. I try to go to bed, and it just doesn't work. You know, I'm mostly awake, and I can't get comfortable. My neck really bothers me. No matter what pillow or bed or what orthopedic comforter or pillow topper we buy to make myself comfortable, it just doesn't work.
Q: Was there a time that the headaches kind of hurt whenever you were using the computer a lot?
A: Yeah, whenever there was any type of video motion, or bright lights, it really bothered me. Very sensitive.
Q: And that's gotten better?
A: Yes, it has. They changed my eyeglass prescription.

Intimacy

The crash also negatively affected his relationship with his partner.

Q: And has this crash affected your ability to have relationships with the fairer sex?
A: Yes. I'm not able to perform and am ashamed to say that I haven't had sex in a couple years. I can't have sex. It's part of the reason why we broke up.
Q: Is that why you are no longer dating your partner?

A: Yes. I felt that she deserved somebody that could be there for her and could take her on dates and be intimate with her because I couldn't do it anymore.

I also had him talk about how his mother had to carry heavy bags for him, do his laundry, make his bed, and generally serve as his caretaker. It was all very embarrassing for a full-grown man, but elemental to his case.

Need for Medications

There was also his medication regimen, which read like a CVS pharmacy inventory.

A: I'm taking Norco, Zanaflex, Ultram, Cymbalta, Neurontin, Fundamental sulfur, testosterone, and human growth hormones.
Q: Were you taking any of this stuff before the car crash?
A: No, I was not.
Q: How much did you pay out of pocket every month for your medications?
A: I pay between $1,100 and $1,200 a month.
Q: What times of day do you take the medications?
A: I usually take it in the morning, probably around 6:00 a.m., and then I take it a little later, probably around 10:30 or 11:00, and then I take it around 7:00 at night. Three times a day.

Next were his medical bills and the financial burden that loomed over him in addition to a physical one.

Q: You understand you have to pay the medical bills regardless of what happens with this crash lawsuit?

A: Yes, and that's the scary thing about it. I didn't ask for this and now it's created an insurmountable amount of debt on my shoulders that I didn't have before the accident. You know, I was hoping to work and save for my son's college fund, and now I have all this debt. It's terrifying. I don't know how I am going to pay this stuff.

My directs aren't usually very long at all. *Johnson*'s direct was pretty quick. And then on their cross-examination, the defense steps in every hole. Under cross-examination, the defense often asks the client what they do all day, since they are injured and out of work. I prep my clients by telling them to focus in on the droning pain they endure. He takes his machine off, he takes pills, he asks for help. He sits around all day. It ended up being the most emotional part of the trial.

Use photos of your client before they were injured in your direct examination. Ask about and show what your client's life used to be like. The good days. In your closing PowerPoint, use that same image. Then slowly have your client disappear from that image. It was taken from him. Coaching basketball for your son? Nope, sorry, that is gone. Enjoying the holidays with your family, cooking the Christmas ham? Nope, sorry, that is gone. Feeling special by caring for that disabled client of yours? Nope, sorry, now you are the burden who everyone else has to care for.

Takeaways

This is your client's hero story. Make it intriguing, interesting, and about a hero your jury can relate to.

18

Cross-Examination

Good news! If you followed this book, your work in cross-examination is already done for you. You read chapters 9 through 13. Now just apply the same ideas to cross-examination. The only thing you need to update is what the expert has been up to lately—you need to track their most recent whereabouts. And cut out the concession and impeachment clips from your tailor-made expert depositions. You are ready to go! Hit them with your haymaker and follow the blueprint below. In expert depositions you can be inquisitive, ask questions you do not know the answers to, and get more information. In cross-examination, it is controlled, shorter, and more exciting.

- Start with your polarizing issue right out the gate (could be challenging the defense expert on causation to a reasonable degree of medical probability or your client faking) right when you have the jury engaged.
- Get your list of concessions (you already know the answers from your deposition, which match your jury instructions).
- Show the jury the witness's severe bias.
- Make the witness look silly with far-out opinions.

- Impeach the witness with contradictions and show the jury some things they were not given or may have missed.
- Re-polarize the witness's big concessions.
- Get out.

Less is more. The most effective cross-examinations are minutes long, not hours.

19

Closing Argument

Let's start with what *not* to do during closings. The last thing you want to do is work so hard for a verdict, only to have it taken away because you violated the rules! Here's your list of things *not* to do:

- *Don't* ask the jury to deliver a verdict in order to send a message to the community.
- *Don't* appeal to the jury's self-interests. "If you side with the plaintiff, your [fill-in-the-blank] prices will go down."
- *Don't* use the Golden Rule argument. You can't ask the jurors to put themselves or their loved ones in your client's shoes.
- *Don't* tell personal stories about yourself. Absolutely not.
- *Don't* say the plaintiff will be poor if the jury doesn't find in your client's favor.
- *Don't* swear (don't fucking do it).
- *Don't* misstate the evidence or law.

Closing is where you tie everything together. This is where you want to tell a story. You only get to talk to the jury twice, once during opening statement and again during closing argument. And a lot of things happen between then, so think of this as the bottom of the ninth inning.

Jurors like attorneys who are efficient, who get right to the point. Jurors hate when people waste their time. Consider the concepts of *primacy* and *recency*. People remember things in the beginning and at the end. Start your argument with your important facts in the beginning, but also end with them. Do not bury the good stuff in the middle.

My closings are about 120 slides, and I am usually done in thirty or forty minutes. I don't bog the jury down with stuff they already saw. The defense usually goes on and on during direct. Every case should have a *theory*. A theory is different from a *theme*.

- A *theory* explains the legal grounds for your lawsuit.
- A *theme* explains the moral story of your case.

Your theory has to be grounded in fact. This is also where you want to refer back to voir dire. Think about your jurors' life experiences.

One major worry we have as trial attorneys is whether the jury knows how to apply the law that's given to them. Connect the evidence to jury instructions that describe the burden of proof. The jury wants guidance. Address this during closing arguments.

There are jurors who've already made up their minds, and there are probably a few jurors who need a little bit more ammunition to make their decisions. That's the powerful part of closings. It's where you win over those swing jurors. In jury selection, if you pick two or three strong plaintiff jurors, you'll win your case. They will sway the rest of the jury.

I usually know from the jump if a juror is in my corner through body movement. But I've certainly been surprised. A lot of jurors don't want to show their cards. I've had jurors with their arms folded the whole time, not taking notes, and then they find for the client 100 percent.

Closing in Three Parts

I divvy up my closings into three parts: jury empowerment, the roads to be taken, then arm them with the law. At the end, the ask.

Part 1: Jury Empowerment

With jury empowerment, I tell them its origin and how uniquely American the court system is. Things were decided in literal courtyards and that's how the name courtroom came to be. Now it's in the jurors' hands.

Example: The *Johnson* Case

From my closing in *Johnson*:

Mr. Simon: So the good thing about our judicial system here, it's unique to the United States. Way back in the day, the king used to be the judge, the jury, and the executioner, until they signed the Magna Carta in the 1200s, and then the people got to decide. And that's what we have here today. Her Honor doesn't have a say, I don't, [the defense], the plaintiff. The twelve of you get to decide. You do. You get to decide this final resolution of this case finally after two and a half years.

My Empowerment Story

This empowerment story I just shared, I picked up from the great trial lawyer Brian Panish. When I was a young lawyer, I worked with great mentors, bringing them in to help me fund litigation, move the wheel, learn, and try cases with them. This included Brian Panish and

Gary Dordick, who taught me many of my jury selection techniques. And I read books from Trial Guides. Brian likes to joke (I hope) that I owe him royalties for using his PowerPoint slides and empowerment talk. I encourage all of you to steal everything from me, too. Occam's razor, two paths, beware of red herrings, and the criminal conspiracy are all ideas that I've worked into my trials by using a process of trial and error. Steal them. I beg of you!

Part 2: Two Roads

I always like to show the jury how ridiculous the defense's position is first. I show them the paths they can take:

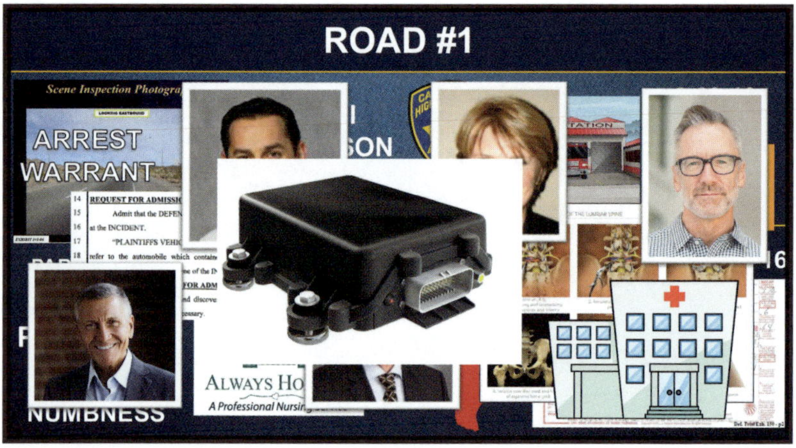

Figure 19-1. Road #1: My client is in a vast conspiracy with many doctors. (Photos have been edited for privacy.)

1. The defense conspiracy theory that my client went through the massive amount of trouble to coordinate with all these doctors to gamble it all away before a jury.

   Or

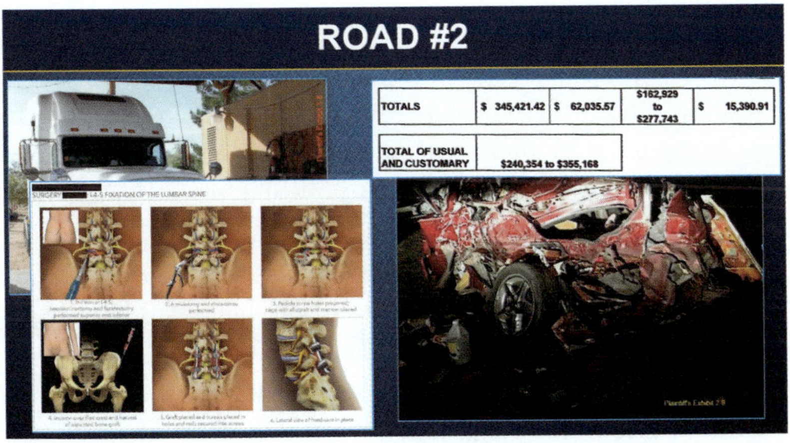

Figure 19-2. Road #2: My client was injured in a crash.

2. That it was simply because he was in a crash that he had no say in and was suffering from pain because of it.

Here's another way to say it: you can believe all of those ridiculous things, or you can believe this—the person was in a crash and they got hurt.

Part 3: The Law

Then I give them the law, which I marry with the facts and evidence to show them a path to winning. Most cases are won on causation because the defense experts cannot say that our clients would have had the same harm without the crash happening.

I'll ask defense experts:

> Q: Can you say, with a reasonable degree of medical probability, that had this car crash never happened, my client wouldn't need spine surgery?
>
> A: Oh I can't say. It's speculation.

Then I point out the jury instruction on that testimony. We've won on that alone. Use actual transcript cites in your closing. But do not bog down your PowerPoint slides with words. Use words to show the jury you are not misleading them by showing the actual evidence. Show them the law. Display the jury instructions and highlight the important parts. Walk them through the verdict form. But the rest should be imagery, photographs, and as few words as possible. You want the jury listening to you, and not reading twelve-point font on the big screen.

There are great jury instructions about pre-existing conditions or the unusually susceptible plaintiff. I show those and show that even if what the defense is saying about degeneration is true, they still lose. Because everybody has a spine, and everybody has degeneration. The defense can't come in and use that as a defense. So I show them the law.

And keep in mind: when somebody has brittle bone disease and they get hit with a car, the driver is legally responsible because they are susceptible to the injury. If something is made worse, that driver is still on the hook. It is all tied back to jury selection. The jury is already empowered to solve this crime for you!

In *Johnson* I asked the defense's doctor:

Q: Do you agree that these changes you saw just because he's getting older could be made worse due to trauma, or made symptomatic or worse?

A: Yes.

I like to tell the jury this is the "yeah, probably" standard.

Mr. Simon: Was the need for surgery caused by the car crash? What's the first thought that comes into your mind? You don't have to be convinced. Don't overthink it. The defense

> is here to try and make you over think. In civil, our burden is more likely to be true. 50.01 percent. No more.

Recently I saw a closing argument on social media, and there it was! My slide on substantial factor with the "yeah probably" standard! I cried I was so happy. The simplified standard, using my method and words.

Arm your jurors with every aspect of the law and show them the corresponding fact that was proven. Here's the law, here's the fact that proved it. We win. And I dare the defense to get up here and do the same because *what attorneys say is not evidence*. I show them that jury instruction.

The Ask

Towards the end of closing, I make the ask, which is where I talk about compensation. This is where I do the "man with a suitcase" story (which I spell out in the next section).

At the end of closing, I always list ten questions in a slide for the defense to answer. These are questions that the jury needs an answer on. Then, for rebuttal, I answer those questions for the defense since they never, ever answer them because they know they cannot answer them.

Here are some of my questions:

> Q: Would this person have needed surgery if the crash didn't happen?
> Q: How are my numbers wrong?
> Q: How do you get around the aggravation, pre-existing condition instruction?
> Q: Where is your spine expert?
> Q: Are all my client's treating doctors wrong?

The questions will vary a lot depending on your case. These are easy questions that we know the defense should be able to answer but that they will avoid. These were the specific questions for Paulina Atlantic's case that we had on a slide and asked the defense to answer during closing:

Q: What date was the attorney hired?

The defense tried to make a big deal that the plaintiff hired an attorney in the first week after the crash. We exposed that she had to because they were blaming her. This question was to again bring up the deceitful acts of the defense attorney for trying to pull one over on the jury.

Q: Why does the defense have her car?

The defense took her vehicle and kept it in their yard for years. This was very strange and they had no explanation.

Q: Why is there no data on the truck's black box?

During the trial, we proved that the box was wiped or swapped out before anyone was able to download the information in it. This is again putting a question to the defense that is so bad for them, they cannot answer.

Q: Is Paulina Atlantic lying?

This tactic is straight from *Polarizing the Case* by Rick Friedman.[1] Dare them to finally come out and say what they are implying.

Q: EDD Form?

EDD (Employment Development Department) is an abbreviation for state disability in California. Our client filled out a form and it had a clear clerical error on the date on the form listed. The defense tried to be sneaky about it, but we used it front and center. We were pretty much daring the defense to fess up to the jury on their tactics.

Q: Does Ms. Atlantic have sciatica?

Even the defense experts admitted that my client had nerve issues in her lower back. The defense attorney kept trying to make it seem like the nerve issues were in her head and she was making it up. The point here is to make the defense attorney either commit to her being a liar or to say he disagrees with even his own expert.

Q: We win based on the pre-existing condition jury instruction, right?

We win based on that instruction, so I keep daring the defense to concede that we do. And to explain to the jury how we do not win using that same instruction.

1. Rick Friedman, *Polarizing the Case: Exposing and Defeating the Malingering Myth* (Trial Guides, 2007).

Q: Is [Mr. Truck Driver] still driving?

We asked the defense if the defendant who caused this crash, to which they were denying liability, is still driving trucks. He was still driving trucks. This is not a good fact for them, and we are again pointing it out to the jury.

Q: Are you suggesting that Ms. Atlantic should have charity care?

This question was to show the jury the extreme opinions of the defense billing expert. He suggested that her bills were too high and she should have gone to a clinic instead a pricey specialist for her back surgery. This makes the defense attorney be a villain with his expert if he wants to double down.

Q: Are you denying that [Mr. Truck Driver] fled the scene?

In this case, the defendant truck driver fled the scene. This is a very bad fact for the defense. They denied liability, so this was all relevant. Again, we are daring the defense to either be reasonable and admit that he fled the scene, or to make another ridiculous excuse.

Q: You are not disputing Ms. Atlantic's future care needs, right?

The defense could not commit to whether they were disputing her future care needs. Their medical expert agreed that adjacent segment disorder exists, but then deferred to treating doctors on future needs because he did not have all the records. So this was challenging the defense to agree with the state of the evidence or again be ridiculous.

Q: How are my numbers wrong?

Here I am talking about my ask for millions for general damages. I straight up challenged the defense to tell the jury this is not reasonable and why. Often, they will just say the numbers are way too high, but they never suggest a number to the jury. I get ahead of it and dare them to be upfront with the jury.

Storytelling Devices

Following are several storytelling devices that I use in many of my closings.

Occam's Razor

The Occam's razor technique is the two paths discussed earlier. Either it's a vast, complicated, multi-year conspiracy theory, or my client was injured in a crash.

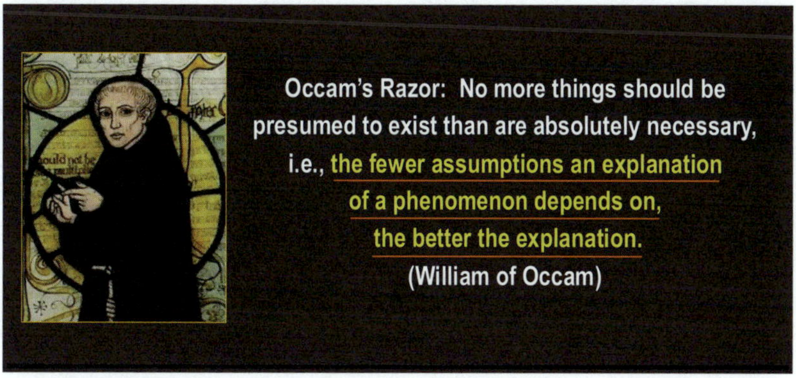

Figure 19-3. Occam's razor slide showing how the simplest answer is probably correct.

Remember Occam's razor: The simplest explanation is always true.

The "Man with a Suitcase" Closing

I first heard this story from trial lawyer, and friend, Nick Rowley. In the "man with a suitcase" closing, I put up a photo of a bad guy (honestly, any bad guy from pop culture that you like) and take the jury back to five seconds before the plaintiff's crash.

I love pop culture from every generation, as does the jury. And by knowing your audience, you can pick any character from their beloved pop culture.

Mr. Simon: Time has frozen. This man with a suitcase comes up to my client and offers him $15 million [*show slide of pop culture villain*]. The client asks, "What did I do to deserve this?"

As the villain, I say: "It's not what you've done, it's what you're going to do, because five seconds from now, time's going to come back into play, and you're going to get hit by a car. You're going to have immediate pain in your neck and back. You're not going to be able to pick up your son that day from school. In fact, it's going to be really hard for you to pick up your son from school for the rest of your life because you're going to have a disc shooting from your neck. And your lower back? Same thing's going to happen here too. You're going to think it's nothing at first but it's going to get worse and worse."

And then I graphically describe everything that he's gone through, every surgery.

"And the people that did it to you are going to call you a liar, a cheat, and a fraud."

What if my client said, "I don't want that money. I want my life back." But he never had a choice because those people made a choice for him.

Rebuttal

In rebuttal, I have several options that I sometimes use.

The *Good Will Hunting* Rebuttal

One of my options is something I made up and I call the *Good Will Hunting Rebuttal.* I look every juror in the eye and go full *Good Will Hunting*, based on the scene from the movie where Matt Damon breaks down in front of Robin Williams. Matt Damon's character, Will Hunting, has had a messed-up life full of poverty, child abuse, neglect, and violence. In this final scene, he breaks down crying when his therapist, played by Robin Williams, assures him that none of the terrible things that have happened in his past are his fault. Williams repeats the line, over and over, "It's not your fault."[2] I start by looking at just one juror. I do this to show each juror I can actually look them in the eye and make a personal connection. You can feel the energy in the courtroom when you do this. You are also empowering the jury to finally tell your client what you are about to repeat through their verdict.

2. *Good Will Hunting*, directed by Gus Van Sant, written by Ben Affleck and Matt Damon (Miramax Films, 1997).

Mr. Simon: All he wants to hear is, "It's not your fault!"

Then I look at another juror.

He did nothing to deserve this. You're a good dad.

Then look at another juror.

You did nothing wrong. None of this is your fault.

Then another juror.

We believe you. We believe your pain is real.

And I keep looking at each juror in the eyes. People break down. I've cried before, too.

The Good Book Closing

I also mentioned the way I end on rebuttal with the Good Book. I got this idea from Ned Good, a former Inner Circle member who recently passed away. I put up a picture of the Bible, and tell the jury that life is supposed to be in three chapters. In the first chapter, you're learning how to be an adult. In the middle chapter, you become an adult and you're giving back to your community. The last chapter is your retirement, when you go off into the sunset during your golden years with a loved one.

> **Mr. Simon:** Life is supposed to be an autobiography, but here the defendant decided they wanted to coauthor the book and change chapter two and chapter three.
>
> But the saving grace of all this is we have twelve citizens here who actually get to rewrite the end of that book. They get to make it right and fully compensate them.

This also empowers the jury to want to help.

Those twelve people deciding your case are your audience, and you better know your audience. I do a lot of research into those people, through social media or whatever means I can to see what they are like. If they have people who were taken away from them, you better be talking about it.

Example: The *Atlantic* Case

Take, for example, the *Atlantic* case, consisting of a semi-trailer truck hitting my client.[3] Of course, the defense wanted a discount. It's one of my favorite closing arguments that I've done. Let me take you through the greatest hits.

First, I let the jury know the power they have:

> **Mr. Simon:** The trucking company in this case does not get to decide who is reasonable, how much they have to pay, if there was a crime that day. They don't get to decide that. Neither does His Honor. Neither do the parties. You do.

3. See "About the Cases in this Book" at the beginning of this book, *Paulina Atlantic v. B&D Transport.*

Then I put up the following slide:

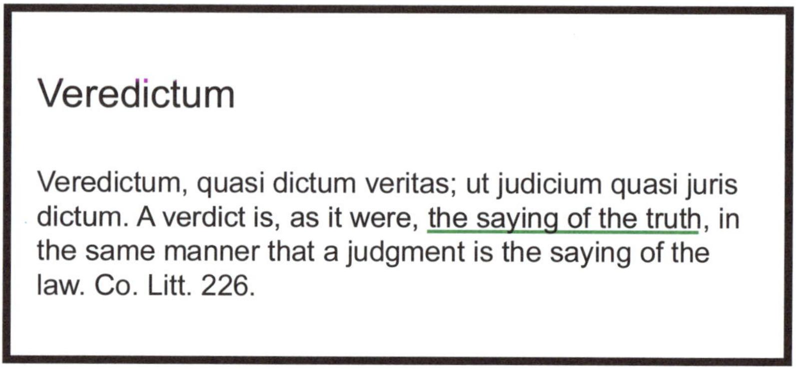

Figure 19-4. This slide shows the power of speaking the truth.

When I put this slide up, I told the jury they get to speak the truth. No more games. No more lies. Then, I relayed back to the jury how ridiculous of a conspiracy theory the defense just fed them, that my client was looking for a payday and orchestrated the whole operation with the police and medical doctors.

Figure 19-5. The two roads.

Mr. Simon: This is the defense road. See, to go down the defense road you have to believe that Ms. Atlantic is a fraud. You see, she has been planning this conspiracy, and she has been planning this crime of hers since she was an eighteen-year-old, when she left home, became a nurse, went out on her own, her and her son against the world, to just fool you that she was living a good life, right; that she was helping people; that she was really waiting to commit a fraud when she was sixty years old.

And this is what she did. She drove down the road on I-40 East, and she saw a trucker sleeping on the side of the road fifteen miles back. And that's when she said, that's my target. Lori is asleep. Let me pull over to the shoulder. I'm going to carefully try to not wake her up, because that's the guy I want to rear-end me at sixty-five miles an hour so I can complete this conspiracy fraud. I don't know how she did it either, but she crossed the rumble strips and drove on according to the defense for twenty-some seconds. Didn't wake up her friend at all. She was driving on for who knows how long.

She fooled the officers at the scene, somehow got them to fabricate the evidence that her tire marks were going straight, something their expert cannot really reconcile with. But she fooled the cops, too. Then she fooled the doctors in the state of Texas as well. She got them to say that, you know, all of this matches up with her medical treatment being from the crash, and they're just recommending surgery for the heck of it. They're misreading the MRIs. She got them all in the conspiracy. That's how good she is. She passed all her DMV eye exams. Maybe she was slipped answers for those, too

She tricked Dr. Samuel, their doctor who said she was telling the truth. She tricked her treating surgeon. She even tricked their vocational expert, who I played clips from. She tricked our life care planner. And she also got all of the hospitals and treatment centers in Texas and California in on the conspiracy to say that she owes these bills in full.

And I don't know how she did this either, but she also somehow wiped the black box of the truck that hit her from behind. She must have crawled into the yard and done that, too. See, ladies and gentlemen, you either believe all of that under the defense road, or that this truck hit this woman at sixty-five miles an hour, causing her to need disc surgery, and she owes this much in medical care.

Then I tell the jurors that they've been conditioned to think way too hard about this.

William of Occam, a famous scholar, once said the simplest explanation is almost always true. I told you from the very beginning, this is a very simple case. Confusion is their best friend. All they're doing up here is throwing shade at you to try and say, well, maybe it's not relatable. Maybe it's something else. This is very simple. This is the verdict form that you're going to get. There are several questions. I'll walk you through them.

The way that we do the scales is if you're weighing evidence, there's just a feather on one side that tips the scales. That's enough to prove our burden. I think of this as the *yeah, probably* standard. If you're thinking in your head, was that surgery caused by this? Was the pars fracture actually caused by this? If you say *yeah, probably* for one second in your mind, that's enough.

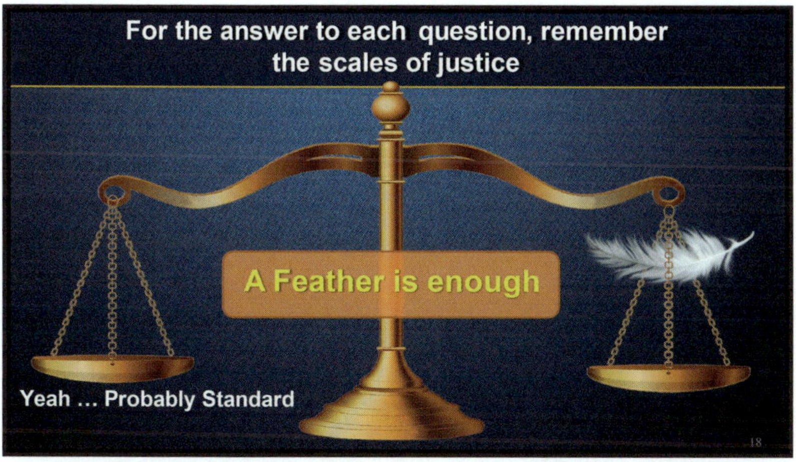

Figure 19-6. I use this graphic to show them that just a feather is enough to sway the scales of justice.

I also give them the law.

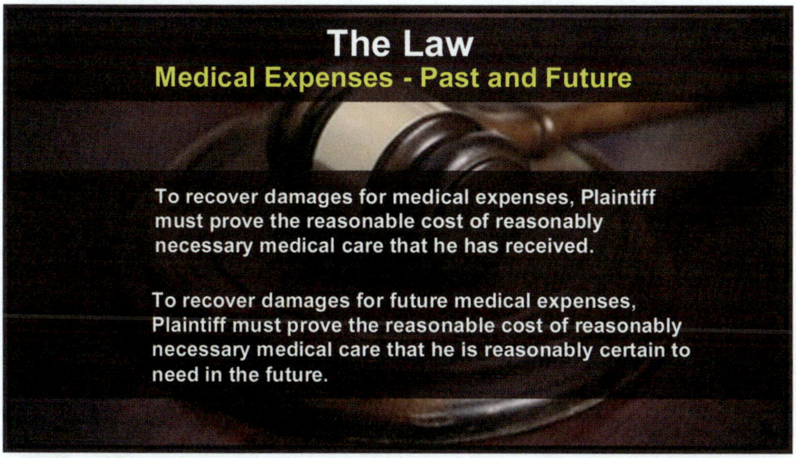

Figure 19-7. This slide spells out the law in an easy-to-read way.

So let's talk about liability. You saw the crashes. You saw the crash. These are all the photographs of the car that she was in. And let's make one thing very clear here, this is a catastrophic crash. These two women are very lucky to be alive. You remember her friend's powerful testimony, the other plaintiff in this case, and she said that she said a prayer over their car before she left. Her prayer was to St. Christopher. We don't know what the prayer was that she said, but it did protect these two women. They walked out of there alive. Broken, but alive. They've been protected all the way up through to get to this courtroom, to get to the twelve of you who will make a decision. But after today it is up to the twelve of you to decide what is fair for Ms. Atlantic and her friend for the rest of their lives.

Because if you're a truck driver, you're coming down the road, any motorist, and you see a car disabled, moving slowly, or slow in the number two lane, you move over or you slow down. He did none of that. And he's a Class A driver. He's a driver of a tractor trailer, 75,000 pounds. He did none of that.

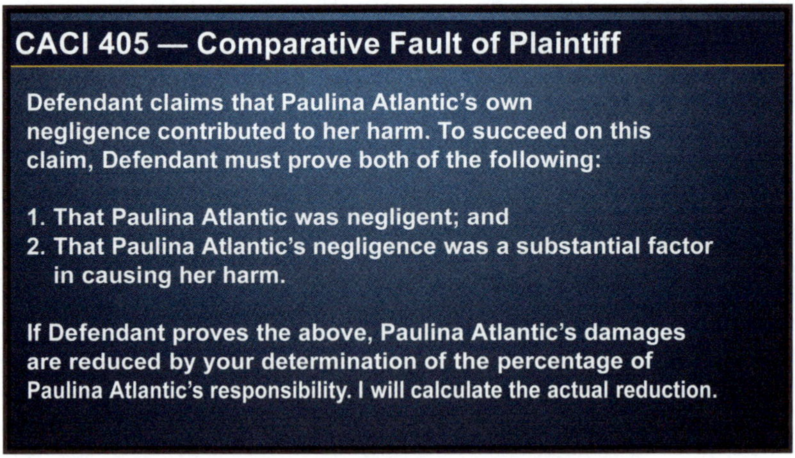

Figure 19-8. The law for comparative fault in California.

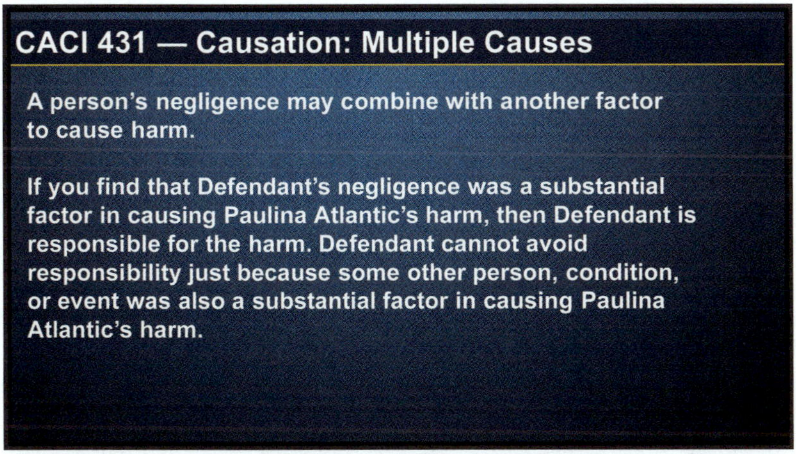

Figure 19-9. The law for multiple causes in California.

What did we also learn? Even though he's on probation, he's still out there driving his truck. You guys get to decide if that's okay or not. Because they're not going to accept responsibility. Never have.

There's a special verdict form. Truck driver is negligent. He caused the injuries. Ms. Atlantic is not negligent. And if nine of you agree on these, you move on. She's not—she didn't cause her own harm. He's a 100 percent at fault. Why else would you run unless you did something wrong, right?

This is a jury instruction that I want to impress upon you; it's called *aggravation of pre-existing condition*. Very important instruction in this case, because the judicial council who makes these jury instructions, in their infinite wisdom, protects every single person with a degenerative condition, every single person with a spine over twenty years old. What this instruction says is if you have a prior condition that is made worse or symptomatic, the person who caused it to be worse or symptomatic is on the hook. And I want the defense, when they get up here to reason with you, to explain this instruction and how they're not still on the hook.

It allows them to not come up here in every case and say, well, she had degeneration in her spine, therefore, we get a free pass. No, use this jury instruction. They have to show you that she would have needed that surgery without the car crash ever happening. They cannot.

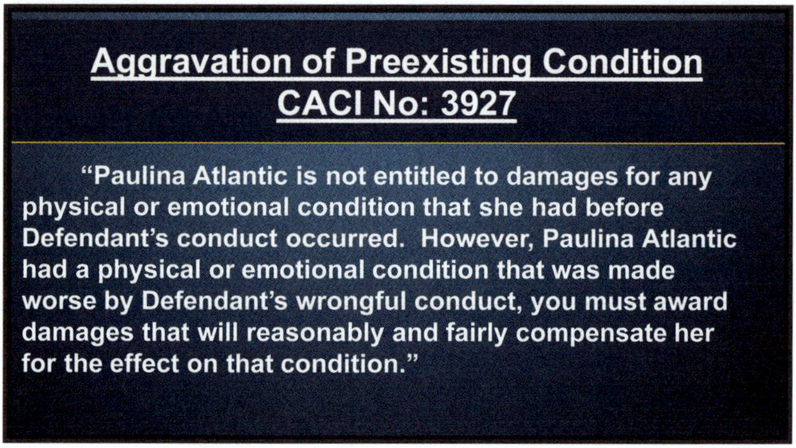

Figure 19-10. California law regarding pre-existing conditions.

Then this is one of my favorite slides:

Figure 19-11. This spells out to the jury the definition of a red herring, showing what the defense is trying to do.

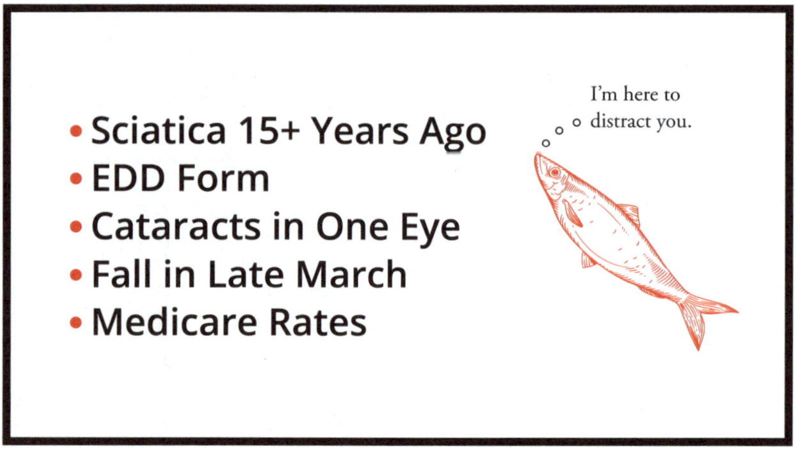

Figure 19-12. These were the red herring issues that the defense was trying to distract the jury with.

And finally, the "man with a suitcase" scene in which an imaginary man approaches my client moments before her accident:

> Imagine this man at a gas station approaches my client and says, "I have something for you." And he pulls out a duffel bag. In that duffel bag is $8 million in cash.
>
> He says, "Ms. Atlantic, this is for you."
>
> She says, "What did I do to deserve this?"
>
> And he says, "Well, it's not what you did, Ms. Atlantic. It's what you're going to do. Because in a few hours from now—you're not going to know—there's a man you're not going to be able to avoid, but you're going to get hit by a tractor trailer. They're going to hit you at a high rate of speed. They're going to push you off in the desert. And for the first time in your life, you're going to be screaming for help. You've helped people your whole life; you're going to be screaming for help.
>
> "But they're not going to help you. They're going to flee. The first time you ask for help, they're going to say no. And from that day forward, you're going to have serious injury to

your back. Instead of a surprise for the grandkids that you were planning, you're going to be a burden to your family. When your parents are dying, and you're supposed to take care of them, that's not going to happen. No more.

"You're not going to be a nurse again. Forget those passions and goals. You've got to figure out a new you at sixty. And, Ms. Atlantic, the people that did this to you, they're going to deny it all. They're going to deny they hit you. They're going to try to flee. They're going to force you to trial."

What do you think Ms. Atlantic would say to that person at a gas station before this accident happened? No dice. No way. The problem is she never had a choice. This happened.

They made the choice for her. So we ask you to write on the verdict form: $2 million for what she's gone through for two and a half years, $6 million in the future. Because anything less than this, their confusion game has worked, and they will be popping open champagne bottles at the end of the verdict. Ladies and gentlemen, we leave this in your hands to decide.

In terms of the ask, I am not one to break it down into categories. I just use whole numbers.

$2 million for past pain and suffering, $6 million for the future.

All you've got to do is ask. Lock eyes with them and say it! You should have all the credibility by now. What you say goes. If the jury agrees with you, they'll start at your number and vote.

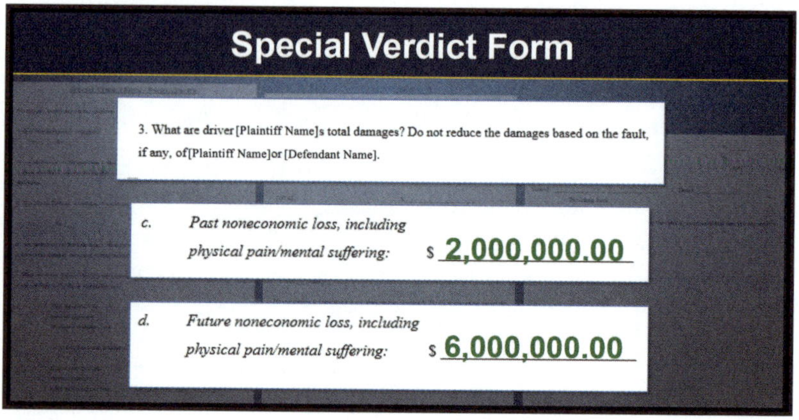

Figure 19-13. I put the whole special verdict form on a slide to show the jury what I want them to do.

Usually during rebuttal, the defense will say the ask is way too high. Then you have to tell them why that isn't true. Point out the high amounts they paid their experts. Mention how ridiculously high things like sports or movie contracts are. The Los Angeles Lakers pay LeBron James $500,000 per game, or $163 per second. Nice! And that's only for four seasons. Meanwhile, your client had no choice but to enter into this situation, which is a crap deal for life. Show the absurdity in all of it. A life-long contract of chronic pain for a measly $8 million? She would have never signed that contract. And that is all we are asking for in this situation.

Then, it's deliberations, the part attorneys hate most! It's the part you have no control over. Enjoy!

Takeaways

The closing is your roadmap to victory. You are arming the jurors who are already on your side with more evidence and law to persuade other jurors who are on the fence, or who were just not paying attention the entire trial. Confidence is critical for closing. Slow down. Look the jurors in the eyes. Many times, I write myself a note as a reminder that solely says, "Slow down."

Conclusion

Every time I do a speaking engagement or teach a class, I usually lead with, "Eff the war stories, I am going to give you some practical advice. Hopefully you get at least one nugget to make your practice better after this is over." Well since this is a book, I hope you are taking a zillion nuggets. I am a huge believer in the whole "rising tides lifts all ships" thing. By all of us being better lawyers, getting better results for our clients with settlements and verdicts, it makes it better for all our clients. The settlements will become higher and more fair. Fewer people will be taken advantage of.

So, as one of my partners and best friends Evan Garcia says, "Crush forth!"

Appendix A

Outline for Plaintiff's Direct Examination

Here is the outline of my plaintiff's direct examination for a non-English-speaking nanny in her sixties who was in a minor impact crash and got a cervical fusion. This outline is a combination of several outlines we use in almost every single case. This was polished and performed in trial by Gabriel Araj with the Justice Team.

Remember, the defense will attempt to paint your client as an opportunist, looking to cash in. They will attempt to confuse your client with the medical treatment timeline. They will attempt to impeach your client, even on collateral issues, over and over again. On direct, you get to control the narrative. Create a situation where your client is the light, has commonalities with the jurors making the ultimate decision, and remember: *Don't Eat the Bruises.*[1]

Throughout this outline, I have highlighted the plaintiff's responses in gray, so they stand out from the lists of questions. I think that her responses are interesting, and sometimes influence the next questions in these sets of questions.

1. Shout out to Keith Mitnik, *Don't Eat the Bruises: How to Foil Their Plans to Spoil Your Case* (Trial Guides, 2015). This book is a great roadmap to discussing these issues not only in jury selection but in the plaintiff's direct examination. Soften all the potential blows that the defense may have.

Themes

- She is a warrior and a survivor. She has an amazing work ethic and is not a complainer, but this crash created significant challenges in her life.
- She loves her job and has always relied on her body and health (she has worked labor-intensive jobs) to support herself and her family, but her injuries have forced her to consider earlier retirement.
- She has lost hope (her middle name means hope). Her goal was to live to one hundred, but not now if it means living with this pain.
- She was active in her family and served as an informal therapist who everyone would go to with their problems.
- She loves being a mom and grandma.

Introduction & Main Points

Jurors pay the most attention during the first few minutes any witness takes the box. I think it is important to drive home your critical points at that time, as well as any themes. Right away. In most cases, the defense goes all-in on pre-existing degeneration. So we pivot the narrative to aggravation of a pre-existing condition. In this case, it was Mrs. Samaniega's uncomplicated prior medical history. In other cases, the defense may harp on the surgery being some kind of conspiracy crime that should never have been done. In those cases, perhaps lead with your client being very thankful for the attorney-referred neurosurgeon, because after the surgery, they are so much better, and so thankful. In another case, they may paint your client as an opportunist. There, you may start with the fact that there are no other claims for injury ever, no crimes, and the good this person has done for the community.

Q: Good morning.

Q: How are you feeling today?

Q: Before [date], the date of the collision we are here to discuss today, had you ever experienced significant neck pain?

Q: Before [date], did you ever see a doctor, physical therapist, get imaging studies done, or have any treatment to your neck?

Q: Let's move to your lower back. Before [date] did you have any treatment to your lower back?

A: Yes. One time about a month before the crash I went to a chiropractor for some mild lower back pain.

Q: Is that the only time you had treatment to your lower back before the crash?

Q: Why did you see the chiropractor that one time for your lower back?

A: I wanted an adjustment for the mild pain.

Q: After that one adjustment, how did your back feel?

A: I felt good. I didn't need any more treatment.

Q: Did you complain of any neck pain at that one chiropractic appointment before the crash?

Q: After the crash, how has your neck felt?

Background

After knocking out the big issues and theme right away, we pivot back to our client's background. We tried to help the jury get to know her. We were building a bond with the jury. We were showing them that our client is just like them. Maybe she grew up in a similar fashion to them, or she enjoys the same type of family or weekend fun activities. As we built up the important things that were taken from our client, we highlighted the precious things about their life they will never get back. We are attempting to create a bond with jurors in general damages.

Q: Ms. Samaniega, what city do you live in?
Q: How long have you lived in Long Beach?
Q: What do you do for work?
Q: How long have you worked as a nanny for the Littleton family?
Q: Are you a live-in nanny?
Q: How often do you stay the night at the Littletons?
Q: Do you have a room at the Littletons where you stay?
Q: What types of duties do you have around the Littleton home?
Q: How many children do the Littletons have?

[Show exhibit that is a photo of the Littleton family and their children.][2]

Q: Are these the Littleton children?
Q: What are their names?
Q: Do any of the Littleton children have developmental disabilities?
Q: Does he require extra attention?
Q: Patience?
Q: What types of things do you do with the Littleton children?
Q: Have you seen them grow up?
Q: Do you feel like a part of their family?
Q: Before the crash, had you been on trips with the Littletons?
Q: Ms. Samaniega, how old are you?
Q: What is your date of birth?
Q: So your birthday was the day before the crash?
Q: What day of the week did the crash occur?
Q: Were you staying at the Littletons that week?
Q: Where were you driving when the crash happened?
Q: Did you have any plans for when you returned home?
Q: How many children do you have?
Q: Is your husband around?
Q: So just you and your sons for the last twenty years?

2. Because the names and locations are changed to protect identities, the photos of people in this appendix are described but not included.

Q: Do you have any grandchildren?

[Show exhibits with pictures of Ms. Samaniega's family members so she can talk about them and identify them to the jury.]

Q: What are the names of the people in these pictures?
Q: How important is family to you?
Q: Did any of your sons live with you at the time of the crash?

Crash Facts

I think it is important to jump around to different topics to keep the jury engaged. Let them know you are going onto another topic. They will perk up and start paying attention again. When discussing the scene and details of the crash, do so with images. Pull up exhibits of the scene, the car, and so on. You want your jury to feel like they are right there.

Q: You were driving home from the Littletons when the incident occurred?
Q: What kind of vehicle were you driving?
Q: Whose vehicle was it?
Q: The Littletons let you drive this vehicle to and from their house?
Q: Would you also use it if you needed to do a task for them, such as get groceries?
Q: Where did the crash happen?
Q: Before you made it to the 101 freeway?
Q: Describe the crash for the jury.

[Show exhibits 16-1 thru 16-5. These are photos of the crash, crash scene, and Ms. Samaniega's vehicle.]

Q: Do these photos show what your vehicle looked like after the crash?

Q: Did you exit your vehicle after impact?

Q: Why not?

Q: Did you call anyone for help?

Q: When did Rick arrive?

Q: How long were you stuck in the car?

Q: How were you feeling in that moment?

Q: Did the police arrive?

Q: Did an officer ask you if you were hurt?

Q: What did you say?

Q: Did the officer ask if you needed to go to the hospital?

Q: Why did you decline?

Q: Did you speak to the driver who hit you at the scene?

Q: Have you ever spoken to him?

Q: Do you have any anger or resentment towards him?

Q: Were you able to drive your vehicle from the scene?

Q: How did you leave the scene?

Q: Where did you go?

Q: What happened when you arrived at the Littletons?

Q: Who took you to the ER?

Q: How long were you in the ER?

Q: Did you complain of neck pain?

Q: Was your neck pain radiating at that point? Describe.

Q: Did you have any bruising on your body?

Q: Did you hit your head in the crash?

Q: Were you administered any medication in the ER?

Q: Did they take any images of your neck at the ER?

Q: Who picked you up from ER?

Q: What did you do over the next few days?

Q: Was your pain getting any worse?

Q: What parts of your body? Describe.

Q: Did you go to work on Monday?

Q: Why did you go back to work with your pain?

A: I needed to support myself and the family needed me.

Q: Did you have to wear a sling or something similar?

Q: Provided by the ER?

Q: How did the Littletons respond when you showed up to work that Monday?

Q: Did you take time off from that point?

Q: How long?

Q: Did the Littletons need to hire someone else to replace you during that time?

Q: When you returned, were you still in pain?

Q: How did your pain affect your ability to work?

Q: Limitations? Light?

Treatment

There is usually so much treatment that it is impossible for even the smartest plaintiffs to memorize it all. I prefer broad strokes. I always use a medical timeline with them, to help refresh their memory and also as a guide for the jury. You usually know the medical visits or issues the defense wants to poke into, such as attorney-referred care or pain being a zero or one out of ten at certain points in treatment. So I try and only concentrate on those with my client.

It is important to pull all these issues into perspective in this section, and explain their treatment and why they had certain procedures. You do not have to overdo it. Remember, use broad strokes. By the time your client takes the stand, the jury will have already heard about the timeline, the treatment, and so on, from the treating doctors or the retained experts. Do not bore the jury. Less is more.

Q: Did you eventually seek further medical treatment for your pain?

Q: Chiropractor?

Q: Name?

Q: How often would you see Dr. [Chiropractor]?

Q: What types of treatment would she administer?

Q: Did it provide lasting relief?
Q: Did Dr. [Chiropractor] refer you to obtain an MRI of your neck?
Q: What is your understanding of what the MRIs showed?
Q: Did you eventually stop chiropractic care?
Q: Where did you go next for treatment?
Q: Who examined you at your first visit at [spine clinic]?
Q: What did Dr. [Neurologist] recommend?
Q: Where was the injection administered?
Q: Did the injection help?
Q: What did Dr. [Neurologist] recommend after the injection did not help?

Surgery

Q: Then you saw Dr. [Surgeon]?
Q: What did you understand to be Dr. [Surgeon]'s specialty?
Q: At your first appointment with Dr. [Surgeon], what did he say was causing your pain?
Q: Did he eventually recommend surgery?
Q: Did Dr. [Surgeon] tell you what kind of surgery he was recommending?
Q: Were you scared to undergo surgery?
Q: Explain.
Q: Did you ask Dr. [Surgeon] any questions about the surgery?
Q: How did Dr. [Surgeon] make you feel about the surgery?
Q: Did he describe the risks?
Q: What were they?
Q: And despite those risks, you decided to undergo surgery?
A: Yes. I desperately wanted something to help relieve my pain. Surgery was my last resort.
Q: Did you tell your family you needed surgery?
Q: How did they respond?
Q: Who took you to your surgery?
Q: Your sister came to help you?

Q: Do you recall the date of your surgery?

[Show exhibits 3-83 through 3-85 to refresh. These exhibits are medical timelines that help refresh their recollection as to dates]

Q: Can you describe your neck pain immediately before surgery?
Q: Same since the crash?
Q: Can you please explain to the jury how you were feeling the morning of surgery?
Q: You eventually arrived at the surgery center?
Q: What happened next?
Q: Anesthesia?

Post-Surgery

Q: How did you feel when you woke up after surgery?
Q: Were you able to leave the surgery center that same day?
Q: Who took you home?
Q: Were you wearing a neck brace?
Q: How long did you have to wear the neck brace?

[Show exhibit, a photo of Ms. Samaniega's sister who came to help after surgery.]

Q: Can you describe this photo for the jury?
Q: Is that your sister?
Q: How long did she stay to help you?
Q: What did she do specifically to assist you?
Q: Did your grandchildren help too?
Q: How did it make you feel needing that assistance?
Q: Were you prescribed any medication to help with your pain after surgery?
Q: Do you recall what it was called?
Q: How often would you take it?
Q: When did you stop?

Q: Did you go back to see Dr. [Surgeon] after surgery?
Q: About how many times?
Q: Did he order X-rays of your neck?
Q: What is your understanding of why he wanted to see X-rays of your neck after surgery?
Q: Did he say the surgery was successful?
Q: How was your neck feeling in the couple weeks following surgery?
Q: Were you happy you underwent surgery?

Physical Therapy

Q: Did Dr. [Surgeon] recommend anything to help with recovery?
Q: Physical therapy?
Q: What types of exercises did you do at physical therapy?
Q: Were you wearing your neck brace at that time?
Q: All the time?
Q: Did the physical therapy help you recover from surgery?
Q: When did you finish PT?
[Use the medical timeline exhibit to refresh Ms. Samaniega's memory.]
A: I finished physical therapy on [date].
Q: After physical therapy, did your neck pain return?
A: Yes. I would get flare ups of pain in my neck. Spasms in my neck and shoulders.

Current State of Health

You are now getting into future pain and suffering and future general damages. Again, let the jury know you are moving onto a new subject. Remember the jury will have been watching your client all during trial. Watching her take the stand. Seeing if she winces, or if it seems like a show. Do not overplay your hand. Much of these cases are about the future, not just right now in the present moment, but the future breakdown of the adjacent levels of the spine, future treatments, future disabilities. You want the jury to root for your client. Your client is doing everything they can to get better. They will not stop living life. But they need help and are struggling.

Q: When did you last see Dr. [Surgeon]?

[Use the medical timeline exhibit to refresh memory.]

A: I last saw Dr. [Surgeon] on [date].

Q: At that time, did you tell him what your symptoms were?

Q: Neck and back?

Q: What did you tell Dr. [Surgeon] at your appointment in June?

Q: Will you continue to follow-up with him?

Q: Did Dr. [Surgeon] tell you what will likely happen in the future in terms of your pain levels in your neck and back?

A: He said I will never be completely healed. I have to live with my back pain. He said I will probably need another neck surgery because the levels around where he operated are going to get worse.

Q: Are you worried about your future?

A: Of course. My neck is getting worse. My back pain is there and I'm just living with it. I'm worried that my pain will keep getting worse and I will need another neck surgery.

Q: How does your neck feel now?

Q: How about your back?

Q: Have you experienced back pain since the crash?

Q: Have we discussed all your treatment thus far?

Q: Did the pandemic affect your ability to get treatment?

Q: How?

[Show exhibit 29, that details all of her medical treatment since the crash.]

Q: Now that we've gone over your treatment, is Exhibit 29 an accurate compilation of all the doctor's visits you've had since the crash?

General Damages—Work

A person's ability to earn gives them self-worth. Pride. The inability to work, or the hinderance of doing it well, greatly affects a person's mood, state of mind, and pride. This is where you drive that home. Not knowing if they can continue doing what they love, or what puts food on the table for their family, is powerful and most jurors understand it.

Q: Did you tell the Littletons that you had to undergo surgery?
Q: Did you take time off while you recovered?
Q: How long?
Q: Did the Littletons need to hire a replacement nanny during that time?
Q: How did it make you feel knowing you couldn't do your job?
Q: When you returned, were you limited by your pain?
Q: Please describe.
Q: Are you still limited?
Q: Before the crash, what were your plans in terms of how long you would nanny for the Littletons?
Q: Did you have any plans to do something else after working for the Littletons?
Q: How have those plans changed since your injuries?
A: I wanted to start my own housekeeping business, but with my injuries I can't do it. I won't be able to teach my workers how to do things right. I move too slow and I cannot supervise them.
Q: You mentioned your neck pain before surgery radiated into your arms and hands, is that correct?
Q: Did that affect your ability to hold things? Please describe.

Walking, Hiking & Active Travel

You are in general damages once again. As you can see, a lot of the plaintiff's direct examination is building those general damages in different aspect of their life, such as family, work, and fun. Make your client relatable. I like to use images of my client being proud, or having fun, or being with their family. Then in the closing argument, use those same photos but crop out your client. Show the jury all that was taken from them. It is important to get the photos all into evidence so you can use them again in closing argument.

Q: Before the crash, can you describe your level of physical activity?
Q: Did you go to a gym?
Q: How often?
Q: After the crash?
Q: Did you hike?

[Show exhibits that show Mrs. Samaniega hiking and being active with her family.]

Q: Describe these photos. Who are these people? When were they taken? Where were they taken?
Q: Have you hiked since the crash?
Q: If yes, what are your limitations?

[Show exhibits that show Ms. Samaniega traveling with her family and with the Littleton family, her employer.]

Q: Where were these taken? Who are these people?
Q: Did you ever go on trips with the Littletons before the crash?
Q: How has the crash impacted your ability to travel?
Q: Are you worried about not being able to travel in the future?
Q: Before the crash, would you go on walks?

Q: Where did you like to walk?

Q: How often?

A: Did you walk with [child from Littleton family] when you would nanny?

Q: Do you have dogs, Ms. Samaniega?

[Show exhibit that shows Ms. Samaniega with her dogs.]

Q: What is this?

Q: Is this what you use to walk your dogs now?

Q: Have you tried to go on walks after the crash?

Q: How have you felt when you tried?

Q: Have your injuries affected your ability to drive?

Q: Do you drive anymore?

Q: When you do drive, how do you feel?

Q: Do you prefer if somebody drives for you?

Q: Who usually drives you?

Q: Do you take Uber?

Family

Q: Ms. Samaniega, you mentioned before that family means everything to you?

Q: Does your family usually get together for special occasions?

Q: Does your family like to dance together?

Q: Do you enjoy dancing?

Q: Do you like going to parties?

[Show exhibits showing photographs of Ms. Samaniega dancing at a party or family gathering.]

Q: Is this from before the crash?

Q: Where is it?

Q: Who are these people in the background?

Q: Did you usually wear heels when you went to parties and danced?

Q: How have your injuries affected your ability to dance?

Q: Looking at exhibit 11-8, it looks like you're wearing some nice heels there?

Q: Do you wear heels anymore?

Q: Do you still go to as many parties?

Q: Why not?

Q: Do you feel fragile?

Q: Have your injuries affected your relationship with your sons?

Q: Please describe.

Q: How does that make you feel?

A: I feel like a bad mom. I am angry and short-tempered, especially after work. I feel terrible.

Q: Have your injuries affected your relationship with your grandchildren?

Q: Describe.

Q: How does that make you feel?

Q: Have your grandchildren made any comments to you about your limitations?

Q: How does that make you feel?

A: They say, "I miss you."

Personality

Q: Ms. Samaniega, have your injuries from the crash affected your personality?

Q: Please describe for the jury.

Q: How is your self-esteem?

Q: Do you feel depressed?

Q: Have your injuries affected your ability to sleep?

Q: Before or after surgery?

Q: Do you still struggle with sleeping through the night?

Goals & Dreams

Q: Has this crash and your injuries affected any goals you set for yourself?

A: I wanted to live to one hundred, but not with this pain.

Q: Why did you have this goal for yourself?

A: So many people in my family, especially the women, lived to old age—in their nineties. So I thought I would live to one hundred. To be honest, I really don't think I can do it with my pain now. I don't want to live thirty-plus more years with this pain. But I will for my family.

Appendix B

A Deeper Look into the Radiology Room

By Orlando Micheli, MD

Why do radiologists disagree on interpretations, or miss things outright? And how important is this variation? Based on my diagnostic and procedural involvement with back pain patients, as well as my experience with quality assurance and quality control, medical legal review, and the published literature on the topic, there are two broad categories of radiologic errors: cognitive and perceptual.

Cognitive errors (also called *interpretive errors*) occur when a finding is identified on an image but the person reading the image misunderstands the relative importance of the finding, resulting in an incorrect diagnosis. *Perceptual errors* are the most common and account for around 60 to 80 percent of radiologist errors. Perceptual errors typically occur during the initial phase of assessment of the imaging and are thought to exist when an abnormality is present but not observed or detected by the radiologist.

If you find yourself with a patient that has obvious and believable pain, with an MRI that does not identify an adequate source, the first thing to consider is a perceptual error during interpretation. This means in the study of the patient, a particular finding was present on the images, but for whatever reason was not identified in the report.

Diagnostic Errors in Radiology

I am going to let you in on a relatively well-kept secret—something that all radiologists know: we all miss things. Quality interpretation of the spine isn't exactly easy. This is especially true if we are talking about very subtle findings that a very busy and possibly stressed radiologist could easily overlook. It is part of life, and no one is perfect. Most of us keep a mental log of our own personal "misses" that still haunt us from as far back as our days of residency. For me, the miss was a subtle sternal fracture on a trauma patient. Though it was by far the least severe of the injuries that were present (for the record I did identify the other more severe injuries correctly), it still provokes me to look at the sternum and the adjacent regions *twice*. I don't want to miss another sternal injury!

The next question is, how important is this variation? As a radiology department director, quality is at the forefront of my mind. The diagnostic error rate in the field of medicine is a significant factor in patient harm and bad outcomes. Incorrect or missed diagnoses are thought to be as high as 15 percent. In another study, autopsy information (when available) was found to have identified potential major discrepancies in up to 20 percent of cases. Because medical imaging makes up such a vast component of most working diagnoses, it is very reasonable to conclude that many of these errors are at least in part due to mistakes in the realm of radiology.

- In 2001, according to Goddard et al., clinically significant radiology errors were identified in 2 to 20 percent of cases, depending upon the type of imaging.[1]

1. P. Goddard, et al., "Error in Radiology," *British Journal of Radiology* 74, no. 866 (2001): 949–51.

- In 2008, Siewert et al. found discordant interpretations in 31 to 37 percent, with resultant changes in radiological staging of cancer in 19 percent, and a change in patient treatment in up to 23 percent.[2]
- In 2007, Briggs et al. found that central nervous system evaluations utilizing CT and MRI had a 13 percent major and 21 percent minor discrepancy rate (undercalls, overcalls, and misinterpretations).[3] In the Briggs example, these differences were identified by specialty neuroradiologists performing a second reading of studies initially interpreted by non-specialty radiologists.

So, if these differences and errors are relatively common, and they are often significant, how can they be minimized medically, and correctly evaluated medicolegally?

A Look at Radiologist Training

In order to answer that question, it is important to step back and outline the training and certification of radiologists. To become a board-certified radiologist, the applicant must graduate from an accredited medical school, complete an internship, and then successfully complete a four-year residency. After that, the physician may pursue a fellowship in an area of interest in order to achieve specialty and/or subspecialty training. Fellowships range from research to the imaging of a particular body system to "procedural" radiology, which is formally known as *interventional radiology*.

Within the field of radiology there are multiple specialties. According to the American Board of Radiology, as of March of 2019, certifications are offered in:

2. Bettina Siewert, et al., "Missed Lesions at Abdominal Oncologic CT: Lessons Learned from Quality Assurance," *Radiographics* 28, no. 3 (May–Jun 2008): 623–38.

3. G.M. Briggs, et al., "The Role of Specialist Neuroradiology Second Opinion Reporting: Is There Added Value?" *Clinical Radiology* 63, no. 7 (2008):791–95. DOI: 10.1016/j.crad.2007.12.002.

- Diagnostic Radiology
- Interventional/Diagnostic Radiology
- Radiation Oncology

Arguably, those best suited to interpret spine imaging cases would be those who have been specifically fellowship-trained in spine evaluation and routinely perform interpretations of the spine in their clinical practice. In my opinion, board-certified musculoskeletal radiologists, neuroradiologists, and interventional radiologists (provided they perform diagnostic and therapeutic spine procedures) are the best suited to interpret spine cases. However, all radiologists *can* and *do* interpret spine cases. That being said, while some radiologists without specialty or subspecialty training interpret spine imaging quite well, others not so much.

Pressure on Radiologists

An analysis of Medicare mean adjusted reimbursement trends from 2007 to 2019, published in July of 2020 in the *Journal of the American College of Radiology*, reported a significant decrease in reimbursement for CT and MRI studies. Specifically, noting a -45.1 percent mean total percentage change in CT reimbursement and a -64.1 percent mean total percentage change in MRI reimbursement. These numbers are significant.[4]

Like most physicians when faced with decreasing Medicare reimbursement, radiologists have elected to compensate by increasing volume. What does this mean? Without prolonging the workday, radiologists are forced to interpret more studies per unit of time. This means the radiologist, while interpreting your client's study, is likely subject to added pressure to read the study quickly. This is a potential setup for possibly missing a subtle finding.

4. S. Kumar, et al., "Trends in Diagnostic Imaging Medicare Reimbursements: 2007 to 2019," *Journal of American College Radiology* 17, no. 12 (2020):1584-1590. DOI: 10.1016/j.jacr.2020.07.003.

In addition to increased pressure due to decreased reimbursement, the typical radiologist is under other pressures. As an example, if your client's study was performed in a busy, high-volume ER, the radiologist will be pressured to get through all of the studies on the list as efficiently as possible, but predominantly to identify life-threatening situations. Furthermore, in a busy radiology practice, the radiologist will be subject to interruptions from a variety of sources. These interruptions can range from urgent consultations from surgical physicians to questions from radiology technicians to technical issues with computers. Distractions in the reading room are common and occur frequently. Again, if the findings on your client's exam are subtle, it is possible that the interpreting radiologist just simply missed them.

I can speak from personal experience that I was involved as an expert in several cases in part due to correctly identifying the appropriate findings present on the study, and ultimately making a correct diagnosis. Choose your expert carefully!

The Four Points of Detective Work

My method of analyzing a medical legal case is what I call the "four points" of detective work. The specific categories that I closely assess are:

1. The clinical record
2. Imaging
3. Minimally invasive/procedural information
4. Surgical information

Ideally, I want there to be supporting evidence in each category. Also, if there is an obvious deficit in one category, I try to find an explanation.

1. The Clinical Record

The clinical record is where I typically begin the investigation. We learn in medical school that we can make up to 80 percent of diagnoses just using the patient's history and physical exam. Therefore, this is the most important section. Using the "*reasonable medical probability*" standard required in legal settings, *a history and examination can be sufficient to determine causation*. The remaining three categories provide additional support for probability and increase a doctor's *certainty* of both causation and the patient's diagnosis.

Completeness

The first issue that I usually review is the completeness of the records. I need to have all available records. Do I have pre-incident, incident, and post incident records? If not, I need to acquire them. I read the patient's deposition (if available), and then evaluate *all* available clinical records. I typically begin in chronological order, starting with the earliest available.

- If the patient was assessed two years prior to the incident for a sore throat, did they mention anything regarding the area of injury?
- Was a physical examination of the area performed prior to the incident?
- What was the physician's assessment?
- Is there evidence of chronic pain in the region?
- Is there any evidence of prior injury to the area?
- What does the demeanor of the individual seem to be?
- Is this person a hypochondriac, seeking medical attention for every little issue, or are they more reserved and avoid contact with a doctor at all costs?

The first significant question that needs to be addressed in my mind is the reliability and completeness of the record thereafter; is there anatomic and pathological credibility? In other words, does the clinical presentation make sense? At this point, if something seems fishy, I still will assess the remaining records but will do so with a much more critical eye.

Making Notes of the Clinical Record

As I assess the clinical records, I typically take notes in a Word document to keep track of pertinent negative and positive findings, as well as clinical questions that I need to address or understand. I have discovered that taking electronic notes is helpful because it allows for a search feature, and it promotes the easy access of retrievable data. During deposition, I have found that my electronic notes promote a more organized experience that is much more efficient. In my opinion, as an expert, it is my job to know the clinical record thoroughly. Knowing the record and keeping electronic notes promotes a more comprehensive understanding of the individual presentation and therefore further promotes a more in-depth understanding of the pathology and mechanism of injury.

With a large volume of clinical information in the current electronic age, I have found that sharing clinical records via encrypted electronic sources is very helpful. This not only protects the patient's clinical record (and is mandated by HIPAA, the Health Insurance Portability & Accountability Act), but also allows for instantaneous transmission of information. As an example, Dropbox or Google Drive provides file encryption protection and also allows users to enable a two-step verification process, making it more difficult for hackers to access patient protected information. I strongly prefer sharing clinical records (with the exception of the actual imaging) via electronic means.

2. Imaging

Getting back to the four points, the next phase is imaging.

Image Formats

When I acquire imaging from a facility, that imaging uses a standard format known as Digital Imaging and Communications in Medicine (DICOM). This is an international standard, and allows for transmission, storage, retrieval, processing, and display. The each image is typically each labeled with the appropriate patient information, the type of study, the location of the study, and the date and time. Its universal and convenient. If I have DICOM formatted information from Whiskey Tango Foxtrot Radiology Clinic in who knows where, I can load the images into my own system and evaluate, analyze, measure, and process those images as I see fit with software that I use every day in my own practice.

As opposed to the medical records, I insist on having the actual imaging submitted on CD. It's the only way to verify that I get the imaging and nothing else. I'm also trying to protect the patient's privacy (I prefer not to use online systems, even if they're HIPAA secure). Typically, Whiskey Tango Foxtrot Radiology Clinic will also have installed on the CD some sort of viewing software. In my experience, this software is low quality and usually contains a disclaimer that it is "Not to be Utilized for Diagnostic Interpretation." I adhere to this recommendation. The software is also usually slow, cumbersome, and lacks the appropriate assessment tools.

Reviewing the Imaging

I review imaging from before the date of the incident with the clinical records; particularly if abdominal or pelvic CT scans were taken in the past for unrelated reasons, and the lumbar spine is the area of interest. When I can obtain CT scanning of the abdomen or pelvis, the spine is invariably included on the exam and I can evaluate it. Prior exams are very helpful, particularly if I can identify the interval of time between the most recent imaging and any imaging secondary to the incident. These can be very useful clues to the case.

Once I have reviewed the clinical record up to the date of the incident, I proceed to assess the pertinent imaging. The first level of evaluation involves the quality and appropriateness of the acquired imaging.

- Was the appropriate type of study obtained?
- Was the study performed technically well, utilizing the correct field of view?
- Are artifacts present?

The most significant artifact is motion, and it can significantly degrade the quality and diagnostic power of the exam. If a patient has back or neck pain and they are asked to remain still within a very uncomfortable MRI scanner, there is a tendency of the study quality to be degraded because of the patient's motion. In lieu of this information, depending upon the technique that the MRI technician used, if the entire spine is to be evaluated with MRI (cervical, thoracic, and lumbar levels), this usually means over an hour of scan time. If a patient is very uncomfortable and in pain, and multiple scans are necessary, I will typically ask the MRI technician to communicate with the patient and offer a break in between exams to limit the possibility of motion artifacts. In an urgent setting, a very uncomfortable patient (or one who has claustrophobia) may require medication or sedation in order for an MRI to be performed.

Why Review the Clinical Record First?

One obvious question at this point may arise: why do I review the clinical record first and then look at the imaging? Why not just save time and go right to the imaging? There is a good reason. It has been well documented in the literature (with the exception of imaging the chest), that radiologists interpret imaging more accurately in a setting of relevant clinical information. In the majority of studies on radiological errors, researchers have found that an accurate and relevant clinical history can improve diagnostic accuracy. A study performed by Loy and Irwig evaluated sixteen studies of radiology report accuracy with and without clinical history and found that the presence of relevant clinical information improved the sensitivity of findings, without an associated alteration in specificity.[5] A similar study performed by Leslie et al. discovered that when referring physicians provided a clinical history, radiologists altered 19 percent of their CT reports, and more than half of these changes were considered to be significant to the impact on patient care.[6] In short, radiologists are more accurate when we have the relevant clinical information.

Back to the assessment of the imaging. The first and the most important question that I like to address is "Can the patient's clinical presentation be explained by the imaging findings?" This is important. Integrating imaging findings with the clinical state (signs and symptoms) that the patient demonstrates adds significant weight to the argument regarding causation. More importantly, the patient's imaging findings plus clinical state give ideas for further management or what to do next. Ideally, we should be able to identify what can be done to help the patient. After all, this is why most of us became physicians, right? To alleviate the suffering of others.

I typically read and evaluate the imaging of the patient just like I would in my normal practice. I produce a report and create a findings and an impression section. If a procedure, surgery, or additional investigation is necessary, I generally place that in a third section at the bottom of the report titled "recommendations." I write all of my reports in this manner.

---

5. C.T. Loy, L. Irwig, "Accuracy of Diagnostic Tests Read with and without Clinical Information: a Systematic Review," *JAMA* 292, no. 13 (2004):1602-9. DOI: 10.1001/jama.292.13.1602.

6. A. Leslie, A.J. Jones, P.R. Goddard, "The Influence of Clinical Information on the Reporting of CT by Radiologists. *British Journal of Radiology* 73, no. 874 (2000): 1052–5.

3. Minimally Invasive Procedural Information

Now onto number three, minimally invasive procedural information. There is diagnostic information in the correct application of image-guided procedures.

Epidural Steroid Injection

As an example, let's say the patient comes in and has low back pain. The MRI shows multiple levels of possible pain generation that could be the cause. Based on the combination of the location and type of pain, as well as what the MRI shows, we then can make a clinical decision to perform an epidural steroid injection at a certain level or levels. Provided the needle ends up in the right place and the procedure is a technical success, based on intra-procedural and post-procedural findings, we can often deduce the levels of pain generation. This is incredibly useful.

During the procedure, once the needle is found to be in a satisfactory position, the infusion of medication begins. At this point, during gentle infusion of the injection (which contains preservative-free anesthetic and an anti-inflammatory agent) into the epidural space, I like to ask the patient some important questions.

Q: Are there any symptoms associated with the injection?
Q: Is this a typical location where you normally experience pain?
Q: Usually, the most common answer is "yes." If the answer is "no," I like to ask:
Q: How is the location dissimilar?

At that point, the patient will usually say it's higher or lower. I like to keep track of this information. Based on how the patient does in the interim, I will potentially alter the location of injection (if necessary) on the next visit. After one, two, or three visits, with a high degree of certainty, I can usually pinpoint the location of pain generation.

See the Imaging

Back to the imaging and clinical assessment of a personal injury case. In reviewing the procedures performed, I like to see the actual imaging obtained during the procedure. The first obvious question at that point is: "Are the needle or needles in the right location?"

In other words, was the procedure a technical success? I also often ask myself if those are the particular levels that I would have injected, given the observed clinical and imaging information. If the patient reported no temporary or chronic benefit after the injections, as mentioned above, in my mind there can be relatively few possibilities.

The first possibility is that the patient's disease process was too significant to benefit from epidural steroid injection. Though possible, I find that this particular scenario is relatively uncommon in my practice. The vast majority of my patients report at least some benefit.

The second possibility is that the procedure was in some way unsuccessful. Perhaps incorrect levels were injected, or an insufficient amount of medication was infused into the desired location.

Another possibility is that the procedure could have unmasked other areas of pain generation. This scenario can be somewhat difficult to assess. It is critical that, if the procedure unmasked other areas of pain, the patient is a good historian and reports the changes in symptoms accurately. Before a series of three visits for epidural steroid injection, I often discuss all of the above scenarios at length; and I encourage the patient to use a pain journal, keeping diligent notes regarding the location of the pain, the severity, and *any* experienced changes in location or type of pain.

Was This the Right Procedure?

The other questions that need to be addressed in the evaluation of the procedural information involve if the procedure was indicated or not.

- Was there perhaps a better procedure to perform?

- Was the standard of care followed as well as useful, relevant clinical information?

A typical example that I encounter involves the treatment of lower extremity radicular pain. I have found that many pain specialists or orthopedic surgeons perform facet injections in the treatment of lower extremity radicular pain. (Recall that *radicular pain* is defined as pain that starts in one location and extends away from that location to another location, characteristically along the course of a nerve.)

Facet joints are innervated by a small branch of the nerve which heads posteriorly towards its target. Stimulation of this particular nerve would result in localized back pain without radicular pain involving an extremity. A facet injection will not test for pain radiating down the leg.

Based on simple neurology and anatomy, in general, a transforaminal epidural steroid injection or a dorsal interlaminar injection (or a combination of both) are far better diagnostic and possible treatment procedures in this setting to target the affected nerve that is causing radiating pain down an extremity. A dorsal interlaminar injection approaches the spine from a dorsal (posterior or behind) approach and targets the nerves (there are more than one) within the canal. A transforaminal injection approaches the spine from the side and targets the nerve (one single nerve) that exits the spine at that location. The idea is to get the medication closest to the source of pain, which is the nerve that is most inflamed or irritated. In summary, the nerve travels inferiorly (down) the spinal canal, passing multiple levels then exits through a space known as a foramen. The foramen is located anterior (in front) of the facet joint, but posterior (behind) the vertebral body near the level of the intervertebral disc.

4. Surgical Information

The final step is to check for any surgical information. But first, let's review. At this point, we have examined and discussed the clinical record. We know what the patient has said. We also know what other physicians have determined based on the patient's history and physical exams. We have the imaging. We also know if a minimally invasive procedure was performed, if it was done well, and the outcome. We have a good amount of information at this point, and we can likely make a conclusion.

But there could be more. If a surgery was performed with strong associated documentation, we will have another level and type of information. This is the direct visualization of the anatomy and the suspected injury.

Example: Lower Lumbar Spine Injury

Let's say for example that we have a patient who has sustained an injury to their lower lumbar spine. Here's what we know:

- The patient's clinical presentation supports an acute injury to the L4–L5 level.
- The MRI shows evidence of abnormality at the L4–L5. The patient experienced at least some transient benefit after an epidural steroid injection at the L4–L5 level.
- However, after the epidural steroid injection, the pain returned and is negatively affecting this patients' activities of daily life.

The patient then sees a surgeon who concludes that medical, conservative, and minimally invasive treatment strategies have failed. A surgery of whatever type is scheduled and performed. During the surgery, the surgeon makes a variety of incisions and directly examines (eyes on target) the L4-L5 level. The surgeon notes a disruption in the annulus fibrosis and disc material contacting the adjacent nerves. This is the final nail in the coffin.

The findings observed during surgery are important. It is the first time that we can claim that direct visual confirmation of the disease process is present. This allows for a very high degree of confidence in our final conclusion at this point. Lastly, provided the surgery is a technical success, we follow the clinical outcome and the postsurgical course. All this information further adds to the strength of the argument.

Performing surgery of the spine is not without risk. There is plenty of risk. I have heard some spine surgeons claim when speaking to their patients and explaining the risks that, "There is a chance that you could be better and a chance that you could be just different, with a similar level of pain." Provided a technical surgical success occurs, and a comparable clinical course is observed after the surgery, we now have further evidence to support with a high degree of medical probability (and perhaps certainty) regarding causation.

Clinical versus Non-Clinical Radiologists

Radiology over the past thirty years has changed significantly. This is for a variety of reasons but mostly the advent of newer and better technology. There is significant breadth to the field with many niche environments. In my opinion, at one time, radiology offered (and still does at some places) an escape from the clinical (direct patient care) environment and allowed for safe harbor for those who did not wish to be in contact with patients. This further promoted the idea among non-radiologists that radiologists are therefore not clinicians. To an extent, this could be somewhat true. However, the notion that radiologists fail to routinely engage in physical examinations and participate in a clinical environment in most arenas is false.

In many fields of radiology, we routinely do procedures, and as a result, we interact with patients. We perform physical examinations and make clinical judgment calls. In the pain management portion of my practice, I spend a significant amount of time physically examining and talking with patients. In total, this amount of time in interview and physical examination is usually more than I spend performing the actual procedure.

Find a Clinical Radiologist

Why am I bringing this up? As noted in the *Johnson* case, you need a radiologist that is comfortable with clinical information and possesses a complex understanding of the pathology involved in your client. Therefore, when it is time to hire your expert, find a radiologist who is clinically competent and who is very, very comfortable with the clinical side of being a physician. Some are not and will never be comfortable with this.

There is a ton of information available in the medical record besides just looking at the pictures. My advice is to find an expert who is comfortable with examining all of the available clinical information, has a strong ability to interpret the acquired imaging, and most importantly, understands and has the ability integrate the two. Also, make sure your expert is able to answer and thoroughly address questions like:

1. What was the suspected cause of the injury or injuries that you are seeing?
2. Does the mechanism of the incident make sense with respect to the injury or injuries that are observed? Have your experts provided you with justifications for the decision-making process and opinions. If it doesn't make sense, it should! Ask for clarifications.
3. Do you agree with the interpretation of the imaging studies that the patient received? If not, what is dissimilar and why? What about the timing and type of imaging work up that the patient received was that reasonable?
4. Was the care rendered to the patient appropriate? Believe it or not, all radiologists are tested on treatments! It is on all of our board exams! So please, ask away! If the radiologist is simply diagnostic (nonprocedural) in nature, you might get an answer

like "refer to a neurosurgeon," this is fine. However, I am hope that by now you realize that a radiologist who does procedures on the spine, like myself and Dr. Lowry, should have more insight and input. Please tap into that knowledge and expertise.

5. Were the medical decisions made reasonable?
6. What should I ask the opposing experts? This is important. Those of us that have been involved in forensic work long enough know the typical strategies of the opposite side. Get the intel on this from your expert. Typically, in my experience, the defense cases seem to omit the clinical records or you get a radiologist that is "uncomfortable" with discussing the clinical findings. This, however, does not negate the importance of the clinical records; it just means that the radiologist isn't comfortable with it. Therefore, the actual clinical information becomes arguably more important here. Most of the defense cases that I have done only come with the diagnostic images and no clinical records. This is unacceptable. There is a wealth of knowledge in the clinical records! In the past, but not always, when I have been hired by defense firms, I still always ask for the clinical records.
7. As a defense expert radiologist without the clinical records, the favorite flower in the garden often becomes the hedge. "It could be X, it could be Y, it could be Z" etc. Or, they may just call it "normal." Therefore, when you encounter a defense expert radiologist that has only looked at the pictures and *not* the clinical records, make sure to ask why and shed light on what your expert tells you with respect to your line of questioning, tailored according to pertinent clinical findings. The more specific your expert can get, the better results you can expect.
8. Lastly, if your client is still in considerable pain, ask your expert what else could or should be done. Quality of life is important, and we—as experts—can and should be able to help in this regard.

If you ask your expert the above questions and you are met with awkward silence, a blank stare or answers that don't make sense, consider finding another expert.

Conclusion

In conclusion, interpretation of diagnostic imaging by radiologists is not a perfect science. As noted above, according to the combination of the studies mentioned, the error rate ranged from 2-37 percent and many of these errors were found to impact the appropriate course of patient care. If you believe your client's injury claims and there isn't apparent support in the final report of a diagnostic study, it is very possible that either a perceptual or cognitive error was made in the interpretation of the imaging by the radiologist. All radiologists (for a variety of reasons, including training, a lack of clinical information at the time of interpretation, degree of specialty, pressure in the reading room, and others) make mistakes. (I am included in this.) There is no such thing as a "perfect" radiologist. However, in my opinion and as noted above, a clinically oriented radiologist performs far better in this medical legal arena.

Any expert that you hire should be very comfortable with clinical information and be able to integrate all available sources of data to include imaging findings in such a way that leads to a confident and justifiable diagnosis. Details are crucial and your expert should know your client's clinical course, imaging findings, and procedural/surgical information as well as pertinent negatives. Potential deficits in the clinical records, the imaging, and minimally invasive procedural and surgical information need to be able to be explained.

Your expert should be able to answer complex questions about your client and the disease and/or injury course. If your expert is unable to explain and/or justify the integration of the available clinical information and formulate a diagnosis, find another expert who can. Experts are paid well; the expectation should be that of excellence.

Appendix C

Glossary of Medical Terms

Directional Terms

Anterior: Refers to the front of the body or nearer to the front.

Posterior: Refers to the back of the body or nearer to the back.

Superior: Indicates a position above or higher than another part of the body.

Inferior: Indicates a position below or lower than another part of the body.

Lateral: Refers to the side of the body or away from the midline.

Medial: Refers to the middle or center; closer to the midline of the body.

Proximal: Nearer to the point of attachment or to a given reference point.

Distal: Farther from the point of attachment or from a given reference point.

Anteroposterior (AP): Directional term meaning "from front to back." Often used to describe the orientation or view of an imaging study (for example, X-ray or MRI) where structures are viewed from front to back, or as a direction of measurement of a structure on CT or MRI images.

Craniocaudal: Directional term meaning "from head to tail." Used to describe orientation or alignment of structures along the axis of the body, such as the spinal cord within the vertebral column, or as a direction of measurement of a structure on CT or MRI images.

Transverse: Refers to the direction across or perpendicular to the long axis of the body or a structure. In anatomy, it is used to describe cuts or planes that divide the body or organs horizontally, (for example, transverse sections in CT or MRI), or as a direction of measurement of a structure on CT or MRI images.

Spine Anatomy Terms

Annular Ligament: Ligament comprised of strong bands of fibrous tissue which forms the outer segment of the intervertebral disc, providing structural integrity and containing the nucleus pulposus.

Anterior Longitudinal Ligament: Ligament that extends longitudinally down the anterior aspect of the vertebral bodies and limits extension of the spine.

Axial Loading: The application of force along the long (vertical) axis of the spine, such as gravity acting on the spine when upright.

Axial Pain: Pain that is localized to the spine itself.

Cauda Equina: Long bundle of spinal nerves and nerve roots that arise from the lower end of the spinal cord, usually at approximately T12–L1; name means "horse's tail" in Latin.

Cerebrospinal Fluid (CSF): Clear fluid found within the tissue which surrounds the brain and spinal cord, acting as a cushion and providing basic mechanical and immunological protection.

Cervical Spine: The upper portion of the spine located in the neck, consisting of seven vertebrae (C1–C7).

Craniocervical Junction: The region where the skull base meets the cervical spine.

Cervicothoracic Junction: The level where the cervical spine meets the thoracic spine, at C7–T1.

Disc Extrusion: Form of disc herniation where the herniated portion of the nucleus pulposus extends into the spinal canal and is larger in craniocaudal dimension than the disc, but still remains attached to the disc.

Disc Herniation: Condition where the nucleus pulposus extends through a rupture in the annular ligament of the disc.

Disc Protrusion: Form of disc herniation where the herniated portion of the nucleus pulposus extends into the spinal canal but remains the same size or smaller in craniocaudal dimension than the disc.

Disc Sequestration: Form of disc herniation where the herniated portion of the nucleus pulposus breaks completely free from the disc and migrates into the spinal canal or neural foramen.

Dura (dura mater): The outermost of the three layers of the meninges that surround the brain and spinal cord.

Epidural: Situated or occurring outside the dura mater; often refers to the injection of medication into the epidural space of the spinal cord.

Extraforaminal: Directional term used to describe disc herniations which occur lateral to the pedicle.

Facet Joints: Small joints located between and behind adjacent vertebrae that allow for movement.

Foraminal: Relating to the neural foramen, which are openings between adjacent vertebrae through which spinal nerves exit the spinal canal and branch out to other parts of the body. Also a directional term used to describe disc herniations which occur between the medial and lateral borders of the pedicle.

Interspinous Ligament: Ligament that connects the spinous processes of adjacent vertebrae.

Lamina (plural: Laminae): Bony segment of the posterior elements of a vertebra which connects the spinous process to the transverse process.

Ligamentum Flavum: Ligament that connects the laminae of adjacent vertebrae from the axis to the sacrum.

Lumbar Spine: The lower portion of the spine, often referred to as the small of the back, consisting of five vertebrae (L1–L5).

Lumbarized S1: Anatomic variant in which the first sacral vertebra is not fused and behaves more like a lumbar vertebra.

Lumbosacral Junction: The level where the lumbar spine meets the sacrum, at L5–S1.

Midline: Imaginary line that divides the body into left and right halves. Structures or conditions that are described as midline are typically located along this central axis of the body. For example, the spinal cord runs along the midline of the vertebral column, and the spinous process extends posteriorly from the junction of the laminae in the midline.

Neural Foramen: Openings between vertebrae through which nerves exit the spinal canal. Often just shortened to "foramen" in spine reports.

Nerve Root: Initial segment of a nerve leaving the spinal canal. Nerve roots exit the spinal canal by passing through the intervertebral foramina.

Nucleus Pulposus: Soft, jelly-like inner core of an intervertebral disc that provides cushioning and flexibility to the spine.

Paracentral: Directional term used to describe the location of disc herniations just lateral to midline.

Pedicle: Bony segment of the posterior elements of the vertebra between the transverse process and the vertebral body.

Posterior Elements: The parts of a vertebra located at the back of the spinal column, including the laminae, spinous process, transverse processes, and facet joints.

Posterior Longitudinal Ligament: Ligament that extends longitudinally down the posterior aspect of the vertebral bodies and limits extension of the spine.

Radicular Pain: Referred type of pain that radiates along the path of a nerve due to irritation or compression.

Sacralized L5: Anatomic variant in which the fifth lumbar vertebra is at least partially fused to the sacrum.

Sacrum: Triangular-shaped bone at the base of the spine, articulating with the lumbar spine and pelvis.

Spinous Process: Bony process originating in the midline extending off the posterior (back) part of each vertebra.

Spinal Canal: Bony ring formed by the vertebral body, pedicles, and laminae through which the spinal cord runs.

Spinal Cord: The cylindrical bundle of nerve fibers and associated tissue enclosed in the spine, which connects nerves from all parts of the body to the brain.

Subarticular: Directional term used to describe disc herniations which occur lateral to the spinal cord and medial to the medial border of the pedicle.

Subdural: Situated or occurring beneath the dura mater.

Supraspinous Ligament: Ligament that connects the tips of the spinous processes from the seventh cervical vertebra to the sacrum.

Thecal Sac: Membranous sac of dura mater, located within the spinal canal, which surrounds the spinal cord and contains cerebrospinal fluid.

Thoracic Spine: The middle portion of the spine located in the upper and mid-back, consisting of twelve vertebrae (T1–T12). Rib-bearing vertebrae, which is a defining characteristic of thoracic spinal levels.

Thoracolumbar Junction: The level where the thoracic spine meets the lumbar spine, at T12–L1.

Transforaminal: Referring to the path that passes through a neural foramen. Often used to describe the procedural approach used for epidural steroid injections.

Transitional Anatomy: Variant in the normal spinal anatomy where a vertebra might have features of another region (for example, lumbar vertebrae with sacral characteristics).

Transverse Process: Bony process extending laterally from the vertebrae.

Vertebra (plural: Vertebrae): The individual bones that make up the spine.

Vertebral body: Cylindrical anterior portion of each vertebra, separated from adjacent levels by intervertebral discs. Provides axial weight-bearing support throughout the spine.

About the Authors

Robert T. Simon

By the Author

Robert T. Simon is from Pittsburgh, Pennsylvania but now lives and practices in California predominately, with offices in Arizona and Texas.

When he was a kid, his uncle was suddenly struck by a drunk driver and lost the use of his legs. This accident forever shifted Robert's career trajectory. He made it his mission to fight for the injured and the less fortunate. He is known for getting massive verdicts on spine injury cases.

He has won Trial Lawyer of the Year awards up and down the state of California over several years. But what he most proud of, professionally, is starting the trial lawyer careers of many others. Robert started his own solo shop with his younger brother Brandon in 2009 after getting the seed money from winning a game show and being inspired by his then fiancée, and now wife, Christine Bullock. In 2010 they were so busy that Brandon went off to law school, and Robert's BFF and womb-mate Brad Simon partnered with him to start the Simon Law Group also known as the Justice Team. The firm grew to dozens of attorneys, and many notable 7-, 8-, and 9-figure verdicts.

Besides cofounding his firm, he also cofounded Justice HQ with his brother Brad, and head of creative Teresa Diep. He is also the founder of Attorney Share. His mission is to change the practice of law in its entirety. He wants to get the best cases to the best lawyer for that specific case and give lawyers a high qualify of life along the way.

Robert considers his quality of life very high, with his wonderful wife and also like-minded serial entrepreneur, Christine Bullock, and their three beautiful and funny daughters Remington (Remi), Penelope (Poppy), and Josephine (Josie). Every day he is surrounded by the rest of his family both professionally and personally as his sisters, Nicole

Prince and Julie Gossett are directors at Justice HQ, and his parents Big Bob Simon and Linda Simon work for the law firm.

For some lighter fare, Robert can be heard and seen hosting the Justice Team Podcast with his brothers, and his whiskey-fueled, legal talk show—Bourbon of Proof.[1] All media can be found at The Justice Team Network.

Dr. Orlando Micheli

By David Lopresti, MD, Interventional Radiologist

Dr. Orlando Micheli is one of those physicians that immediately comes to mind when you think about your favorite colleague or the physician you would want to care for your loved ones. I've had the privilege of working alongside him and am honored to call him my friend.

His early life was instrumental in shaping his pursuit of medicine. You would never guess by his appearance now, but he was plagued by several chronic medical conditions as a child. His mother also suffered extensively from back pain throughout her life and endured two particularly grueling spine fusion surgeries. The memories of helping her recover and conquering his own ailments sparked his fascination with medicine and healing that guided his journey and ultimately led to his graduation from New York Medical College class of 2008.

In his final year of medical school, he found himself looking for a specialty that offered continued intellectual challenge, innovation and growth. Dr. Susan Rachlin was instrumental in mentoring him during this time and he chose the field of radiology. Shortly after his graduation, his mother was diagnosed with colon cancer. This provided further clarity and resolve for his path. The pioneering spirit of interventional radiology (IR) fellowship training offered exactly what he was looking for. Since 1973, the subspecialty field of IR has been the birthplace for minimally invasive procedures and surgeries that influence, support,

1. https://www.bourbonofproofseries.com

or drive almost every single medical specialty today including interventional spine/pain management and interventional oncology. After becoming board certified as a radiologist in 2013, he started his medical legal consulting practice and entered fellowship at the University of Southern California which he completed in 2014.

He then joined a radiology practice in Yuma, Arizona that summer. The opportunity was exciting because the community had a great need for care, but service and capabilities lagged far behind demand. The environment was just the challenge he was looking for and his impact was immediate. Within six months he became the director of Quality Assurance/Quality Care (QA/QC), the Radiation Safety Officer and the interventional radiology section chief. Meanwhile he continued to grow his medical legal consulting practice. In 2016, he took over management of the entire radiology department.

The department he has built at Yuma Regional Medical Center is the best I've had the pleasure of working with. You will not find a more skilled, compassionate, efficient, and fiercely loyal team of nurses and technologists working in an interventional radiology department anywhere. This is a direct reflection of the dedicated physician, role model, and leader that he is. He attracts the best and makes them better.

With this book, he shares some of the wisdom he has learned. It is another testament to his continued impact on the lives of people and patients, making us all better.

Dr. Peter Lowry

By the Author

My introduction to musculoskeletal imaging came through looking at X-rays and MRIs of my own shoulder, knee, ankles, wrist, hand, and ribs. Recalling these injuries here explains my deep appreciation of ibuprofen today. Athletic performance and the mechanics of the human body has always intrigued me. Inspired by my dad, an anesthesiologist and polymath who is famously undefeated in Trivial

Pursuit, I checked all the undergraduate pre-med boxes and enrolled in medical school. There, the variety of imaging and procedures available to musculoskeletal radiologists proved an irresistible combination and led me to the University of Florida for residency and then the University of Colorado for fellowship.

My career has since focused on sports and trauma imaging, with a heavy focus on the spine. I've been fortunate to work on cutting edge spine imaging and intervention techniques, and to teach residents and fellows who I see pushing the field forward in amazing ways today. I'm luckier still to have met many patients who shared their lives and experiences; I'm a better physician and person because of them.